GROWING UP IN COUNTRY AUSTRALIA

GROWING UP IN COUNTRY AUSTRALIA

EDITED BY RICK MORTON

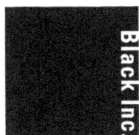

Black Inc.

Published by Black Inc.,
an imprint of Schwartz Books Pty Ltd
22–24 Northumberland Street
Collingwood VIC 3066, Australia
enquiries@blackincbooks.com
www.blackincbooks.com

9781760643065 (paperback)
9781743822326 (ebook)

A catalogue record for this
book is available from the
NATIONAL
LIBRARY   National Library of Australia
OF AUSTRALIA

Cover design by Akiko Chan
Text design and typesetting by Typography Studio
Cover image of Milky Way by ms pics / Shutterstock
Cover image of rain drops by Midstream / Shutterstock

P. 277: reproduced by permission of the poet / Alan Gould, 'Flying over the
Australian Alps', *Years Found in Likeness*, Angus and Robertson, Sydney, 1988

Contents

Introduction

Rick Morton

In high school, I had one job.

A handful of friends and I spent three nights a week folding the local newspaper, the *Fassifern Guardian*, and two other publications that served surrounding districts in regional Queensland. It wasn't especially glamourous. Some shifts we would work after class until almost midnight, black ink staining our hands and school uniforms. We folded rigs with the pages stacked into different levels and would pull newsprint from the top down, collecting everything at the bottom and creasing it with our soft little hands.

It was the best job, even at $6 an hour, and I never wanted to be anywhere else.

Still, I like to joke that I knew the threat of redundancies that haunted the legacy media years before I became a working journalist. The owners had long ago bought a machine worth tens of thousands of dollars. It was rumoured this contraption would replace us – if they could ever get it working. Every year, from the new millennium until I graduated in 2004, there were whispers that the Machine was close to ready. My friends and I felt like blue-collar workers from the '80s, anxious and suspicious of the great automation that would soon be upon us.

On weekends, I also cleaned the *Fassifern Guardian* office and the workspace out back, which housed the Machine, the printing press and the compositor's desk. I cherished this access; on deserted shifts I would take breaks in the archive, which was stacked with hardcopy newspapers, bound by year, going all the way back to 1901. In regional Queensland, where we still didn't have machines to fold our family-owned newspapers (no, not *that* family), there was a degree of charm about the enterprise of searching through a town's history.

It was always the same names: the Mullers, the Wimmers, the Nykvists, the Neuendorfs and what felt like a hundred other names of German origin. Some of the same stores too. In the main street of Boonah is Maynards, a clothing store from another era, which is still run by the titular family and still filled with product in boxes stacked on shelves stretching almost to the double-height ceiling. Ask Erroll for any size in any garment and he'll eye off a dusty package in a distant quadrant and bring it back. He does this as if communicating with a part of himself hidden in every part of the store. If you visit more than once, you won't even need to remind him of the size you're after. Erroll remembers.

One of the big stories from the middle of the twentieth century was a local government election that was marred by the appearance of a ram at a polling booth. The big boofhead was being a menace and preventing the citizenry from casting their votes. I can't remember how it all panned out, but there was a fuss and it now remains in print for all time.

Later in my young adult life, I returned as a journalist to the newspaper. One afternoon, when everyone else had gone home, an old gentleman from a neighbouring town walked into the office holding a pawpaw and coughed expectantly until I popped my head out from another room.

It was an especially large pawpaw. Mum had some pawpaw trees in her yard at the time, but I had never seen one like this.

'It's 4.3 kilograms,' the man said.

And I said, 'That's great. A phenomenal achievement.'

And then he said: 'Are you going to photograph it?'

So, I did. The story ran in the following week's edition.

Now, there have been bigger moments in my career. Times where things changed. Stories that helped someone and stories that didn't. There were assignments that were just plain fun and some that were so moving I wept. But as far as great days go, this one left me thrilled.

It seemed to me a perfect distillation of the country Australia bargain. Yes, everyone will know your business. Secrets are hard to keep. And when things go wrong it feels as if the strain is magnified. In return, however, there are 4.3-kilogram pawpaws, curiosities, artefacts; the full breadth of the natural world.

When I was just a boy, living on a remote cattle station five hours west of Charleville in Queensland's channel country, this world was endlessly fascinating. In my mother, Deb, I had a guide who was herself curious and kind (except when it came to snakes).

Don Watson once wrote: 'Deep in the Gippsland subconscious there lay coiled a snake.' I thought this applied rather nicely to all of Australia, especially the regions, and it certainly governed a lot of our life. When we weren't fretting about them, Mum was showing me the different kinds of birds – glorious wedge-tailed eagles, peregrine falcons, Major Mitchell's cockatoo, brolgas, finches – and small mammals. My brother, Toby, and I made cubby houses in the scented mulga shrub that erupted with sensation after the rain, chased feral pigs into the dry creek beds filled with opal and lined by river red gums.

Sometimes I wonder who I would be if I didn't see the world in such detail from such a young age. Perhaps flatter, in my dimensions. This early connection to the land is a shadow of what this continent's First Peoples know to be an overwhelming imperative. To be and stay in communication with Country is not just a matter of culture but of personal health.

It is also a privilege.

My family and I saw the other stuff, too. The addiction and crime; the heartache of losing friends to accidents, which are more common in the bush; the small-mindedness and periodic rejection of minorities. Despite being able to see the horizon, we realised how suffocating our lives could be. How denuded of opportunity, or so we felt.

This collection of writing is, I hope, a way to be honest about all of it. Having spent half my life now living in cities, it is increasingly the country life that I crave. Others may have been formed in rural areas but will never return because of the scars left by those experiences.

Ask anyone what growing up means and they'll assume it refers to an exit from childhood. That is not the definition we have taken here. At thirty-five, I am still growing up. People have encountered foundational moments at the age of forty, sixty and eighty. There have been times when children have been the most grown-up people in a room full of adults.

There were hundreds of submissions to this collection and although it is impossible to include all of them, the themes were striking to me. Of loneliness or belonging, sustenance or degradation; or even the particular politics of the country school bus. Unlike public transport in the cities, these buses are a pre-programmed ride for the same kids on the same route every day. Whole fiefdoms are given the chance to develop in this closed system. I didn't even get to use a school bus until I started Year 3 – when we moved to Boonah and I had to go to a 'real' school – and I had largely blocked out those forty-five-minute-each-way trips where the older kids would hoot and holler and I would try to look out the window and be small.

Nothing seemed to illustrate the far-reaching powers of the school, or its status as a panopticon in student lives, than when special assemblies were called to *discuss what happened on the bus yesterday*.

Much of what we see about life in the bush is coloured by the romance of days long behind us. I wanted this anthology to be a more modern account. One thing that has always fascinated me, as a white boy raised in an almost entirely white part of the world, was how migrants found life in the country. Especially when they skipped the big cities altogether and arrived from their home-lands to settle in the regions. What does that do to the soul, to lose a common language and culture and in doing so find that the ability to remain in the background also vanishes? No one person's account is the same as another's, of course. You will find in these pages a colourful and gripping pastiche that updates the experience outside Australia's cities and large regional centres. You will find, despite the absolute variety in these essays, that there is still something ineffable about life in the country.

Perhaps that is the one secret we get to keep.

Slow Life

Sami Shah

There was a moment, halfway through Melbourne's extended lockdown of 2020, when I realised I had my four years in a country town to thank for my ability to cope with isolation. There was something familiar about the sudden lack of activity; spending long days with nothing to do but consider how long until the next meal, the next shower, the next time I could reasonably crawl back into bed. Instead of finding the sudden brakes applied to the hectic forward motion of life in Melbourne upsetting, or even traumatising, it felt comfortable. I knew how to do nothing. Northam had taught me that well.

It wasn't always like this. I grew up in Karachi, a city of twenty-four million people, all of them vibrating with the need for the now – get to work now, pay the bills now, meet your friends and family now, party hard now, run for your life now. Sleep is a waste of time. While you sleep, everything can change. A friend can be shot and killed, a terrorist can blow himself up, a riot can bloom. Or, alternatively, a family member can get married, a new restaurant can open, friends can suddenly appear with rolled joints of hash, a trip to the beach can eventuate. Karachi is a city that thrums with restless, even manic, energy and if you don't sync to that frequency you will be left behind. And being left behind means you'll always be catching up. You work from nine a.m. to nine p.m., then spend your earnings in the hours between. Until I was thirty-five, I knew no other way of living, and if you'd asked me – shouting your question over the din of life – I'd say there was no other way worth living.

Then, I ended up in Northam, Western Australia, with a population of 4000. I'd been to weddings with more people in attendance. It wasn't the plan of course. The plan was to leave one big, mad city and move to another big, mad city: Karachi to Melbourne, keep the momentum in place, ride the adrenaline from kebab rolls at two a.m. on Tariq Road to Laksa at three a.m. on Russell Street. Except the immigration department had another plan, which superseded any plans I might have bothered aspiring towards. Melbourne would have to be earned, a gift given only after my family and I had spent four years in a country town in WA. Instead of revelling in the hyper-existence of urban twenty-first century, I was sentenced to 1950s pastoral. Rural Western Australia is what happens if quaint British towns take a nap and never wake up.

Once, years after I'd finally escaped to Melbourne, comedian Rhys Nicholson was touring through WA. Having finished his show in Northam, he called me and asked where he could find some dinner. It was just past nine at night, and I answered, 'The servo should be open.' Rhys laughed, called me a sarcastic prick, and went off looking for grub. An hour later he called to apologise. Dinner had been crisps and a Diet Coke from the servo, because nothing else was open. That was my first big surprise after settling into our rental in Northam; everything closes early, and there isn't much of anything in the first place. There was a single Chinese restaurant, two pubs and the aforementioned servo. And frankly, the food in the servo might be a bit better than what the others had to offer. I was used to eating whatever I wanted, whenever I desired it, and realising that this debauched Roman emperor lifestyle was no longer accessible was deeply upsetting.

Another adjustment: the silence. Karachi is cacophonous: millions of trucks and millions of buses and millions upon millions of motorcycles without silencers on their exhausts, roaring and raging at millions of cars, and donkey carts, and cursing pedestrians. There is a dull roar even before you reach the city, rising like a migraine the closer you get. I was so accustomed to it all, it didn't register for me, as unnoticed as the heat of summer, or the ever-present threat of violence. Then, in Northam, I learnt how deafening silence can truly be. Standing on my porch on a clear night, I could hear nothing. No traffic, no angry shouts, no distant gunfire. The silence, in those first days, was a reminder of being isolated from all I knew, of having left behind all I loved. 'You're not in Kansas anymore.' At least Oz still had singing and dancing lions and tin men. Northam was the kind of quiet that forced philosophical considerations of the insignificance of trees falling in abandoned forests.

In the first months I struggled with the stillness of my new surroundings. I raged against the injustice of having ended up in a place so bucolic, cursed the fates for having forced me to slow my life until it was barely moving at all. Then, slowly – of course, slowly, because there was no other speed setting – I learnt to adjust. I learnt that not everything has to be done right away. That having no place to go can mean learning to appreciate the place you're in. And that I was able to find peace not in productivity but in peacefulness itself. I learnt to cook the foods I craved, spent afternoons walking through fields of canola and wheat, watched sunsets on the back of a ute with a six-pack of beers between myself and a friend. I learnt that hungering for the next wasn't necessary, when the next would be the same as the now. The sameness of each day stopped being a frustration, and instead became something to savour.

Einstein explained the relativistic effects of time using a minute for a hand on a hot stove contrasted against an hour spent with a pretty girl. The former feels like an hour, the latter a minute. He could have used Northam and Melbourne for the same illustration. Four years in Northam felt like forty years, in the same way that four years in Melbourne now feels like just forty days. Except when the lockdown came. The propulsive force of Melbourne ground to a halt, and work-filled days and comedy club nights suddenly evaporated. A city of four million people were relegated to contemplating their own existence. It was like sending us all to a silent yoga retreat to find ourselves, and once we'd done that, we discovered we were stuck with ourselves for several months more. Friends grew suicidal, others learnt to cry. Marriages collapsed, relationships soured, and we were given a lesson in the fragility of the world we'd worked so diligent and tirelessly to construct. We'd convinced ourselves that always having things to do, places to go and people to see was good for us. And for many, the lockdown was evidence of the truth of that lifestyle. For me, however, it was a reminder to slow down before I fall, to sit in silence so I can hear myself think. The silence of empty Melbourne streets and endless Melbourne days felt like being back in Northam just for a little while again. And to my surprise, I savoured that reminder.

Mousepocalypse

Annabel Crabb

Growing up on a farm teaches you some fairly brutal lessons about life's realities. One of them, of course, is 'Where does meat come from?' A matter settled fairly early on for me, given that ours was a sheep farm, where my Dad would occasionally do his own butchery. This explains my thirty-year stint of vegetarianism, or pescetarianism at least; my own slightly wonky approach to matters dietary is that I am prepared to eat anything I would also be prepared personally to kill. I'm okay with knocking over a fish, even happier to deprive a prawn of its life. Crabs can expect no nomenclatural solidarity from me or my family. But a chicken: nope. You can go on your way, friend. I like your beady little eyes and your innate sense of physical theatre with that comb. You and your four-legged acquaintances need fear nothing from me.

Another lesson you learn on a farm is the sharp limits the natural world imposes – sometimes summarily – on human effort and agency. There is nothing that pops you right back in your little box as a human more than watching the crops you spent countless hours planting frizzle in the sun. Or be washed away by a flood. Or get some weird disease that makes the harvest impossible to sell. Or not grow at all, something you do see from time to time if you grow up – like I did – in the driest state on the driest continent in the world.

Direct experience of how crisply and with what sadistic resolve the forces of nature will render your toil unto dust is enough to give the farm-raised person a lifelong ultra-sensitivity to the elements.

To this day, the sound of rain brings me a mindbending rush

of relief, even now that I live in the city and rain means mouldy washing and kids going berserk indoors.

I was forty-seven years old when I learnt there was a name for the smell of rain on dry earth: *petrichor*. It's a Greek-fragranced and lovely word, drawn from *petra* (stone) and *ichor* (the fluid said to flow in the veins of the gods). I was happy to learn the term; it's not often that something so magical turns out to have a suitable name. And in an even more satisfying development, it turns out a couple of Australian scientists coined it. Richard Thomas and the exultantly named Joy Bear – both CSIRO scientists, Joy the more unusual owing to her gender – established in their 1964 research paper 'Nature of Argillaceous Odour' that the intoxicating smell of rain on dry earth was caused by the release in moist conditions of a fragrant, yellowish oil contained in rocks and minerals. They called it 'petrichor' and the name stuck. Joy Bear (Joy! Bear!) kept working at the CSIRO until her late eighties, and died very recently, in the autumn of 2021.

What does *petrichor* smell like? It smells like luck changing.

To a kid who knows how adults feel about drought, *petrichor* smells as rich as fruitcake; the dense and sweet assurance that better times are ahead.

It's the intoxicating feeling of dicing with elements that are larger and more powerful than you, and winning a round.

And, look, dealing with the weather is one thing. It's a mighty and worthy foe. No one should ever feel bad about being bested by drought or floods or hurricanes. They're all bigger than you. There's a reason why, in an increasingly secular society, we still recognise the concept of 'acts of God' as grounds for why bills won't be paid, services delivered or concerts performed. It's a formal acknowledgement of our own ultimate puniness in the face of a greater power. We poor bare-forked animals, despite our rapacious exploitation of the planet, still know to fold em when the planet occasionally hits back.

But what about when the enemy is smaller than you? What about if the adversary that's grinding you and your business and any chance you might have at prosperity into the dirt weighs, say, about 20 grams?

The common mouse (*mus musculus*) was introduced to Australia with the arrival of the First Fleet. Mice and rats were an inescapable part of seafaring at the time, and it's likely no one noticed or cared when a handful of the creatures were hauled ashore in boxes of provisions and zoomed off into the vastness of the scrub. Getting on for a century later, the first reports of a mouse plague emerged; the *Queanbeyan Age* published in 1871 the testimony of a landowner near Walgett: hordes of mice feasting on 'rice, flour, starch, bacon, meat, hides, tallow, boots, clothing ... the vegetables – which this year have been a great crop – are now being devoured by these pests ... nothing comes amiss to them, and what we are to do I know not.'

White Australia was not – at this point – sufficiently self-aware to take a sip of its tea and think with any perspective about how annoying it was to have a throng of uninvited mammals show up and decimate its stuff.

But mouse plagues would go on to become a regular part of Australian life. Here's a weird thing I didn't know until very recently: Australia and China are the only two countries in the world that experience mouse plagues. Why? No one has any firm idea. The mouse is thought to have originated in India, which remains the second-biggest producer of wheat in the world, but the cropping expanses of Uttar Pradesh do not experience the regular depredations of the Mouse Warriors the way that Australian farmers do.

I was seven years old when I first encountered a proper mouse plague. My mother and father, who as newlyweds moved to Lower Light on the Adelaide Plains, recall a minor invasion in 1969, during which time my mother says they could *hear* the haystack outside their bedroom window at night if they left the window open, so alive was it with teeming and feasting invaders. How was my elder brother conceived? Some questions are best left unanswered. But 1980 was the big one. By that time, my parents

7

had three children. The littlest – my brother Tom – was two. My clearest recollection of that infestation is opening my drawer and seeing brown bodies ricocheting about in a panic among my underpants. The mice would jam themselves into anything that afforded cover. Cupboards were alive with them. They'd scuttle along curtain rods. The yellow armchairs next to the fireplace wore a frill of tails sticking out from under their skirts.

The stench was incredible and multilayered; the sort of smell you'd run at top speed to evade, except it was everywhere. Top notes of acrid rodent urine, with deep feral undertones that infiltrated everything from paper to food to upholstery. Mice love cheese, as everyone knows from *Looney Tunes*. But they also love soap, and candles, and shoes, and electrical wiring.

We had cats, but they surrendered quickly. Like diners who have peaked too early at the all-you-can-eat seafood bar, they spent their days lying nauseously in the shade while mice skittered around them completely undeterred.

The haystacks were heaving with mice; every piece of wood or sheet metal on the place, if turned over, would send hundreds of creatures zooming crazily for somewhere else to hide.

Like any seven-year-old, I was constantly whining at my parents about getting a pet. But this oversupply of tiny furry creatures was something else. The thing is, one mouse is cute. Two mice, even, are cute. But when you factor in the unstoppable evolutionary ambition of *mus musculus*, things start to get less sweet, rather swiftly.

The common mouse becomes sexually fertile at six weeks of age. Its gestation period is three weeks. Two mice can become ninety mice in just three months. And in the space of one human gestation period, two mice can become *five hundred mice*.

My brothers and I were assigned the task of seizing mice by the tails and dashing them to the ground. So, yes, I have probably thousands of tiny deaths on my conscience. And, no, I would not eat a mouse, notwithstanding the murder/edibility matrix outlined earlier.

In May 2021, when the scriptwriters of *Planet Earth: The Reality Series* sent Australia a mouse plague to add to the already-quite-Biblical pandemic, bushfire and climate Armageddon storylines, a spokeswoman for PETA created uproar when she criticised farmers for using poison to control the marauders, counselling that 'humane traps allow small animals to be caught gently and released unharmed'.

Now, on the whole I'm not in favour of city/country sledging, but I do have some sympathy for mouse-besieged farmers catching wind of PETA's well-intentioned advice. If you imagine how annoying it is to be asked 'Have you switched it off and on again at the wall?' and multiply that about four million times, you will approach the level of fury a person might feel when – overrun by tiny gnawing stinkbombs – they're asked by some distant bozo if they've considered chivvying their persecutors into a carry-cage and dropping them off at a nice farm.

(Side note: The myth of the 'nice farm' is a hypnotic one. We once had a terrifying sheepdog called Ginger who had a mean streak a mile wide; he used to chase and bite us when we walked home from the school bus. It was like being walked home by Cujo. One day, we came home and Ginger was gone. Dad told me that Ginger had gone to live on a nice farm. It took about ten years before the realisation crystallised that *we* lived on a nice farm.)

The PETA lady's words, of course, became an opening for Nationals leader Michael McCormack to sound off about inner-city latte sippers; in parliament, he suggested that the creatures be rehomed into the apartments of animal rights activists so that *their* children could be bitten at night.

(Look, in Mr McCormack's defence, he was at the time holding off a challenge from former leader Barnaby Joyce, who is himself in some respects not unlike *mus musculus*, in that he's very difficult to eradicate humanely and is a surprisingly prolific breeder.)

But calling on the gods to send mice to bite the children of your opponents is … not very grown up, is it?

And that's the greatest demand that living on the land makes of you, in the end, I reckon. You have to be a grown-up. Which means coming to peace with your own helplessness, sometimes, in the face of natural forces that are bigger than you, even when they are tiny rodents.

This is a bloody tough lesson to learn; it involves humility and strength and humour. I have met city people who are very clever and highly educated and successful in their own lives but who would struggle mightily if called upon to make peace with their own place in the natural universe. Come the Mousepocalypse, we shall know their names.

The Hunter

Joo-Inn Chew

Forty-two degrees. Heat radiating off dusty windows onto the hot carpet where we are flopped, wet cloths around our necks and ankles. Everything is itchy and irritating, especially younger siblings. I want to kick my snotty brother and slap my skinny sister, smack their bored, whiny, sticky heads together and emerge an only child again. I want to, but I'm supposed to be mature and reliable so I order them around instead. I'm make them take turns to re-wet the washers, even though the tank water from the kitchen tap is almost warm as blood.

We squabble until it's time to go. Mum has the water and snacks, Dad the bucket, bait and net. We grab our faded towels and remnant bucket and spades. Closing the door, the handle burns my hand. Outside, the throb of cicadas pulses in shrill waves against our eardrums. The sun bites our skin and sucks away sweat. We hobble barefoot over the hot yellow stubble of the paddock, avoiding anthills, jostling for scraps of shade under the limp gums. Heat shimmers and warps the baked earth, blurs the distant hills. Grasshoppers flick away right and left. Our noses wrinkle at the stench from a shrivelled lump of fur and bone.

We climb the final ridge, and there below us is the dam. The water level is low, the edges are slimy, and there is a sheep carcass splayed on the far bank – but to us kids it is a muddy oasis. We drop our towels and run down to splash into the squelchy shallows. Gum leaves, sticks, velvety mud underfoot, an occasional flick at our ankles as an unseen creature swims away. We wade deeper until the warm brown water circles our waists and our

legs find the glorious cool depths. Sinking under at last is such
relief. Our closed eyelids are red-yellow and then brown-black
as we kick down deeper, the shrill beat of cicadas muffling to a
distant throb. Right at the bottom it is still and cold and dark
enough to bring on a delicious fearful shiver. We stay as long as
breath can hold, heartbeats quickening in our ears, until finally
we push up to the surface, gasping into the noisy sunlight again.
We drag up handfuls of red gold-flecked mud and paint our
faces with it, then wash it off again. We dare each other to swim
out to the pump in the middle of the dam, touch the machinery
that fills our hoses and animal troughs. We take turns singing
songs underwater and guessing what they are. We float and float,
stretched out in the warm skin of the dam under blinding blue
sky. We paddle and somersault and dive until we are limp and
dizzy, until our blood feels as light and skimmed as the water.
When we clamber out, our legs wobble and our ears ring. We
collapse onto towels in the warm shade of gum trees, and guz-
zle from our drink bottles.

Mum wades in and out of the shallows, wearing a batik hat
and reading a book about India. She seems happy today. She has
brought the soap so we can wash our hair at the end, to save on
tank water.

Dad has the big white bucket. He knots string around a lump
of old meat and tosses it into the water. For a long while nothing
happens. We watch the limp string until it twitches and tightens.
Dad wades in and slowly, slowly draws it in. The string shortens
until a ripple appears and two fine antennae break the surface.
Dad freezes and sneaks the net in sideways through the water,
gliding under the line until, with a sudden flick and pull, he yanks
it up, dragging with it three big greeny-brown yabbies clinging
to the bait. He flips them into the bucket and pulls the meat free.
The yabbies clatter and crawl over each other, blue claws waving. Dad picks up each one behind the claws and turns it over.
One has a mass of tiny black eggs hoarded under her transpar-
ent tail; she gets to be thrown back into the dam. The others

are returned to the bucket. We poke at them until another two are caught. They circle and grapple with each other, not realising their common danger. We give them names and backstories, tribes and histories. Mine is big and battle-scarred, a seasoned warrior now sworn to peace. My sister's is an orphaned princess with a crooked claw, and my brother's is a cat in disguise who only speaks in miaows.

Dad squats at the shore in his loose cotton shirt and pants, tying up more meat. His hands are brown and strong, his face impassive. He sheds years of toil, loses his working stoop, moves like a boy hunting mud crabs in the mangroves of Malacca. He feels the underwater twitch, senses the shadows around his toes, bewitches the crustaceans into his trap. Sometimes he catches them just to throw them back in again. Sometimes he catches them for the boiling pot. Sometimes he catches them to thrill his children, wave wet claws under their sunburned noses.

Sometimes I see a dark hunter in Dad. Something outside the ordered streets of his hometown, the generous lands and calm waters. A small thing struggling attracts the predator, the one who likes to feel the cringe of the prey. The dark hunter is alert to pain; a humiliation or hurt can draw him out. He is there for the thrill of it. He takes trust and breaks its bones. Sometimes he stares at me and his eyes are black and gleaming as stones. Then he blinks and becomes my ordinary father again.

I feel sorry for the yabbies, can't stay in the kitchen when they are plopped in the big simmering pot, or crack their crimson backs to eat the white flesh underneath. I like them best when they first emerge like green-backed prehistoric monsters dripping muddy water, triumphant claws around the meaty prize, heedless of their fate. I like it when Dad, the capricious hunter, decides on a reprieve and tosses a particular yabby back, the way it cartwheels through the hot air and splashes down to disappear beneath the brown, rippled water. I imagine its dim crustacean feelings – shock, alarm, relief – as it escapes the alien dry dazzle and welcomes the muddy liquid embrace of home again. I imagine it scuttling back down to the familiar depths, brushing trembling antennae against another yabby, transmitting an unbelievable tale, like an astronaut returning to earth who can never be truly understood.

A New Home

Fiona White

The Australia of my early childhood was a hard-baked land from which I came and went. With itchy-footed Australian parents, my brothers (first there was one, then two, then three) and I saw Australia as a holiday destination. A land with two gentle grandfathers and a beautifully spoken, worldly aunt who sent me wonderful books.

We returned to Australia every three years; that was Dad's promise to Mum when they left to live in New Zealand. *We will always come home to see our families, and we will stay long enough that you are happy to leave again.*

But my grandfathers grew frail, and the land of eucalypts and wide-stretching skies called to my mother, an artist, in a way that no travelling adventures could silence.

I was thirteen when Mum told Dad, 'If we don't go home now, our fathers will be gone and our children will settle in foreign lands.'

It was as simple and as complicated as that. They sold our two-storey house on a North Island peninsula between Eastern Beach and Bucklands Beach. They sold the cars with their lace-work of rust etched by the briny sea air. We rehomed the guinea pigs and the loud white duck that lived in our murky paddling pool beneath the fruit trees.

'The dogs will come, of course,' Dad said, 'and Mum's Siamese cats.' Then he levelled me with his solemn blue gaze. 'But you'll have to sell your horse.'

Sell my horse. This was no ordinary horse. This was Nimbus – I'd fallen in love with him at the riding school where I volunteered.

I'd been the only one who could catch him and get his bridle on. Mrs Oates, the owner of the riding school (yes, that was her real name), said he was probably ear-twitched when they broke him in.

'The trainer loops a thin weave of string around the horse's ear to force them to behave,' she told me.

A fierce ache grew in my heart and I vowed I would give Nimbus all the love and protection he deserved.

'Horses aren't like dogs,' Dad said. 'You don't bond with them the same way, and besides, it'd cost thousands to fly him across. I've already checked.'

Dad was an economist and a practical man.

I wrote poems. I cried. I advertised Nimbus for sale, like my parents told me to. People came. They saw a wild, naughty pony no-one could catch. I saw one of my greatest loves. Eventually (due, I suspect, to Mum's quiet but relentless campaigning) one of my grandfathers came to the rescue. He'd found out that ship fares were much cheaper than planes. He got out his cheque book and paid half of the $900 fee to transport that $400 pony to Australia, while Mum and Dad paid the other half.

Nimbus arrived on the Melbourne docks in May 1981, narrowly beating the major wharf strikes that left animals and shipping containers stuck at sea for weeks on end. He travelled there in a wooden box with an expensive broodmare on either side. It took three days for his ship to cross the ocean. Three days during which I woke every morning sick with dread that he'd somehow been put onto a livestock version of the *Titanic*.

Nimbus always made a ridiculous song and dance about everything. I'd lost count of the number of gymkhanas we'd missed or turned up to late because he wouldn't get in the hired float, no matter how many buckets of food, threats or spiky brooms I used to persuade him.

That horse transport mob, though, took no prisoners. Nimbus was whisked out of the crate and onto a fancy blue truck before he had time to blink. They drove him to our new home in Macedon, bouncing up the narrow gravel driveway, gum-tree branches scraping the truck roof while Nimbus shifted and stamped inside. What was this nonsense? What had his crazy owner done this time?

He came off the truck, head high and eyes white-rimmed, snorted at me and the bracken-dotted paddock, flaring his nostrils at this ancient land abundant with kangaroos, koalas and snakes.

We went for long walks. I had started a new school, and I told Nimbus how hard it was to make friends when everyone had known each other forever and no-one needed to meet anyone new. I explained to Nimbus that it turned out I had an accent and all the kids thought I sounded funny. I leaned into his solid shoulder and told him I wished we could go home. He sighed heavily, as if he wished we could, too.

Nimbus and I spent our weekends exploring. We galloped the bush tracks beside the railway line; he froze in horror the first time a long red rattler trundled past, kids' faces pressed to the windows.

We met a snake and there was a millisecond when the three of us – Nimbus, me and the brown snake with tiny, dark eyes – stared at each other in equal shock. The snake may have met a horse or two in its time, but for Nimbus the existence of this slithery creature must have left him wondering how long the list of exotic creatures in this new land was going to get.

We discovered the pine forest and swam in the dam on hot summer nights. Frogs and crickets sang songs while kookaburras guffawed and cockatoos wheeled and screamed. I told Nimbus about the boys I liked and he listened and sighed and then frowned when I made him wear a fly fringe. The flies in New Zealand were not nearly this persistent and rude, I'm sure he thought.

He adapted amazingly well, my little kiwi horse, but then came 1983, a ferocious summer on the back of years of drought. Nimbus was in the neighbour's paddock the night the Ash Wednesday fires roared through the ranges. He'd jumped over there to eat their grass – his paddock had so little.

The fire sounded like a freight train. It lit up the sky. The wind threw sparks and ash like bombs. He was trapped in that paddock. Inexperienced and unprepared, dressed in a tank top, thongs and a miniskirt, I ran to Nimbus, vaulted onto his back and tried to make him jump the fence. Fire inhaled the forest behind us. Nimbus was too spooked to listen to reason. He couldn't see the fence, couldn't understand my frantic pleas. One of my brothers came down and demanded I leave.

'We have to evacuate,' he said. 'Everyone is in the car – even the cats and the cockatoo.'

Evacuate meant going without Nimbus. It meant leaving him there in that paddock that was already starting to burn. I dismounted and ran, sobbing, smoke thick and acrid in my eyes. There would be someone – police, firefighters – who could come and save him, surely?

This horse, the greatest love of my childhood, I left him. I let myself be stuffed in the back of the old, grey Falcon and be driven away.

Our neighbour's house was already burning as we inched our way down the dirt road, through smoke so dense it was like a solid beast.

We spent the night in our car in the nearby township of Gisborne. We were given food from the supermarket shelves, even though we had no money with us.

Next morning, as the roads reopened, we drove home to a razed world. Where there had once stood houses now stood shells. Animals lay, black and bloated, in bare paddocks. A mantra had played in my head all night, over and over until it was knitted into my cells and looped around my heart. *Please give us a miracle. Please let him survive.*

We passed our neighbour's ravaged block and the crumpled mess of their home. Drove up over the rise and onto our driveway. There, grazing on a tiny patch of green, a defiant look in his eye, was my Nim – a survivor.

I tumbled out of the car and ran to him, throwing my arms

around his neck before he had time to bolt away. Mum, Dad and my brothers got out as well. They were staring up the driveway at our house; it too had survived. Later, I found out 157 houses had burned down in our area alone, and many more across the state.

Our town was patched up. Fences and houses rebuilt. It was my VCE year. I went to blue-light discos and tried getting into the local pubs underage. Nimbus and I took long meanders through a scarred and blackened land. Dad took photographs of gum trees reshooting, small blue-green tufts sprouting on charcoal trunks. Mum painted landscapes, as though she could rebuild our world with a paintbrush.

Our neighbours drew up plans for a new home.

The following year I took an accidental gap year and met a boy. I introduced him to Nimbus and they eyed each other warily. By then I'd added another horse to the family, a part quarter-horse bushfire survivor called Poppy, so all four of us headed out together on the tracks. We were plodding along beside the railway line when Nimbus shied at some hidden thing, a snake perhaps. He threw my new love off and galloped away, farting.

I married that boy and we moved to a nearby town while Nimbus stayed in Macedon. I had children and I took them to meet Nimbus, who still grazed in that cracked-clay paddock, frowning at the flies and whisking his tail impatiently. I sat my boys on Nimbus's bow back and told them that once he was fast. That once, if he did not deign to be caught, there was nothing anyone could do. Nowadays, though, I could run faster than him.

He was my first friend. My great friend. Head-shy and difficult he might have been, but there was something when we met that ignited in my heart and the flame never went out.

I was at home with my boys the day I got the call. Mum and Dad had just come home from a movie. Nimbus – old, slow and sleepy – had fallen dead in the paddock. Just like that. The vet suspected it was a heart attack. Though we never knew Nimbus's age, we worked out he was probably about thirty-five. We had been friends for twenty-four years.

We buried Nimbus at Macedon. A friend from the pub brought his digger and carved a deep hole in the paddock. Nimbus is beneath the bracken, held gently in the heavy clay arms of this dry bushland he and I had both come to call home.

Grafton's Derry Queen

Bridie Jabour

When I was fifteen, I worked as a waitress. I was atrocious. I knew nothing about the menu, I couldn't read the orders I wrote down in my notepad, I could barely carry two plates at a time and I certainly couldn't do that elegant thing waitresses do where they balance four plates on one forearm.

One night at the restaurant I worked at in Grafton there was a party of about twenty people seated at a long table. We were taking out all the mains and as I was putting a meal down in front of a man, with the other hand I accidentally tipped the sauce from the other plate I was holding into the lap of the woman sitting next to him. Later that night this woman tipped me $20. It was 2003. I was the daughter of two nurses, the oldest of the five children living at home at the time. That $20 was roughly equivalent to $650 in today's money to me.

'You're Philomena's daughter, aren't you?' she asked as she pressed the money into my hand, telling me not to put it into the 'shared tip' jar, which the owner also got takings from for some reason. As soon as she said Ma's name, I knew what was coming next. 'She delivered both of my daughters. She stayed with me until the end with both. She is an amazing woman.' I nodded, slightly bored.

In a family of minor town celebrities, my mother was Madonna. Everyone knew her, everyone loved her, everyone had a story to tell me about what she meant to them. Our family was used to her sometimes not returning from a shift as a midwife at the local hospital for more than fifteen hours, such was her devotion to women bringing their babies into the world.

Mum migrated to Australia from Derry in the north of Ireland the day before her thirtieth birthday and still has an accent so strong I sometimes have to translate for her at the bakery. She is about 5 foot 2 with jet-black curly hair, is still much prettier than any of her daughters and always has been, and has also always been absolutely terrifying in her own specific way.

If a woman was distressed, she would not leave them halfway through their labour just because there was a shift change; she would stay until the baby arrived safely. It meant that a lot of women in Grafton felt very close to her. She was the person they trusted in the most terrifying moment of their lives.

It could not be more boring for my brother and sisters and I to constantly hear this from them at the shopping centre, at Mass, at school pick-up. *Yeah, yeah, yeah, Philomena is an angel, yeah, yeah, yeah.* But I was more than happy to parlay her legendary status in the community into $20 hard cash for me when the opportunity arose.

I also worked the checkouts at Coles, and it was not uncommon for a shopper to ask if I was a Jabour, such was the significance of my nose. Well, I always assumed it was my nose. Once, an older woman looked at me as I weighed her bananas and said, 'Norma would be so proud of you' – and I started crying. Norma was my nana, who I had been very close to before she died and to hear that from one of her friends who I did not know was so meaningful.

As well as all the stories of Philomena holding women's hands, holding their legs, catching their babies, holding them as they brought their children into the world, I occasionally got a woman telling me that her daughter was also called Bridie.

I would love to see census data on the concentration of Bridies across Australia. If you made a heat map of it, I reckon there would be tiny little dots over most of it (Bridie was the second least popular baby name in 2018 in Australia) and a giant purple patch over Grafton. Mum would often tell people the names of her own children when she was delivering their babies: I don't know if the names of my siblings had much influence but there were certainly a surprising number of Bridies as a result.

When I was thirty-two, I was home in Grafton for Christmas. At the supermarket with my ma, I walked out to take something to the car and as I reached the entrance I heard Mum yell out, 'Bridie! Briiiddddiiiieeee Jabbboouuurrr!!' Face burning, I turned to face her and she pointed to a teenage girl standing two metres from her. 'Her name is Bridie too!'

A middle-aged woman standing next to Mum called out excitedly, 'Your mum delivered her!'

Teenage Bridie and 32-year-old Bridie stood, mortified, both of us a bright red and nodded to each other. 'It's a good name,' I yelled back and promptly ran away. The brute force of the embarrassment mothers can wield is an incredible phenomenon that physicists should try to measure.

My ma was not the only town celebrity in the family. Everyone also knew my grandfather, my dad's dad, who was mayor in the 1980s. One of ten children born to Lebanese migrants, he took his obligation to the community very seriously and was known around town for various deeds. I loved him immensely. In my twenties, I went to Mount Druitt in Sydney to interview some people about work being done by an Aboriginal-run organisation. A man in his eighties happened to be there and someone mentioned that he was visiting from Bundjalung. I brightened. 'I grew up on Bundjalung country,' I told him, 'in Grafton.' He had lived in Grafton for years, on and off. 'Did you know Gordon Jabour?' I asked.

He laughed.

'Did he have a shop in South Grafton?' He did.

'We used to drink at the post office hotel, and they wouldn't let blakfellas drink in the main bar, we had to sit out the back. Gordon used to always buy me red wine and bring it to me because they wouldn't serve me.' He paused. 'I think it's because he was Lebanese.' I had to turn away because I started weeping unexpectedly.

My grandfather was famous for giving chickens away for free at his shop. I heard a lot of jokes about the tabs kept by mothers of big families – they probably would've owed thousands if these were tallied. He owned some houses in South Grafton and my aunt, a nun, used to go with him to collect rent in person. My siblings and I ended up with some very random stuff as a result. One day my aunt gave us two sets of wind chimes, which at the time I thought were the coolest things I had ever seen. The top parts were crocheted – one red, the other blue. Then the chiming bits were made of different kinds of clay painted in rainbow colours. I asked my aunt where she got such amazing objects. 'Oh,' she said. 'Marlene couldn't pay rent this week because she slept in and missed the markets. So I bought these wind chimes from her.' My aunt had given her money for the wind chimes which was given straight back as rent.

One of the wind chimes hung in our kitchen for years.

*

I used to finish my waitressing job late and I would often have to go to the hospital and wait in the staff room of the maternity unit for Mum to finish her shift so we could go home together. Usually someone else could give me a lift from the restaurant to the hospital but one night nobody could, so I walked to one of the only taxi ranks in town. I got in the car and in all my teenage honesty said to the driver, 'I only have $7 in coins. Can you drive towards the hospital and stop in $7 and I will walk the rest of the way?'

The man started driving and asked me how my night was. I was tired and Grafton was not a very well-lit place: if it was dark enough it could be difficult to tell where you were even if you had lived there every year of your life. The driver was maybe in his fifties, although teenagers are not the best at guessing ages – everyone looks ancient to them. He was definitely a lot bigger than me, well over 6 foot, and broad. He was squeezed into the front seat. I would've barely been 50 kilograms at the time. He asked me questions and I responded a little gruffly as I leaned against the window, eyes drooping, tired after six or so hours on my feet at the end of a school day. And then the car stopped.

I looked out the window and saw that we were in front of the maternity ward. He had known exactly where I needed to be taken. The meter had not been turned on.

I tried to give him my $7 of change but he wouldn't take it. 'Do you think I would let you walk at 11.30 p.m. at night?' he asked, shaking his head. 'You're one of Philomena's aren't you?' I nodded and thanked him. 'She delivered my children,' he told me as I got out of the car.

The taxi driver's kindness was not particularly exceptional. I was used to strangers looking after me in a town where it felt like everyone knew my name. When I told Mum, she berated me for even thinking about walking at night to the hospital.

This is what it was like growing up in a country town. The fabric of the community was so strong – for me, at least. There were bad parts, for sure: there are always bad bits. Even worse, there were incredibly boring bits. But overwhelmingly, it was good people, doing their best, looking after each other.

When I had my first child, in Sydney, at the end of an extremely difficult fiftteen-hour labour, I finally understood what my mother meant to all those women in Grafton. I will carry my midwife forever in my heart, a supremely special woman, without whom I might have had a much more difficult birth. I will probably never see her again. The difference in a country town is you get to see someone like that every few weeks, randomly. And tell them 'Thank you! thank you! thank you!' – for as long as you want. You can even tell their uninterested kids how incredible they are.

When I look back on growing up like that, it is easy to imbue it with a happiness that was not really there. I *was* happy, but I also thought I was going to lose my mind with boredom. I felt on the edge of a big, wide world that I could not wait to step into. In the meantime, I was stuck with people who did not understand me or my sophisticated outlook (an outlook that went only as far as cities = glamorous, Grafton = not). I grew up in a place where people could guess my name from looking at my face, where I was always put in the context of my mother, my father, my grandparents, my uncles, my aunts, my cousins, my brother, my sisters – and even on occasion my dog. I grew up in a place where I never knew how the person watching might know me. Growing up like that can make you crave anonymity like nicotine, but it also gives you a sense of self within a community. It's a good way to learn you are not the most important person in your life, and sometimes you are not even an important person. It teaches you to look out for other people and that community is important. It's important to care about other people, not just yourself and be able to place yourself in something that is bigger than you. I actually think it is the rock my astonishing (believe me, it is astonishing) self-confidence is built on. If you never think you're the centre of the universe, then you never have that notion ripped away from you.

Being part of a proper community means you can score $20 even if you are a shitty waitress.

$Q\&A$

Tony Armstrong

ABC News Breakfast *sports presenter and former AFL footballer Tony Armstrong, interviewed by Rick Morton.*

Q: You moved to a country town called Brocklesby when you were still in primary school. It had a population of about 200 people, which is a bit of a change from Western Sydney where you were before that.

A: Yes, Western Sydney was, and still is, a bit hectic. I loved it. I had the best time ever. But it's such a different pace. I went from a school of 1400 kids to a school of twenty-five. It was culture shock. I went to Year 6 in Brocklesby as one of three in the class. There were two teachers. My mum taught in the junior room.

Q: Thank God for that.

A: Right? I was in the senior year. As if the only child of a single mum didn't have Stockholm syndrome already. You leave home to get taught by your mum [Margaret Armstrong] and go home to get told off by your mum. When I was at primary school, we lived at the teacher's house. I would literally step over the back fence and be in school.

Q: And then your mum had to drive you to the bus stop when you were in high school.

A: Yes, it was a half-hour bus into Albury to go to high school. I loved it. You'd be up at sparrow's fart getting ready, Mum would get you out the door, drive you 10 kilometres over to the nearest town and you're standing there at this country bus stop in this town of 250 people called Burrumbuttock. You've got a couple of kids from your school, a couple of kids from the other high schools in town, and everyone is just messing around, kicking the footy to each other or whatever. And then the bus arrives. And the thing about the hierarchy in the country buses, I found, was that part of being cool was how far you had to travel on that bus.

Q: That's amazing. I love these equations.

A: So the two factors were 'are you cool' but also 'how far is your trip'. So, clearly, the kids who were already on the bus when we got there, which was the next town out at Walbundrie, they were really, really cool from a distance travelled point of view. They weren't the coolest kids traditionally, but in this country matrix they ended up being sort of three-quarters towards the coolest kids.

Q: It sounds kind of like a congestion tax. If you were to get on after some of those kids but you were objectively cooler, did you get to kick them out of their seats?

A: Yeah. But then basically because everyone is on these buses all the time – the same bus, every day, there and back – your seat never got taken if you were at a certain apex of coolness. I was always two from the back on the left-hand side of the bus and I always used to sit on my schoolbag with my feet on the seat next to me, so I was the same height as the backseat but not *on* the back seat. I used to like ripping yarns; it felt like I was holding court. It was almost like a lectern. The people on the backseat became like those on the bleachers.

Q: Almost like a proscenium arch theatre.

A: Exactly. But yeah, it was so funny. Everyone used to give each other shit but then we'd all play footy against each other on weekends.

Q: Did you have enemies on the bus?

A: I was someone who always tried to get people on side. Mainly because I couldn't fight my way out of a wet paper bag. And I realised it was way easier winning people over with gags and being nice than being adversarial. But it was always good to have the super-adversarial, farm-strong kids on your side.

Q: The Praetorian Guard of farm kids.

A: Like, this guy could lift eight bales of hay. He could throw you *over* a bus. You reckon Finchy is strong chuckin' a pair of shoes over a pub – this bloke will throw you over a double-decker bus!

Q: How old were you around this time?

A: From about twelve until I was fifteen, and then I went to boarding school.

Q: And you mentioned playing the other kids on the weekends. What did football look like for you there?

A: I used to play football 'in town' because we used to drive from Brocklesby into Albury, where I played on a Saturday morning, and then we would drive back out and run the boundary for the reserves in the local team. I'd get my ten bucks and then I would play senior footy. Where has all this energy gone? I get winded taking the bins out now.

Q: I get winded walking up my stairs. How good is local sport though?

A: What I loved about it is the sense of collegiality between the whole town. The whole town would turn out to local footy. Ten bucks on the gate. We had a community pub that was only open on the weekend when everyone would come into town and go to the footy. It was super-gendered roles back then. Ladies worked in the canteen, men ran the bar. The ladies would make all the spreads and that would all get sold and go back into the footy or cricket club, depending on what sport was being played. I was probably too young to understand why that was fundamentally problematic. I just thought 'this is great'. It's super nostalgic for me. It was a time of no stress. Your mum was stressing about you because you were being a little dickhead, but you were just being carefree riding your Mongoose [bike] from the footy club down the park, dinking someone.

Q: Dinking someone?

A: You know, dinking someone, you've got someone on the front of the bike sitting on the handlebars.

Q: I thought you meant like Double Income No Kids or something!

A: [*Laughs*] Yeah, we were really worried about our segments back then.

Q: What was the name of the footy club?

A: It was the Brocklesby Roos, and the town next to us was the Burrumbuttock Swans. Then the two clubs ended up merging because they were both so small.

Q: Were they deeply unhappy about it?

A: Oh, they were fierce, fierce rivals. It's so funny. And they couldn't decide which town's name would go first. The most famous footballer to come out of there was number two draft pick Justin Koschitzke. He played 200 games for the St Kilda Football Club, and the way they decided was that when he came back up one year, everyone went down to the footy club and he flipped a coin. And so now it's the Brockburrum Saints. Country towns are gold.

Q: They really are great names aren't they. Burrumbuttock is phenomenal.

A: There are three small towns east to west, all of them about 15 kilometres away from each other. Burrumbuttock, then Brocklesby and then the last one is affectionately known as testicle valley. Because the name of that town is Balldale. How good is that?

Q: That is amazing. But nothing affectionate for Burrumbuttock?

A: Nah. We'd probably just call it the arse-end of the world. Honestly, I've just made that up.

Q: You didn't have a licence at this point. What did you do for fun?

A: I went to Murray High in Lavington, which is a suburb of Albury, for a few years and I had no friends after school because everyone was on the farms. So I literally had to get on my pushie and ride my bike 10 kilometres to go and hang out with someone. What a loser!

Q: The pushbike is everything in small towns isn't it?

A: I used to build bike jumps. I got fully into BMX. I was a bit of a nutter and I would just go for it. Thinking 'oh yeah, I can make that gap'. Like, Dave Mira couldn't make that gap, Tony. You're twelve. I made this one jump and, you know how next to some country roads they have the fallaway part, almost like the drainage part? Perfect kind of jump, right? I spent a whole weekend building a jump to get from one side of the main road to the other.

Q: [*Laughter*]

A: How dumb is that. And on the other side of the road, it was the same thing, it was the perfect landing. So I was building up to it and then I was like 'I'm going for it' but I tried to jump so hard I pancaked myself on the road. And as I've done it, I've heard someone go [*car horn noise*] and this car has had to swerve to miss me. I wasn't even watching the road. I was so unused to traffic. Like, I could have had dinner and sweets on that road and a car wouldn't go past. So I wasn't looking left or right. And I'd stacked it so hard, one half of me looked like Two Face because of the gravel and then they [the driver] got out and dressed me down. They didn't ask me if I was alright. They just said: 'You're a fuckin' idiot, Armstrong.' Because it was one of the local guys from the footy club. He dressed me down and went to drive off before going 'Nah you're actually hurt'. He took me to Mum who said, 'Tony, you're a fuckin' idiot.'

Q: I love this about country towns. Everything you do is known to everyone else. No secrets.

A: If I had any secrets worth keeping, they would have come out. Some of these stories, when you talk to people in the city about them, they don't get it. They don't understand how big some of those little things can be in the country.

Backstage

Laura Jean McKay

Why not ask? Why not? I balance on pedals hung over the wind. Why not? I am hung like fear. Rain singing down like nothing hurts and that sky, the height of the wind weighing down. My trumpet ears. The lane ahead a rocky hall spindling off through the paddocks. Many more turns of the pedal before I get there. On the side of the road the old drive-in's white metal boxes like soldier's graves – but markers for music, for words and pale dresses. I am flat shoed, school skirted, old biked. My knees purple and arced like the road. Move. If I don't I'll fall.

A dark time to be alone and why not? Why not ask her? Perhaps if I tell her I've changed. I have changed on this road. I was far and now I am near. Weaving from gravel to grass just to get to where it is quiet. It's quiet. I heard a cow cough here once. In the paddock at the lane's entrance. It was polite, a respectful sound. Nothing like our horses – all hoof and bone. Between the potholes is a cream-coloured dirt. If I ask she will say no and worry: will parents be there? But I can ride, I can ride all the way from the school, up the Princes Highway and past the pocked paddocks to the lane. I am thirteen soon. A panting at my heels. Move fast, faster along the dirt. A voice breaks from the house next door: *Rollinsgetin'eryafrigginmongral.* Our dog killed her chickens last year. She was nice and shrugged about it. We live on a farm. It is thirty-seven and a half acres.

Our horses canter about in this weather. They kick and splinter, their heads a fire of hair and bile. The line of trees on the drive bend as the sun comes out over them – suddenly hot, suddenly busting – branched out at right angles, I cycle past. The wind sings around the edges of the house and through the empty driveway and the sun disappears as though never there. I hate my bike. I kick it and nothing breaks. My bag eats through the cotton of my shirt and into my back. The sides of the house are pink dirt stained, creeping up. In summer, fat redbacks line the concrete block it sits on. I need to pee. There are no boots at the door but a key under the mat. Safe place. My shoes are caved and tortured from being scuffed away from my feet at the muddy doorstep. Inside, the floor is vinyl dressed as slate. Mum says, why have carpet? I slide along it in socks sometimes. I notice that the big grandfather clock in the hallway is gone.

Even when everything is there the lounge room has an emptiness to it that begins mid-morning and stretches long through the day. So that by now it is almost lonely there. Mumbling to itself. Even when the chairs and tables are tucked into each other in their right spots, cushions arranged, dog-bitten recliners upright, there is an echo to footfalls. A hollowness to laughter. Mum and The Farmer painted the walls peach and passionfruit and lemon meringue. The windows at the top are supposed to bend the sun into the corners. The cats chase it and lay on the sills. Today, though, it is dull. The walls dank like rotting fruit. A dry room in a windy place. All I want is a white wall now and some heat. To warm the stolen noises. Something important is gone. What is it? The small clock ticks frantically on the wall – trying to fill the void with seconds bigger than its hands. What is it? There! I know: it's the photographs from the wall. The trophies from the glass cabinet. A plate with dogs playing cards. Videos. A vase. They are gone and other things moved sideways in their place. The chaise longue (embroidered chocolate with wooden legs) gone too. In place of The Farmer's recliner: a newly swept piece of floor. Someone there for the first time mightn't notice that these things are missing. They might glance out the window to the tank – the ivy knotted up its side. They might notice that the sheets and towels on the line are bore-water pink.

They might glare or stare at the walls and the room around them would harden. Settling new skin.

I am stopped in the door. I am both feet stood apart, turned slightly in. Fawn socked. Our cat watches – hunched on a chair back. My brother said that at share houses in the city they steal each other's beds and couches and pile them all up in a cupboard somewhere. So that people come back to their rooms and an emptiness. A lack of things. For a joke and a fun and games. Maybe that's what happened here? The Farmer got bored halfway? I am peddling fast. Running on. A wind in my face in this quiet room.

Mum and The Farmer got tin for the roof so we could hear the rain. Now, when it comes, it is a roaring. A racing down the sides. When you get closer and the wind is strong a prickling starts. From hairline to hairline. A can't-wait-to-be-there pain. Above the door the roof caves in creative angles that speak of light and things that have been done here. In the family room where the chops are served. Where the dog begs and the TV squalors. Dare move in? The games we played with the cracks in the floor – step on them and you love Rodney Jones! Step on them and it's real. I've taken a photo in here: The Farmer sleeping with his legs stretched out and his double-chin snores. I've been told in this room that the missing cat was found behind the shed, poisoned and stiff.

I lift my bag and it peels away. The floor from here to the kitchen is wide and long. The cat whispers past my feet. Outside the drumming stops. My damp socks squeal on the vinyl and bits of dirt and hair coat them – the things that are picked up in this cool light. Weightless. I am wheeling about to the curtains. Touch the top and down again. A bubble of excitement bursts and falls flatly in my gut. In primary school The Farmer would pack my lunch and leave it on the kitchen bench in a brown paper bag with a joke or cartoon drawings – grey lead on the top: *What did the one-legged donkey say? Threeee-mooore, threeee-mooore.* My friends would read and laugh. I would hate and love them. Now, in that same place, three letters. One for Mum. One for me. One for the house. It needs one too. A cloud outside breaks and sputters clumps of rain at the big windows. The drops slide down knowingly as I open my letter and find two small thin sheets – the kind that are sent overseas. I do feel a long way away.

What is there to recall? Something about where fault lies. A quake and a tremor. The paper fragile in my hand but thick, also, with meaning. Like church wafer. Like hair or skin. The blades of the Sacred Grass at our school. Between classes, walking to and from, you're not allowed to touch it. If Mr Smith sees you on it out of lunchtime you are warned. Your name is written down. But the seniors stroll across it, school colours like nooses dangling from their necks. They call, *Hi Mr Smith, big weekend?* And he laughs, says, *I've got your number, McGraff!* We will do that too. Our socks huge. Lank hair against our cheeks. Bums moving big under cotton dresses and we'll call and laugh on the grass there. One day we will know the sacred things, like this and that and they do.

Here, holding papyrus and on it is neat, slanted blue pen. This wasn't written this morning but thousands ago. Millions. Before the grey road, before the lane. Before the market gardens that have left crockery and Chinese coins scattered throughout the horse yards. Before the Brayakaulung stories, which I've never heard. I have found part of a gun that was younger than this. Some letter! *One day*, it says, *I hope we can sit down and talk about this.* That day has come now. More blustery, perhaps. Colder than expected for this time of year. My nanna will be at the window with her arms wrapped around her sides, watching the cloud rise over the ocean. I can't see the mountains, they are hidden by the pale. It has settled everywhere, over my dress and elbows. A white that conceals the bench and the two letters left there. The geraniums growing by the window shine only a vague green through it. My feet gone, I am only a nose above. We have driven through this fog to perform in the Amateur Maffra Theatre Society's production of *Annie* – I was Annie. Put the beams on high and let other cars pass like ships. A lonely sort of a feeling. The wig spiralling plastic to my neck. It is hard to remember how the day is supposed to go. Television? Milk? Cereal or bread? Another song. Annie smiles, flings her little arms. To the cold. To the other orphans curled in the home. Maybe. Again and again, like a spell. She also says, tomorrow. Tomorrow is only a day away. I was the one who could act, they said, the other Annie could sing. We took turns making the audience cringe in the hall. The red dresses. All that dancing with fake, rich men. Mum in four parts: a beggar, a lady, a flower-woman, a maid. Scene to scene.

Late last night in the gloom they fought. Up the corridor I cried in my bed. There was indignation snaked up the walls. A banging of doors. I made it loud, let them know I was angry, and why not? Why not be loud too? The Farmer peeked around the door in a red dressing-gown and told me to be brave. The room lit by the hallway. A house too big for the small hateful words, slithering room to room. These things must happen. They change. Mum, a shadow in the background, those emerald, stinging eyes, *No, don't be brave, I'll be here. For you.* A green dream. A who-do-you-know-best? The Farmer and his dressing-gown cord slunk away. We stared after him. Held hands. Boys! Who knows about them?

He never played music so the records are still there. Just had a huge silver radio always on the crackle, usually horseraces, politics, the news. If I looked to where it was plugged in in the shed would it have vanished? The saddles and the linseed oil and the straps and bridles too? The horseshoes hung frowning, tipping their luck to the floor? He couldn't take the wind away, though. The feel of chaff mixed with molasses. That strange smell of winter coming, even when the days are still warm and snake rumoured. I find myself wringing my hands and realise that this is what older people do. Some ancient me in a time far from mine – not school uniformed, school haired, wringing. Living in backwaters. Wrinkled hands twisting the family name, dramas far worse than mine. Pacing too. I am like a foal newly dropped from beneath its mother's tail, shaky leg and tongued, scorching for milk. Outside the stallion carves dints into the fence with his hoof. His doodle flops grey, almost to the ground. He raises his lips and shows his teeth to the mares, paddocks away, who swing their tails towards him. Only Sunrise is missing – last year she came in first. By a nose. We have watched her since then, how she moves and is special. The only winner on a flailing farm.

Two dinted horse trucks usually out there. Only one now and it lies crooked. Without the car it is lame. Limp in the long grass. A window at the front so that you can see the horses watching you through the screen. How they hoof the ramp and the car jolts and sways. When you stop they are shiny with snot. Once I saddled Sunrise and she took off. Wilding through the trees – pines flicking past like gunshots. The Farmer's laugh far behind me. I leant down low so she would go faster. Terrified but knowing. That horse. Her wide rump. Her ears braced orange and backward. When she stopped she was crazy with the smells. But the only scent was her. Mid-winter The Farmer would pick me up from school – the truck huge and flamingo with horse poo or mud-smattered sides – he thought it funny to blow the horn. So did the Tech kids. They know my mum; they swagger in her library and out on the street. They say *Sucked in* and don't know how to ride. To always put your hand on a horse's rump when you walk behind. To let her smell your hand.

But I have a question. Some questions about all this. Dusty and unsettled like the stables, the pock-marked paddocks to the side. Damply folded, a letter, a prized envelope. A kitchen tipped so the luck runs out. What a step-farmer says in a room with a pen. How to fit it all onto the two small sheets? Was there a title? An end? A middle and a start. What to say? How to put it? The night before I kept open my sore eyes and listened to the silence left by the fighting. An uneasy space. The light from the kitchen that spilled onto the dirt. That light making squiggles and darts of my curtains. Letter light. Light that stayed on until after three or four. Perhaps he wrote drafts. *I am going but will be back ... If you don't understand now you'll never ... One day I hope we can sit down and talk about this* … It was coming. The Farmer bought me a watch with a moon and a sun that spin to show whether it is night or day. Engraved. I flick my arm. It is still day.

A car door slams outside and I am nervous. How will I tell her? Or maybe the house will. Maybe that last envelope has all the instructions for what to do. Paint the walls a colour you can't eat. Rearrange the chairs. Turn the clocks back to another time other than quarter past four. Plant strawberries in the manure. Boil coffee. Get that smell of horses out. Change your clothes. Move away. I arrange myself on the cream-coloured chair. It is warm. From The Farmer? Did I pass him on my bike with his trailer full of chaise lounge and horse? Head down, chaffing against the wind? Is it him outside? Rushing home, embarrassed. Those letters on the bench, a joke, a week-too-late April Fools'. Silly, nasty, didn't mean a thing. *Did ya laugh? Did ya get it?* My heart jumps, flattens. I still have the note. It is folded in the envelope with the frayed edge. Footsteps crunch on the wet gravel outside. I have never looked so staged.

The Country Club

Lech Blaine

One of my earliest memories is watching my mum scrub blood from the beer-soaked carpet in the front bar of The Country Club Hotel. I was four, and it must've been a Sunday morning, because every other day we paid a cleaner.

'Blood?' I asked.

'No, honey,' said Mum. 'It's ... raspberry cordial.'

'Yum!' I said, lurching close enough to touch.

'Don't!' she said.

'Why?' I asked.

'The raspberries were ... poisonous. That's why they spat it out.'

Mum spent many Sundays scrubbing forbidden fruit from the floors of the run-down pub. My father had secured the three-year-lease for a song. So we shifted from tiny Wondai to the metropolis of Toowoomba.

Leading up to the new millennium, Toowoomba replaced Adelaide as the murder capital of Australia. In 1997, the wife of a Jehovah's Witness minister was found floating by a fisherman in Lake Perseverance. That same week, there was a stabbing in the Mort Estate, directly opposite my kindergarten. A woman was slashed to death inside her flat at a boarding house. The murderer claimed that Satan made him do it.

I was oblivious to all of this. At the pub, Dad counted the takings from the pokies, while my brothers blasted the beer lines with bleach. It was a badge of honour to switch on a neon sign beside the cigarette machine that proclaimed: *LIFE'S A BEACH – WATCH OUT FOR THE CRABS.*

'Many hands make like light work,' said my mother.

'But too many cocks spoil the broth,' said my father.

The most popular option on the jukebox was 'Duncan' by Slim Dusty, closely followed with 'Rock Lobster' by the B-52's. This was a different kind of 'Country Club' to the ones in Hollywood movies. Ours was Toowoomba's roughest pub, amid some legitimate shitholes. A guy got 'glassed' before anyone called it that. The glasser called it self-defence. The wounded came back the next day for Happy Hour with blue stitches in the skin around his bloodshot eyes and a sheepish shrug of the shoulders.

'It's all fun and games 'til the dumb pricks get on the drugs,' said Dad.

Later, politicians tried to pacify such violence with the 'One Punch Can Kill' campaign, as if this was a disincentive to those Darwinian degenerates. Where I come from, a punch that couldn't potentially kill someone was called a slap.

*

Nate – short for Nathan – was my first best mate. His mother, Rhonda, was a cleaner who moonlighted as a barmaid. She was seventeen when Nate was born, and seemed impossibly young compared to my mum, who was thirty-eight when I arrived. Nate and I slid under the tarpaulin factory beside the railway line and deposited rocks into shopping bags like they were nuggets of gold. We cleaned them with Coca-Cola stolen from the bottle-o.

'You're my best friend,' said Nate, apropos of a successful expedition.

'We're best *mates*,' I said, correcting him. 'Friends are for girls.'

Nate was short and thin with black hair, pale skin and a smattering of freckles. I was short and fat with black hair and hazel-green eyes. Nate was shy with permanently terrified blue eyes. Whenever he got too fretful, I sang an ode to our mateship, which drew hysterics.

'I'd love to have a beer with Nate,' I sang, 'cos Nate is me mate!'

We went to a local public primary school and played rugby league for the Lions, two places where white kids like us were in the minority. Neither Nate nor I were good enough to sever our allegiance to each other. One time, the coach shared around some raspberry cordial before a game.

'Don't drink it,' I whispered to Nate. 'It'll kill you.'

'Says who?' he asked.

'Says my mum,' I said.

Nate's eyes were frightened, like always. We both tipped out the cordial and water from the white styrofoam cups when the coach wasn't looking.

'Nobody got sick,' said Nate after the game.

'Not yet,' I said.

*

Besides my siblings' social worker, the only white-collar regular at The Country Club was a real estate agent named Richard Breeze. Dad secretly nicknamed him 'Dick Cheese'. He drove a maroon Volvo over the railway tracks dividing Toowoomba between the haves and have-nots. Dick Cheese had black cowboy boots and shades that he wore indoors like a pro poker player. Nobody knew he had a different pair of sunglasses for the City Gold Club, or that the blonde pocket rocket rubbing Dick's thigh wasn't his wife.

This was the man who twisted my father's working-class arms into becoming a belated property investor at the age of forty-eight. My mother believed that anyone who owned someone else's home invited bankruptcy.

'Negative gearing!' my father begged, a password to the middle class.

My father was a recovering gambling addict. Now, thanks to Dick, he learnt that the government would gift him a tax deduction for betting with the bank's money on horses made of bricks and mortar. Or fibro and asbestos, in the case of the four fixer-uppers he quickly snapped up. It was just before John Howard halved the tax for capital gains from property and made mugs like my father look like economic Nostradamus's.

Rhonda rented one of those fibro shacks for $120 a week. My mateship with Nate was on borrowed time from that moment. He must've noticed me regarding the sandpit in his backyard with a possessive pleasure.

The new power imbalance in our kinship remained inadmissible until Nate's ninth birthday party. I can't remember the theme, although I've got an old photo of me wearing a red tinsel wig and Oakley sunglasses. It was all fun and games until Nate hit me with a high tackle in backyard footy.

'You're a grub!' I said.

'Whatever, fatty,' said Nate.

I listened to the laughter of the other boys. Then I looked between Nate's unapologetic smirk and my parent's proximate investment property.

'This is my house!' I said.

'No, it's not,' said Nate unconvincingly, pale cheeks reddening.

We had to be separated, and I left without a party bag. I was accepted into St Mary's College for Grade Five, and subsequently signed up to play for Brothers, the Catholic rugby league team. Nate and I disappeared from each other's lives like tomato sauce from a tablecloth in a bucket of bleach.

*

Murder was part of the furniture on the Darling Downs, like drought and Christianity. On Christmas Eve 2001, a man was struck twice in the head with a tomahawk at a public toilet just off the highway in Helidon. The victim's head was placed inside the boot of a blue Subaru. His mother and brother were shot when they stumbled upon the scene.

In May 2002, the torso of a heroin dealer was found floating in Helidon Creek. His head and hands were located in the boot of a car up the range. Two brothers were arrested for the dismemberment. One of them had gone to school with my brother Steven.

That same year, a regular customer at my parents' corner store was found one block away. She was naked and strangled. The proximate homicides were accompanied by a glut of drug busts in the Mort Estate. One night, used syringes were scattered on the footpath outside the shop. Dad railed against the littering junkies on the front page of the local newspaper.

'Drugs are bloody un-Australian!' he said.

Those who could afford it fled, including my upwardly mobile parents. They bought a brick home with a security system in aspirational Glenvale using the growing disposable income from their property portfolio. Drug dealers didn't live on cul-de-sacs, or so it seemed to us.

On one side was a vacant block of land Dad plotted to buy and fill with an in-ground swimming pool. On the other side was a house owned by an ageing boxing trainer named Buddy, a doppelganger for Elvis Presley. He survived an axe attack as a teenager, and was notorious for breaking people's faces during his heyday as a municipal standover man in the 1980s.

A decorated boxer named Troy occasionally sparred in Buddy's garage. Troy was the younger brother of a jockey. In 2002, Troy spent eight months in prison for breaking a man's jaw in a street fight. The warden called him 'a calming influence'. And now he soothed me. Occasionally, we passed a footy across the cul-de-sac. I'd never felt safer than while rubbing shoulders with members of a suburban fight club.

Once I hit high school, Buddy kept badgering me in his taciturn way to come over for training sessions. He told a story about how his son 'wouldn't hurt a fly', but that boxing saved him from getting 'his ass handed to him' by an older bully at a high school social.

'You need to know how to swing your fists,' he said. 'Or the universe will make you look silly.'

I lasted three sessions before blaming shin splints for my lack of attendance. Buddy gave up chasing me. Meanwhile, Troy won the world title.

*

Toowoomba suffered from split personalities. There was a tectonic discrepancy between the serene landscape and the rages of the citizenry. In 2005, two boys – aged sixteen and seventeen – went on a murder spree at a flat on the northside. They tortured three of their mates to death and raped a sixteen-year-old girl while her baby slept in the next room. Police laid spike strips across the Warrego Highway to derail their getaway van at two a.m.

The civilised conservatism of an R.M. Williams wearing upper crust turned into something much bloodier the further you ventured into the surrounding country towns. Christian fundamentalism and white supremacy festered. In 2007, a teenage boy named Anthony was recruited to the KKK by his high-school guidance counsellor, an Evangelical minister named Graeme. The KKK had been letterboxing the Garden City with anti-Sudanese pamphlets. Graeme – the Imperial Kluk – was the father of my classmate. A crucifix and suitcase didn't win Graeme's son any popularity contests.

Now, Graeme gave Anthony a laptop. Anthony's brother Robert found Ku Klux Klan material on the laptop and threatened to dob on him. On the family farm, Anthony approached Robert from behind and shot his brother twice in the head with a heavy-calibre rifle. Then he immediately called his guidance counsellor. Graeme helped his protégé dispose of the corpse under a bridge. The shooter gave his guru the bullet casing as a souvenir.

I grew desensitised to the regular demonstrations of bored and angry men with deadly intentions. The dark heart of the Darling Downs wasn't as far away as I liked to imagine. It was frequently close enough to touch.

*

The last time I saw Nate was on New Year's Eve in 2008. It was the end of Grade Eleven. My parents had separated a year earlier, and I was given free rein to do as I pleased on the weekends. A St Joseph's boy hosted an open house party on his farm just past Withcott, a little town at the bottom of the Great Dividing Range with a reputation for cleanliness. Besides organised sport, those egalitarian bush doofs were the only time private-school kids mixed with public ones. Six hundred teenagers showed up.

I bumped into Nate at the invisible ringside for the main fight of the night. Two boxers from Buddy's gym punched the blood from each other's orifices over a mutual ex-girlfriend. Years later, one ended up going to jail for king-hitting someone; the other for dealing drugs.

'Hey, bra,' said Nate afterwards. 'That was sick.'

'Fuckin' oath, bro,' I said. 'Happy New Year's.'

Police were beaten to the scene by the news crews. They shot footage of the ageless adolescent rage. The coppers evicted everyone onto dirt roads just after midnight. My mate Big Red and I walked half-an-hour from the farm to the Warrego Highway. Taxi drivers were occupied by nightclub patrons. Our parents – rich or poor – were equally oblivious. What seemed like a million blistering teenagers began an uphill pilgrimage from Withcott to Toowoomba.

A mate of Nate's threw a star picket at us like it was a spear. Red's pop had played prop for the Australian Wallabies, and was famous for knocking out a rival farmer who attacked him with a tomahawk. His flame-haired grandson was 185 centimetres tall and weighed 110 kilograms, so I had no fear about fighting. But Red had a rugby scholarship at Brisbane Grammar to protect. We hailed down a lift from a Hilux.

'Drive,' Red shouted at the startled motorist, as the rear view darkened with shadows rushing towards the dual cab ute. 'All those guys are on ice.'

The middle-aged bloke was on the way back from watching fireworks in the Big Smoke. He was recently divorced and bursting with free advice about life and love.

'Stay young,' he said. 'Growing up is for mugs.'

*

Two New Years passed. I moved to Brisbane for university. Buddy died of throat cancer. His family put the house up for rent. Whenever I came home for visits, I watched a constant stream of visitors to the new neighbours. The boxing gym had been replaced by a suburban meth lab. I didn't find out until later that Wayne – the father of the family – had once been charged with taking his mother-in-law hostage and injecting her with meth.

At the time, police paid little attention to my mother's complaints about the constant domestics next door, or the suspicious thoroughfare of traffic. They were wiretapping Wayne's phones as part of 'Operation Ice Winnebago'. He was a protected species until the bust finally happened.

Rhonda and Nate were evicted from their rental. My father sold his investment properties and leased a three-star motel in Bundaberg. He negotiated a sweetheart deal after the landlord got viciously assaulted by drug dealers. Bundy was possibly the only place in the Sunshine State with a worse ice epidemic than the Darling Downs.

Dad slept with the bedroom door open and kept an English Willow cricket bat beside his pillow. He nicknamed himself 'The Nightwatchman'.

'One of these junkies will kill me before diabetes does,' he said.

He was being a bit optimistic. In the first week of spring 2011, my father suffered a catastrophic aneurysm. I caught the Sundowner from Roma Street Station. The main street smelled like cigarettes and KFC.

'I'm so sorry for your loss,' said the sex worker renting one of the honeymoon suites. Her king bed had mirrors on the ceiling and lace curtains draped from the awnings. She handed me two crisp $50 notes and a bag of cherry tomatoes donated by a local fruit farmer. 'You come and see me for free.'

'Cheers,' I said. 'But I'll be right.'

The funeral was at the main rugby league stadium in Toowoomba. Dad timed his extinction to overlap with the Carnival of Flowers. Jacarandas shat their daks over the brick walls surrounding the football field. Hundreds of mourners came from across the state to pay farewell. At least a quarter of the crowd were heartbroken bar flies and employees from Dad's various dives.

My eulogy received a standing ovation. Afterwards, I kept shaking hands and saying, 'It is what it is.' I was lying. *It* was so much more than this.

I wasn't expecting to see Rhonda, the mother of my ex-mate Nate. She hovered wanly behind more confident mourners until I had a brief availability. 'I'm so sorry, bud,' she said, hugging me.

*

Rhonda didn't come to the wake. It was at The Country Club Hotel. Too much time between drinks. Too many happy memories to get drunk and sullen about. A former NRL star had bought and renovated the run-down pub, seeking to rehabilitate its seedy reputation. That scintillating spring day, a congregation of my father's most repugnant customers descended to drink for free at the gentrified establishment.

'I'd love to have a beer with Tommy,' they kept singing, 'cos Tommy is me mate! We drink in moderation. And we never ever ever got rollin' drunk ...'

One of the wake-goers was Rick, a plasterer with a dark side. He was a heavily tattooed gym junkie with a high-pitched voice. Rick became a bar fly and Keno enthusiast at my father's last tavern after he got banned from the CBD for fracturing another man's skull in a nightclub fight.

'All these cowards keep dying on me,' he said.

This wasn't a place for small talk. Rick regaled me with a graphic description of grief. He was best mates with Troy – the boxer – and Troy's jockey brother. Roughly a year earlier, the jockey – blood awash with vodka – overdosed on a fatal cocktail of ice and ecstasy. Rick had been at that last bender. Troy subsequently became addicted to ice himself. Rick got the jockey's name tattooed across his chest, like a password to the hereafter.

'I could've saved him if I wasn't so fucked up,' said Rick.

My father's wake was a fast-acting solvent for nostalgia. And not just because the new publican had rendered the brick facade and tiled over the carpet. Everyone was either breaking up or breaking down, whether they escaped the Mort Estate or not. Some of us were just better at faking being okay, or more capable of paying for painkillers that didn't promote psychosis.

Rick took my phone and entered his mobile number.

'If anyone ever messes with you,' he said, 'I'll fucking shoot them.'

I grinned and stirred the lime in my rum and dry to pass the time. Rick's eyes flashed with an elated rage. I was dealing with someone on a different kind of drug to the one I snorted in the disabled toilets of Brisbane pubs. Rick grabbed the brimming drink and splashed it across my face.

'Don't laugh, cocksucker,' he said. 'Or I'll punch the piss out of ya.'

My nuts jumped into the stomach region. No one nearby blinked an eyelid at the casual intimidation. The wide-eyed tyrant shrieked like a hyena.

'You'd go to water in a blue, wouldn't ya?' he giggled. 'Don't worry, brother. I wouldn't waste my fists on a skinny piece of pelican shit like you.'

Someone put on 'Rock Lobster' for old time's sake. Rick got a fresh round of rums and generously added it to the tab funded by my father's estate. I grinned with a brittle insincerity. It was hard not to see all these laughing clowns from my youth as masking sociopaths and basket cases.

My brother John moved to Bundaberg to run the motel. A gang of junkies armed with knives held up the office while his partner was working. Screams alerted my hypervigilant brother to the disturbance. John – a 120-kilogram front rower – mowed down one of the muggers on Bourbong Street and delivered a textbook cover tackle, followed by a flurry of punches.

Retirees cheered from the verandahs of their Queenslanders. The police blamed the assailant's broken nose on the footpath. The vigilante small businessman became a local hero. Drug dealers kept renting motel rooms, but there were no more muggings, and they only attacked each other.

'Sometimes you need to take matters into your own hands,' said John.

I was backpacking indefinitely through Europe, America and Asia, where I cultivated the careless air of a person escaping their fate. Toowoomba and Bundaberg were places to flee from, not seek comfort.

I arrived back in Toowoomba November 2012. That month, a teenager named Max murdered his best mate. Max went to the same high school as Nate. His single mum had been the social worker for my foster siblings. They lived two blocks away from us in Glenvale. We used to visit for afternoon tea. Mum pleaded unsuccessfully for me to play Xbox with her friend's socially awkward son.

The murderer and victim met on Facebook. Max arranged the execution with an accomplice over text messages. Then, while the trio were playing Xbox, Max stabbed the target 102 times with a carving knife. He was sentenced to life in prison. Mum stopped receiving visits from the social worker.

'But he was such a nice boy,' she said.

I rushed back to Brisbane and culled anyone too Toowoomba from my Facebook profile, which included Nate and Rick.

The following year, my mother was diagnosed with a terminal brain disease. I moved back to organise a nursing home placement and sell the house in Glenvale. My father wasn't alive to complete DIY renovations. John suggested that I get Rick to do the replastering in the bathrooms and the laundry.

'The guy who threatened to bash me?' I asked.

My brother explained that Rick nursed a general grudge towards the universe following the overdose of his best mate, and a specific grudge towards the police. He made a heap of money in the drug-trafficking trade but couldn't do anything with it because the cops were watching so closely.

'You're not really selling him,' I said.

'You're after a plasterer, not a babysitter,' said John. 'And knowing Rick, he'll probably do it for nothing. The bloke's heart is in the right place.'

Rick drove over in a Nissan Patrol dual cab ute, and brought me a carton of piss as a consolation gift. He was even bigger than I remembered. His box head was totally bald now, emphasising cauliflower ears and a broken nose.

'Sorry about your old girl,' he said. 'Life can be a real cunt.'

I hadn't seen him since Dad's wake. He didn't bring up the fact that I'd deleted him on Facebook. And he refused to take a wad of fifties from me.

'Keep your money, brother,' he said. 'This one's on me.'

'You're a good man, Rick,' I said, feeling bad about writing him off, although I still felt slightly terrified whenever we made eye contact.

*

In 2017, I moved back to Toowoomba for the home stretch of my mother's illness. The Country Club had burned down in suspicious circumstances, shortly before the owner was arrested for cocaine trafficking. Due to ongoing investigations, the cremated remains of the pub hadn't been bulldozed.

Mum was slowly dying at a short-staffed nursing home. I lathered my thumbs and fingers – thin like hers – with industrial-strength sanitiser.

The name of the brand was Glad Hands.

'Propaganda,' I thought.

Occasionally, I found my mother lying sideways on the linoleum, moaning quietly to avoid making a fuss for the underpaid orderlies. The pain was plain in the red rims around her eyelids. She was too sick to make friends with the other patients, so I was it, and I wasn't feeling particularly friendly.

'Must be tough,' said the Sudanese nurse, no older than me, who had scars on his scalp from a past life as a child soldier. 'You're so young.'

'It is what it is,' I said.

I pushed Mum in a wheelchair to visit the grave of her dead ex-husband. We trundled past a lush City Golf Club and dusty cattle yards and rusted grain silos. The cemetery was surrounded by conveniently located stonemasons.

'I don't want a burial,' said my fading mother at the shady gravesite, where I plied her with contraband Longbeach Menthols. 'Please cremate me.'

My heart broke, but my brain was bent out of shape, so there was no sharp pain. I was in the middle of nowhere and at the centre of everything.

*

I spent most of the nursing home visits compulsively scrolling through social media. One afternoon, Rick's naked skull and tattooed torso popped up on my Facebook feed, like a deranged guardian angel. He was wanted for pouring petrol over an ex-girlfriend and shooting a gun during a domestic violence incident. That morning, he called Toowoomba police.

'I'd rather get a lawyer from out of Toowoomba who doesn't play golf with the judges,' he calmly told the officer, before descending into a trademark rage. 'Go fuck yourself you cocksucker, come and get me.'

Later, I watched video footage of his descent into total psychosis. Police officers spotted the plasterer's dual cab Nissan Patrol adjacent to the football stadium, around the corner from the townhouse that I was renting. The cops chased him down the Great Dividing Range. The sky was cloudless: blue and wide and bright. Trees cast silhouettes across the glinting blacktop. The mindful psychopath slowed down through the sixty km/h zone at Withcott.

'Be aware of firearms,' said the police communications centre.

A spike strip was unfurled on the highway at Helidon. The Nissan blithely evaded the stingers. Rick clapped his hands sarcastically out the window. He pulled a U-turn across the nature strip and led three cop cars onto a dead-end dirt road.

Rick hit the brakes. He slipped from the ute in a singlet. Then he lifted his ripped, inked arms to aim an automatic rifle. The general thirst for revenge was quenched with a short, sharp burst of fire. The front vehicle reversed and rolled. A solar eclipse broke through the foliage and the smoke.

'Urgent!' screamed a female police officer. 'Urgent! Urgent!'

The breath in the shooter's chest was useless as a concrete parachute. Death was coming, one way or another, from his trigger or theirs. He intuitively knew this to be true. So he kept going. At point blank range, that patriotic maniac assassinated a male police officer.

Rick retreated onto his Lockyer Valley hideout. Drugs, firearms and a thousand rounds of ammunition had been strategically stockpiled inside a metal container. A twenty-hour siege ensued. The cop killer sprayed bullets indiscriminately towards enemies in the trenches and the chopper above.

The next morning, the blue-collar fugitive stormed from the tomb of the metal container with a machine gun and was shot three times in the chest. He was a latter-day Ned Kelly: part bush-ranger, part Howard Battler. All those redneck rants, battered girlfriends, bar-room bashings and seemingly hollow threats of homicide eventually led to this act of undeniable violence. Who was I to think I could just play dumb and thumb my nose at such close ghosts?

*

A year passed. Mum died fast at the end. Words were too much for her by then. She was four knots of skin and bone in a cot. More like a baby than a lady, if you want to know the truth. I didn't cry at the funeral. You grow a thick hide to this kind of thing. You know that we all go the same way soon.

We sold the motel lease five months later. I moved to Sydney, alive and trying to put the past behind me. Coronavirus scarcely made a dent on my iron psyche. 'Big deal,' I thought. I was prepared for the end to happen at any given moment already. One afternoon, my brother called from Bundaberg.

'Did you see the news?' he asked, before sending through the article.

Nate was Toowoomba's latest casualty. Hikers stumbled upon his corpse in Lockyer Valley bushland, not far from the party where I last saw him, or the farm where Rick went out in a blaze of mayhem. The same Gatton police sent to assassinate Rick were dispatched to scrape up Nate's body.

I immediately looked Nate up on Facebook. His cover photo showed a hundred $50 notes fanned across a white bedsheet. The profile showed him shushing the camera, tattoos from the wrist to the knuckles. Cheeks gaunt like the people I used to evict from motel suites.

I called an old mate currently in recovery for addiction, who used to move in the same nocturnal circles as Nate. He confirmed my first and worst suspicions, and added gory details that were far too graphic for the newspaper.

'Nobody deserves that,' he said.

Soon, police arrested a 36-year-old mother of three from Glenvale, my old stomping ground. She had dyed white hair, dark mascara, a piercing in the lip and the cheek. Less than a year earlier, the suspect was caught trying to smuggle Subutex – a drug used to treat opioid dependence – into Woolford Prison within her vagina, along with six syringes wrapped up in pornographic self-portraits. She was suffering from PTSD and a fifteen-year drug addiction.

Now, the woman was charged with thirteen counts of supplying a dangerous drug and interfering with Nate's corpse. Police alleged that she relocated the body from the suburbs to the bush and suspected that there were other parties involved with the ghastly dumping. The Darling Downs had never seemed closer to home or harder to shake.

Grass in the Wind

Tim Bocquet

Caught between the South West Slopes and the Riverina, caught between the river flats and the Snowy Mountains. Caught in the war in which the gumtree fought the pine tree. The magpies and the hawks.

My blood is from the west, grain country, flat country, AFL country. Quintessential country. I descend from continental Africa, colonial Kenya, full of mystery, full of adventure, the origin of exodus.

I was raised within the long golden grass in the immigrant paddock, there are no trees there, just the granite rocks that the bullock and chain couldn't move. The lazy sheep and shadow-casting cloud. An old man used to tell us stories about the Chinese miners, their deep funnels now just shallow hazards.

The history of the land was white, although we knew the word Wiradjuri. We knew that some of the surrounding hills held power and spirits, although I can't say how we knew, perhaps child intuition. The rumour passed down and along, superstitions to believe and trust.

My sister would point at a plane flying overhead, something never seen up close, and tell me that my aunty and uncle were on it. She would tell me to wave as we stood under our mother's clothesline shielding our eyes from the white sun.

We would swim in our dam – a large muddy puddle of water, deadly and off-limits to the individual. The yabbies would cloud the coldest reaches while our legs would kick the tepid top layer down to the bottom. We would walk home, skin almost orange with the clay that coloured the water, smelling of the winter floods that now lay decaying in the bottom of that country pool.

Every family, I am sure, had a chest freezer. And every family, I am sure, had a bag of frozen bacon, waiting for Saturday morning, waiting for an electric frying pan with fresh eggs. Flies crashing into the wire mesh, cars rolling along the dirt road, covering the mailboxes in fine quartz dust.

Dad at the table, dreaming about finishing whatever work he had to do so he could watch the football. Mum in the garden, dreaming about her days in Africa. My sister dreaming of how to get me in trouble. My dreams full of more bacon, new shoes and fishing.

Spending summer holidays in woolsheds, a cold stone of impatience in our bellies waiting for the pens to empty, the cool breeze finding its way from the mountains over the creeks through the cracks in the corrugated iron. Lunch consisting of stale cheese and green-tomato pickle sandwiches. Getting home to watch the sun set over the tall grass, the pine trees, and the sparrows that dived for the dragonflies.

*

Lying alone in the hayshed thinking of the other farmers and thinking of the future. I would hide urges in the hay, hide the truth, and hide my secret in the dirt of 200 years. In the shame of pale white Christianity that had fought so hard to grow in the hard soil like the tea tree and wattle.

I would never have a wife to beat into the dirt, a woman whose head I would hold at the mirror to watch her youth and beauty fade into the droughts, to melt with the frosts and disappear like a mist into the scrub. I would never have a child to put second for their own good, to make realise the land must come first, to treat as a stablehand, one whose future was decided with a kingdom worth everything to one and nothing to many.

57

Instead, I would leave in my own time, leave like the frogs in the drought, or the birds in winter, I would sing as I kicked at the rocks on the road, sing with the cicadas, gone walkabout, looking for the permanent spring of the summer, the one that tastes sweet and would give birth to a new tomorrow, a new man.

I found the cold concrete of the city and I came across the warm nights of tropical lands, I became used to planes and trains and foreign languages. I spent days within art galleries and museums and people who drank strong wines from crystal glasses. I found men to fall asleep next to, men to embrace, and men to wake up next to in small apartments on narrow streets, in large mansions of the capital cities' wealthy suburbs. I realised I needed it all, so I tried it all, and I loved it all.

I was deep in my drunken, never-ending summer, immersed in some sort of poetic landscape, when I suddenly awoke, remembering and longing for the smell of rust or grain or cow shit in the spring clover. My family had long forgiven my necessary cowardice, my mad attempt to throw myself to the wind with the scotch thistle seed. Better this than throwing myself into the water like so many before.

I made it home a different person, yet the land remembered my bare feet and remembered the awe I held for its mystery and beauty, my love for it. Just as I remembered every rock embedded in the sheep tracks, the hidden gaps in the fences for crossing, I remembered the groves of wild plum and I remembered where I could sit and watch the lyrebirds. I would sit in the autumn and light fires and watch as the smoke slowly drifted around the trees and up and out towards the sky. I would sit and watch the sky as it turned and changed its colours to the night, showing the different patterns and telling the story of the southern hemisphere. Telling the story of a million people just like me.

I would be the land's groom, the bride of the summer stream, married to the burning tussock and the rabbit's warren. I would fall asleep next to the rising and falling chest of the summer storm and the thawing frost. Growing old with the ageless granite of the outlying rocks and hills covered in grass trees and Messmate. To die and join the army of ghosts that drift among the land, the broken and the whole, the empty and content. To lay among the grass for eternity, spinning in the pocket of dead Australiana, dancing with the Wiradjuri, drinking with the miners, working with the shearers, walking to a school long gone, drifting like wood smoke, forever smiling like grass in the wind.

Rain, Rain, Go Away

MA Plazzer

'Mummy!'

Indyana ran to me, eyes widening as her hands reached upwards signalling to pick her up. Immediately.

'Hey, hey … shhhh, it's rain. It's rain.'

I settled her with an embrace. This was the first time my daughter had witnessed the rain. She was three.

The enormity of this country storm was unforgiving as it unearthed the scent of the soils. The screeching winds shook the fragile parts of the old Jeparit hotel, as the thick sand grains we called 'dust' formed pools of mud along the window ledges.

Out here, dust particles were thicker than a grain of cane sugar. Much of the dust travelled a great distance from the dry lakebed of Hindmarsh, or as topsoil stripped off barren farm lots. Some of it might have been gypsum from the local mine, or sandy soil from around the Big Desert, which fringed the community. There was no point dusting out here: after ten minutes, it would be back.

My upbringing in Horsham, about eighty kilometres south of Jeparit, had been firmly religious. Indy was the 'bastard' child, born three months before I married her father, Matt.

I sighed, and my shoulders dropped as Indy clung tighter. The windows were unsettled, rattling in their frames as the water crawled inwards and upwards through the unsealed edges. Indy balanced on my hip as I reached to open the kitchen drawer. Rummaging through it, I found some grey electrical tape.

'Perfect. Now. Where are the scissors?' I asked myself.

Indy sucked her fingers to pacify herself as I hurriedly decided to cut the tape with a steak knife. I secured the windows with a cross shape of tape, hoping it would hold the strength of the storm. The intimidating wind showed no signs of settling.

Indy cuddled in tightly. 'It's okay. Everything's gonna be okay.' I kissed her forehead. For a moment we were still.

The wind was now roaring, as thunder struck. As a child, I was scared of the sound of thunder. My mum would say to me: 'Don't worry, God's moving furniture and restyling up there.' I tried this on Indy, but it made things worse. I'm not sure she could comprehend the concept of God, let alone a mystery being in the sky moving furniture.

*

The Hindmarsh Hotel in Jeparit had a public bar and restaurant, with accommodation on the second floor. It seemed oddly out of place, with Spanish influences in its design: green mosaic tiling and a balcony with endless white-pillared archways that overlooked the community.

Around 300 people lived in Jeparit, including the surrounding commercial farms. The Hindmarsh Hotel was one of two pubs servicing the area. Most outsiders wondered how this was possible, but the area was home to some of the biggest pub-goers in Victoria. The Jeparit-Rainbow football team, the 'Lakers', were famous for drinking towns dry after a game.

We had travelling guests too; stopping over on their way to go dirt-biking in the Big Desert, farmhands assisting with harvest or shearing, and nurses in residency completing training or placements at the local hospital. There was always someone needing company and a good pub feed.

To visitors, I'd often pronounce the town's name as Je-pa-ris, with my best French accent. There's something in the French accent we've been conditioned to find alluring. I guess this place was a little like that too. It sparked a curiosity in those who found it on the map.

In fact, the town's name was an Anglicised interpretation of a Wergaia word, thought to mean 'home of small birds' and pronounced JAH-PARROT by the locals. The longer you lived out here, the broader your accent would shift. Our sweet local tweet. I didn't know much about the traditional owners of the land but there was a lot of talk and whispers over the bar about land rights. It was mostly corporate/government-driven misinformation that circulated, which caused confusion for both the farmers and the First Nations mobs. Some of the local farmers claimed to have found artefacts including spears, middens and bats, (fishing equipment) around Lake Hindmarsh and further up north around Lake Albacutya. The drought had exposed them. But most of this was hidden away and the corporate fearmongering continued to divide over matters that may have been resolved over a yarn.

Our Italian chef, Fabian, was married to a local Wotjobaluk woman, Robyn. He travelled to work from Dimboola (Dimmy), a small town 40 kilometres southeast. Jeparit was thought of as the poorer cousin of the two towns (by those living in Dimmy of course.)

But Jeparit was known as a sacred meeting place for many First Nations mobs who would travel over for fishing along the Wimmera River, carrying their cans and rods, mostly steering clear of the pub. Except for Robyn. When she came by, she grounded most folks with a glance; an ability unbeknownst to her.

For my young family, Jeparit found us when we were looking for a new start. We'd been living in Melbourne and had planned to move to Ballarat, but then we saw the ad: 'Hotel for Sale'. When we enquired, we discovered that the previous publican had drunk the profits and left no accounts. However, by this stage our curiosity had already drawn us in.

We quickly fell in love with the people there and found common ties. Yes, it was a mixed bag out here, but we had everything we needed: personalities and trades that made the community rich. As well as the two pubs, Jeparit had several shops and services, including a cop shop, bank, local council, chemist, post office, independent grocery, hospital, nursing home, public pool, pre-school, primary school, golf club, bowls club and many other clubs. (Any excuse for a meet up!) Oh, and of course the town square, named after Australia's longest-serving prime minister, Sir Robert Menzies, who was born here in 1894.

The hotel was one of the key community meeting places. All goings on round town were reported here first. No need for a local paper. We opened daily to host our regular barflies, tradies, farmers, slaughterhouse workers, shearers, musicians, accountants, lawyers, nurses, massage therapists, council members and bankers. We had small families, large families, netballers, footballers, socialites, bikers, ex-jailbirds, circus performers, swingers, queers, hermits and even a professional wizard (with his staff) who would stop by for a meal and a beer. All welcome.

Although you needed a relative in the cemetery to be considered a true local, the folks in Jeparit made us feel at home on our first meeting. It was important to everyone to keep this venue alive and thriving; so many memories had been made in their 'beloved' Hindmarsh Hotel long before we arrived.

Jeparit was not a town that people came out of their way to visit: 380 kilometres north-west of Melbourne and 390 kilometres south-east of Adelaide. We weren't even on a highway! In fact, we were quite a way off with no clear digital telecommunications signal.

Getting one bar on your phone was a miracle out here so rural landowners continued to use different mobile technology other than what was used in metropolitan areas.

The main attraction, the largest freshwater lake in the state, had been nothing but a dust bowl for several years when we arrived. The odd keen tourist would stop by the hotel asking for directions to the lake, their car loaded with camping and fishing gear, only to be disappointed when they discovered it had dried up. The Four Mile Beach of Lake Hindmarsh was empty of tourists and locals, and the kiosk and facilities closed. So we'd divert them to the local caravan park, where they could camp along the adjoining Wimmera river and fish there instead.

I was twenty-three when we first arrived, three months pregnant with our second child, Taylor. I had a strong will and determination, which I needed to carry out my role as publican. Pouring a good beer and providing warm hospitality only scratched the surface of the work required. But the people of this community, the farming surrounds and neighbouring towns changed the course of my life for the better.

*

Out here, the weather was both oracle and lifeline. It was front and centre in almost every conversation. Everyone owned a water gauge of some sort. Comparing measurements was part of the daily bar banter and top of the list for important gossip topics. Who'd had the most points of rain? The weather was no 'small talk'.

The farmers' reports would come in later in the day and throughout the week after the rain settled. We hoped the heavy rain wouldn't cause more damage for the farmers than the lack of rain had already. When managing the pasture, rain is welcome at the right time when the right amount falls at the right velocity. Rain, sun, wind, frost and humidity all matters immensely and it needs to be balanced and harmonious. I had a sinking feeling that this rain was mostly not welcome due to its timing, late in the season. It would be the devaluing and possible death of many crops.

*

The intercom phone rang three times then stopped.

I'd barely heard the ring over the rain, but promptly headed downstairs to check in with my husband. Three times and a hang up meant he couldn't talk but needed me in the public bar.

We lived on the second floor of the pub and had transformed the building's left wing into a private residence. There, we'd installed my parents' 1970s kitchen after they upgraded. The old brown laminate was in good nick. And having a non-commercial kitchen made it feel like a home, rather than part of the accommodation adjoining.

Our private front entrance and double-brick walls were solid enough to work as soundproofing when the poolroom jukebox sang out. It blocked the smell of cigarette smoke, which crept through the porous walls on the first floor.

I was halfway down the two-flight stairway when Matt burst through the swing doors into the foyer. He was carrying our younger daughter, Taylor.

'There's water gettin' in the cellar.' He placed her awkwardly in my arms.

'Oh. What about the pump?' 'It's not workin'.'

Matt promptly disappeared. He looked kinda excited.

With my two daughters now clinging to me, I kicked open the swing doors and popped my head around to see who was in the public bar. The usual barflies were grouped at the window, looking out onto Roy Street. They were deep in bar yarns about 'the time the town flooded' and they canoed down the main drag.

Stage five water restrictions had been in place for some time now. Things were really dry. The Salvation Army had visited to offer support in the form of clean water deliveries for private use and an additional water fountain we could use in the bar.

It was important as a local to keep your vehicle dirty at all times; otherwise, you were bloody wasteful. Not to mention an egoistic wanker. It was only acceptable to clean your car in Horsham, (the nearest city) as they had a car wash service. But you'd have to be pretty keen, as by the time you got back to town, the dirt would've covered the vehicle again.

Our hotel kitchen herb garden mostly fended for itself. Only the toughest survived. We'd also ran a pipeline from the washing machine to drain the grey water onto the lawn in the beer garden, which kept it an Aussie green.

The water status of any community reflects its health currency. For Jeparit residents, everyone needed a private water tank as the main town supply was not safe to consume. We counted ourselves lucky, as we had a large underground concrete tank, which kept things a little cooler in the dry Jeparit heat, as well as a couple of plastic tanks as back up.

*

My dad, a first-generation Venetian-speaking Italian migrant was good with concrete. He'd learnt his trade in Australia, and he'd worked on everything from the house foundation and laying bricks, to commercial buildings and churches, to water tanks, water reservoirs, and treatment plants.

When we drove through regional towns, I would often play I-spy, spotting the concrete tanks he'd built. E PLAZZER & SONS stamped in red on the side. It was fair to say I was a little biased when it came to concrete water tanks.

I also think that plastic tanks made the water taste like clingwrap, especially when boiled by the sun.

What brought my attention most to the water in this town was when Indy came to me one day unsettled with a sore back. Had she fallen? I held my hand against her: she was burning hot around the kidneys. Five hundred metres from the hotel was the hospital where the local GP single-handedly serviced the community. He said it was an infection, seemingly mild, and sent us on our way with a prescription for antibiotics.

But while I was administering the medicine back home, Indy turned bright red and started to froth at the mouth. I snatched the intercom. 'Pick up, pick up,' I shouted to Matt in my head.

'Hey.' He answered from the bar.

'We need the doctor. Now. Indy's havin' trouble breathing.'

Without pausing, I ran with her in my arms to the front entrance and as I arrived the local doctor pulled up in his car. That was bloody quick. Indy vomited on the pavement. The doctor's sigh of relief was comforting momentarily. The vomit was a good thing.

'Meet me at the hospital. We've got an ambulance due to arrive shortly to transport an elderly patient. Non-emergency, they can wait. We need to get Indy to Wimmera Base Hospital. We are not equipped for the care she needs.'

My face stiffened. The hospital was a 45-minute drive away, in Horsham. There would be loads of slow-moving machinery moving about at this time of year and possibly roadblocks or sheep crossing.

We were soon in an ambulance heading to Horsham at speed, lights flashing. Indy dropped in and out of consciousness, her tiny body fighting hard. She was strapped into the stretcher bed, out of reach where I was seated.

I held tightly to Taylor, balanced on my knee, now almost eight months old. She'd barely made a peep despite having missed her feeding time. I guessed her digestive system was mimicking mine and experiencing a loss-of-appetite in the flight of adrenalin. The wind surrounded the ambulance to assist our prompt arrival. Inside all remained still as the paramedics and I watched Indy closely for any change. Time slowed. Indy vomited once more. Her cheeks flushed of colour. Ahh. I breathed for her. Her eyes opened and closed.

Soon after arrival at the hospital, Indy was given penicillin intravenously. The infection had reached her kidneys. Had we not had a prompt emergency response she may have been a lot worse.

Note to self: *Keep the girls away from the town's main water supply*.

*

When I first saw the yellow-brown water, I thought it must be the pub's old pipes turning it that colour. But the water changed with the seasons – possibly as a result of crop chemicals used, leaving behind heavy metals and making its way to the open channel. Livestock were often found dead in there, too, after escaping their property boundaries for water. It was ripe for infection. Some may say we were living in 'developing' Australia.

There had been many concerns about water contamination and infections dating back to the 1970s – this was not isolated. However, most locals relied on their own water collection that was cleaner, despite paying rates to have potentially harmful and non-potable water connected.

It would be eight years later, in 2010, that the Wimmera Mallee Pipeline was installed, closing the open water channels that supplied water to Jeparit. A welcomed improvement. Add four more years, the Jeparit water was connected via Rainbow's water treatment plant, (a neighbouring town) which filters the supply via chemical treatment.

If you live in a major city in Australia, you are serviced with piped treated water, and you probably don't think about your safety before taking a sip or a dip! The vast majority of Australians have no idea this is reality for hundreds of remote communities. However, being unregulated comes with blessings, too, and many country folk are happy to have their water delivered from the sky, to the tank and to the people without interference.

*

Indy let go of her grip, slid down my body and climbed confi- dently onto a bar stool. Some of the local barflies – Maxie, Lenny and Pete the Pom – turned from their street-gazing to greet us with smiles. Indy treasured these hang-outs in the public bar. If she was lucky her dad might pour her an OJ or order her a bowl of hot potato chips.

The storm continued to command our attention. Lenny and Pete were keen to go for a short drive to check how the town was faring.

'Ahh, I think we're gonna be stuck here for a bit. May as well pour me another drink,' said Maxie, returning to his regular stool and settling into the paper to check the next greyhound race.

Matt returned from the cellar, his face weathered and sweaty. 'Everything's okay, for now. We'll pump the water out once the storm dies down.'

Matt poured Maxie a beer and continued like he'd not missed a beat of the conversation. 'What race is up next?'

Outside the pub, overflowing water tanks around town created temporary ponds. The dry lakebed of Hindmarsh would become a little softened to form a large mud crossing, while the river held on to what it could.

What crops were going to be blessed? What crops would be destroyed? Who had sewn after hearing the curlew birds' nesting call? Who had sewn following the weather forecasts made by the Bureau of Meteorology? Had the selective storm cloud passed or released its load? The outcomes would be different for each independent farmer, stretching across the golden wheat-belt.

As the reports came into the Hindmarsh Publishing House, the rainfall had reached far and wide in varying levels. Some properties had overland flows that washed large amounts of debris and organic material into farm dams. Some crops had been 'lightly sprayed' and others weirdly dry. No report was unworthy of a headline whilst having a beer. I think we may have had close to two and half inches in parts that day. Some crops were now spoiled by the abundance at the wrong time, 'grain shot' that would mould the head of the grain. Any land without groundcover wouldn't hold onto this gift from nature. But the Little Desert and natural parks – wild and untouched – thrived. It was a day to remember, in the great millennial drought.

*

Indy had become intrigued now by the creative storm activity. We moved out onto the porch, mesmerised by the rainfall. Indy held out her hand, her eyes squinting as the raindrops kissed her skin. She had made peace with the rain gods and they were now friends.

*

Rain, rain, go away. Come back perfectly another day.

1983

Olivia Guntarik

By the end of our first week in Bendigo, we'd been kicked out of the house we were in and had twenty-four hours to find somewhere else to stay. I have a searing memory of the bone-dry ground as we marched from the house into a bare and barren landscape. It felt like we were on the moon.

That day, Mum's car broke down and we were forced to lug what we could carry into that colourless moonscape. A cow let out a long bored *mooooooo*, sounding almost pitiful and needy in the stillness. Sheep huddled under a dry stonewall, and a bull watched us through a fence.

I remember my sister grabbing my hand as we hiked through that desolate strip of the world, wondering what the future held. We felt fed-up from all our fighting, felt like the fault was ours.

On both sides of the house was an open field with a track that cut straight down the centre of the property and took you to an elevated embankment. The other side was hidden and as we approached, I imagined a slope with a ridge and a steep drop, as if we could plunge off the end of the world. This was the short-cut we took into town that day. The track tapered into another and another, and I remember Mum telling us we had to keep our eyes peeled for snakes in the long grass.

This sent us into a state of senseless panic. In Melbourne, we had run freely through city parks, where our biggest worries were the odd unruly dog or some new snot-nosed kid who'd pick on us for being Asian.

We monitored each step, afraid that a snake would come

slithering towards us ready to strike like we'd seen in *Raiders of the Lost Ark*, where man and snake face off. My stomach was stiff from the terror churning inside me and caused my palms to sweat, my heart to pound. The track eventually T-boned onto a busy road. We no longer had to stay alert for snakes, but the sense of dread stayed with me for the rest of that day.

We were fugitives on the run. That's how I now picture that period of our lives. Years later when my sister and I compared the events that transpired that week, we came to different conclusions. She saw it as a matter of honour on our mother's part; I saw it as a matter of flight or fight. Yet as I cast my eye over the shoulder of time, perhaps these perspectives were part of the same thing. Rubrics of how we saw our mother.

Something terrible had happened that day.

As time passes those memories become even more vivid, and they whip back when I listen to certain tracks from the '80s. Mournful songs were a delicious pastime. The Smiths' songs mesmerised me. One song has a haunting riff that takes me straight back to those days of moving to the country, of moving in with Bev.

Yep, that was her name.

Bev.

She had been all open arms about us staying with her. On reflection, she wasn't used to living with other people or living with difference. I never doubted her sincerity in trying to help us. We weren't exactly angels.

Bev was a big-bosomed woman with a rattly voice who struggled to breathe when she spoke. Words took effort and assailed her body. She'd shudder, clutch her knees and pant as if she'd run a race.

We stayed in the guest room, which had a view onto a dry garden bed with spikes of lavender and swaying wattle. I watched bees spiralling in and out of purple flowers. They swarmed to form a cluster on a tree limb and wriggled around on the window. We had spent the late afternoon in the backyard on our first day and I remember the sky being bigger than other places we'd lived.

'Don't you two go fighting,' Mum warned us, when she saw the size of the room. Small spaces got us riled and raring to fight. Our movements constricted, we'd prod and pester the other until one of us broke or we broke Mum. But that day, we promised to be on our best behaviour. We wouldn't be staying long. 'Just until we find our own place,' Mum reminded us.

Bev lived alone and it was clear she was a 'kids should be seen and not heard' type.

We made no more noise than we usually did, but my sister throwing me a certain look or me glaring back a certain way might have caused a giggling fit one day. My sister badgering me about hanging out with her or her butting in while I was reading my book might have sent me over the edge on another. This mix on a sweltering day in a squishy room was likely to push us in the wrong direction, and either one of us would erupt. Then there was my music, which Mum said sounded like someone wailing in pain, not singing.

Our bickering was a habit that Mum couldn't curb or tame, nor had patience for. No punishment could rein us in, or it might for a day or two before we were fighting again.

'That's it. No bike for a week,' Mum would say to me. If it wasn't the bike, it was something equally as precious.

'Not fair!' I'd yell. 'What about Melissa?' I demanded, staring my sister down with snake eyes.

'You're older. You know more.'

I may have known more but my sister knew me. She'd use this savvy to measure how much she could push. With increasingly creative insults hurled back and forth, she would edge as close as she dared to breaking me. The unspoken rule was set: chuck a flare and wait. The goal was to prod-prod-prod until the other caved in and imploded. One sister had to be pushed to the brink of a full-scale explosion. And that sister sure as hell was *not* going to be me. Whoever exploded first was the loser.

Back then, we had no way of curing our relentless boredom. I'd begun to build a mental playground of all the places I could escape to. In those last weeks in Melbourne, before our move, Mum insisted on taking us on endless drives from the city to Bendigo and back again in her search for the perfect place.

Finding a place at the right cost in the right location with two kids in tow proved impossible in Bendigo's blistering summer heat. Time was running out and Bev came to the rescue, offering her spare room to us indefinitely. This gave Mum more time to search. She was about to start her first teaching job and school would begin for us in a week. Mum was edgy. She had a migraine and we weren't helping. My sister and I were grumpy and bored. We needed a break from the monotonous work of sitting still. 'Are we there yet?' we would ask, over and over, testing Mum's patience until she finally gave the vital answer when we'd reached our destination.

By day six, our search was proving unsuccessful, so we decided to head back to Bev's. But as we entered her street, Mum's car gurgled to a sudden stop and smoke billowed from the engine.

'No!' Mum cried. 'Okay. Out. Now!'

We slogged the rest of the way to the house.

Bendigo was experiencing a monstrous heatwave. South-eastern Australia was in the midst of a bushfire crisis, and on the previous Wednesday ash had rained down on the streets and dyed the sky with a rose-gold glow. Later we learnt the fires left seventy-five people dead and a trail of destruction. We woke up to thick smoke outside our window and the constant sounds of helicopters and sirens. I could taste smoke and smell it in my hair and clothes. The fires were drawing closer and closer. People were snappy and tense. I have a strong recollection of visiting people's houses. Windows were sealed to keep out the smoke. Suitcases were ready at the door.

At the house we found Bev in a state of distress. Through the window, we saw her cradling her face. I sensed trouble before she flung the door open. One eye was a wet slit. The other we couldn't see. It had been replaced by an enormous red blister, giving her a sinister look.

'Molly,' she shrieked, coughing. 'You left the window open in your room. You let a bee in. I got stung.'

'What? On your eye?' Mum asked aghast.

'Yes! You and the kids need to stop traipsing in and out of the house all day. This would not have happened otherwise.' Bev stooped forward and held her knees, wheezing. 'Come in. Quick,' she ordered. 'You're letting in the smoke.'

'Should we call an ambulance?' Mum's voice was getting louder with each question.

Bev broke into a coughing fit. When she caught her breath, she told Mum that her daughter was on her way.

Mum wanted us to go to our room, throwing us a *don't go fighting* look. We shuffled down the hall but left the bedroom door ajar to eavesdrop. Something else was wrong and it had something to do with us. We heard snatches of their exchange but could not grasp the full extent of our error. We heard Mum placating Bev in a voice I recognised later as the same one she used to calm desperate parents at her work: sprightly, relaxed, focused on the positive.

We got the sense that Mum was defending us or that something had been betrayed. More fragments stirred our curiosity. Bev's panting voice. *No, you can stay another day, another day, I just* ... We heard the words: *blame* and *brats*.

We moped on our beds in the hot, stuffy room. We played the stare-without-blinking game. We lolled by the window, waiting.

'I'm bored,' sighed my sister.

'Tell me about it,' I said, releasing a big breath.

We gazed into the garden but could only see smoke haze, drifting. A bee appeared stuck on the windowsill. It was crawling around in circles like it had lost its sense of direction.

At last, Mum stomped down the hall, telling us to pack our bags. 'We're leaving,' she said, rolling her eyes. Hands on hips, exhaling through O-shaped lips.

'But where will we go?' I asked.

'We'll find somewhere,' Mum replied in that sprightly way.

Just as we were about to leave the house, Bev's telephone rang.

'I'll get it,' Mum hollered. Bev rearranged herself on the couch.

The call was for Mum, and the news wasn't good. 'Do you have anything else?' Her foot was tapping.

There was a long silence. Mum paused. We heard her mumbling, 'Mmmmhmmmm. Aaahhhhaaaa,' and then say, 'Today.'

Had she found a place?

Bev was watching television with an icepack pressed to her eye. We listened to the news about the raging bushfires, the creeping deaths. The reporter's delivery was rapid-fire.

Deadly day ... nervous watch ... Cut off escape routes ...

The reporter lost his lines. *Here's where I have to ask where do I go from here please ... 'Scuse me ... one moment ... these stories are coming through on the spot ...*

Embarrassed, he picked up a phone and listened, eyes diverted. I watched, half listening to the news, half to my mother's murmurings on the phone. The reporter mumbled, *A bushfire at Belgrave. Thank you very much.* He put the phone down.

My sister pinched me on the leg and I went to slap her but Mum threw her arm out to stop me. I was seething. My sister ducked behind my mother and grinned at me, crossing her eyes. I stared her down without blinking until my eyes began to smart.

The reporter's voice wavered and our attention was back on the television.

The shaky footage hovered over a blazing landscape, then cut to a topless man in shorts belting at flames with a jumper, and then slowly panned over a child's toppled tricycle and into the hazy sky. I had a sudden urge to hide, to run away, but saw Bev scowling at me through her available eye, now glowing red and swollen like the other.

My sister and I stood either side of our mother. She was still on the phone.

Melissa was tugging on her dress. 'Mum, can we go now?'

'Sssssshhhhh,' Bev hissed.

I tried to stand as still as possible, imagining the statue we had passed several times that day on our trips between viewing houses.

There were four female figures on a raised fountain, clutching what looked to be flowers or seashells. The women were draped in flowing gowns, each raising an arm to the sky as if they were ready to fight or had won a battle.

We heard Mum ask the person on the end of the line, 'Is it ready?'

And later, she said, 'I'll take it.'

When Mum got off the phone, she asked Bev if there was anything she could do but Bev waved her hand to dismiss the question. Then we trotted out of there quick smart, taking the smoky track as a shortcut into town, to collect the keys to our new home.

Bev had remained on the couch as Mum closed the door behind us. When I glimpsed her through the window, Bev was dabbing her eye with a tissue.

To anyone else it might have looked like she was weeping, but we knew better.

*

To strain back time to capture our former life demands a certain reckoning.

Maybe I was bitter about moving away from my friends. We'd migrated from Borneo's tropical rainforest and had moved quickly between cities, first from Brisbane to Melbourne so Mum could go to university, and then in 1983 to Bendigo after her graduation. It felt like there was a constant roundabout of people to meet, to know and to forget with each move.

Mum wanted more than a hand-to-mouth existence. She wanted to live a full life.

If we thought the cities were a brutal place for Asians to live in the '80s, the country was even worse. Bendigo was inhabited then by a strange mix of farmers, hippies, retirees and rednecks. Over time, the changes have been rapid and unpredictable. Today, Bendigo is a culturally diverse and progressive community like any other, give or take.

Yet looking back, it is hard to ignore what was; the sharp impulse of my Australian youth is what anchors that time in my life.

The sense that the world was caving in, that we were somehow to blame, that everyone was dying, that even my mother was dying, might die, would die in what was a long summer of bad news. All. This. Felt. Real.

We were under the control of Nature.

But the day, the week, the year – none of it matters now, as memories slip into a single panorama of time that lurches to the present. Hindsight catches the light and brings clarity. For it is only now that I can say with conviction, we should have seen the storm coming. In my mind, we're together again – my mother, my sister and me – walking back through that hazy moonscape, when we're suddenly caught in a rip and reeled out to sea. Change was a constant rather than a blessing. I had come to expect it as an absolute. It was all a maze.

But the maze has no centre unless I focus on my mother.

We had moved to Bendigo to chase a dream.

'It's a good job,' Mum sang, when the fires had subsided. 'We could get used to this place.'

Planning.

Progress.

Sheer hard work.

This was more than sink or swim. We had to follow the dream, ride the wave to shore together, and I had to believe the dream was mine too. It was her first real job in Australia, and she had to make it work.

*

Our new home was sun-bleached and sunk into the land. We lived on the highway, with craggy eucalypts dotted along the road. Weeds and wildflowers dipped in the breeze, often an iridescent blue buoying up a sweeping forest view. The house backed onto an old motel with a swimming pool that – except for the kids next door, who snuck in when the summer nights became unbearably muggy – nobody used.

The passing traffic stirred the clay-dust dirt that would always find its way inside, that we saw swirling through the air, that would settle on the walls, the floor, the furniture. That would irk my mother as she scrubbed at it, knowing the dust would soon return.

The house had a pot-belly stove that you could shove firewood into, though this required much effort and created a mess. Still, come winter, it would always be ablaze, keeping the house toasty warm so there was no need to complain about how cold it was or why we had to rise early again or why we couldn't have *real* heaters like other families.

My mother loved firing up that furnace. When she could do something with her hands, when she could bustle about and see things with her own eyes, she loved it. She told me this later, long after I had well and truly left my past behind and made a new life for myself in Melbourne. *Those were the days. The simple life*, she said.

I can picture her now, in that time in our lives. Her recollections of our first week in Bendigo, among other memories, float into the frame.

Molly lay in bed under the blankets with her eyes closed and registered the week, the day, the hour. A Sunday. She wanted to savour the undisturbed quiet time before the children rose. She opened her eyes. Drank in the room, the walls, the faded carpet. Here in this new place, a two-hour drive from the city, she could start over.

Soon, Molly threw herself into work and household chores and life began to change. The house represented a new beginning. It was both a starting over and a slowing down.

I imagine her forcing certain memories to the sidelines, as she'd do with any show of aggression. Once when I came home upset about a school debate where kids were clearly expressing their parents' views that 'migrants take our jobs', she said, 'Pick your battles and your friends.'

Remember what you have, not what you don't, she would say.

When I now look back to the past, I imagine what it takes to *define who you are*. I imagine how my mother saw that time in our lives.

Molly realigned her mind to the definitive. A more plausible picture yawed of her children on their bikes. Then another as they stood beside the highway, watching the oil-shimmer of a semitrailer's faraway haze nearing the town, nudging closer to the house. The children waved, a horn honked. A pitiful bleat in the hush-hush sluggish rhythms of country life.

Molly's brows narrowed. She closed her eyes and felt the blood rushing to her face. Her lips pursed. A sense that something wasn't right. Pity, futility, fatality. All at once.

Outside, the absent sun, the sky like coal.

Later, it will rain. Later, she will have to tell the children. And much later still, there would be more telltale signs in her body, probing, forceful, making the terrible secret known. Her fingers would curl of their own accord. Her muscles would become hard as rocks and altogether altered. The changes she would observe, little by little. The strangeness of it all.

But let's not go there now.

Last night she had loved the feel of the breeze against her body. The evening wind crisp, the sounds of the elms swaying. She knew too well their leaves would not last into the winter. When they lost their leaves, the trees looked dead. As if Mother Nature was crying out and reaching out with her limbs.

It was cold in the room and she shivered, lingering in bed to savour the warmth. The morning light twirled in and out of the trees and stung her eyes. She had hardly slept. Short bursts of interrupted sleep. Eyes smarting, awareness, tumbling fears. Fears that returned, again and again, rose, expanded. Even with the day gone. Another day gone. Every day. More of the same. A snatch of conversation, *listen.* Nothing. The children asleep.

A neighbour's rattling laughter. Sleep. Eyes shooting open. *Don't think about it. It's nothing. Nothing.*

Shift the mind to other things.

Besides work, why did she come here? *To take it slow. To treat the illness. To fight it.* This would be easier in a small town. Smug in its absoluteness for stilling time. For a slow-paced way of life. *Take it easy*, her new friends said, regaling her with accounts of alternative lifestyles. *Take charge. This is central Victoria, not the city.* A quiet life. So she had taken up gardening. Had grown pumpkins, tomatoes, zucchinis the size of footballs. This became a passion, an obsession, one that occupied her time and oriented her mind to what mattered.

The garden thrived, shocking visitors. Of course, this was a barren and hostile part of the world. Impossible for anything but weeds and wild things to grow. Plants that claimed permanency, that were robust, unwieldy. This land disembowelled by mining gold, its *real* history silenced. Its soil compact. Stony tough. This drought-prone land, parched, killed any effort to cultivate a garden, least of all a veggie patch.

'How do you do it, Molly?' someone quipped.

The comment amused and surprised her. The answer was simple enough. Forced her mind to other questions.

How do we nourish the land? How is life from nothing made?

She made different types of compost depending on its stage of decay, knew when to water across the seasons, took advantage of the sun. Nothing went to waste. Things got repurposed. There was a word for it in her native tongue. The land regenerated. The land. A living body. A mystery. This was what she saw and sensed *deep in her being*, but it was hard to find the words to express this knowing.

We moved to another house in Bendigo, a step up from the house with the potbelly stove. 'Watch these seeds grow,' Mum carolled, as she tended to her garden there. She was saving her money in her Starting Over years. The slower pace suited her, she told us, gave her purpose without crushing her spirit.

She could heal.

In those days we were free. There were no extravagant forebodings about our future or our freedom. We coasted through life like there was nothing to it, gazing around at our fellow country folk as if we could behold their lives from a wholly different outlook than our own. There was space and time to listen, to talk, to choose how to live. Most of all there was time to see how other people lived.

How *we* could live.

For my mother, work was a means to an end. She had come here for better prospects after years of study. Work freed her to concentrate on things that mattered. She built new friendships and her social circle grew. People were drawn to her confidence and laughter, which erupted readily and fell around the room like sudden applause.

She enjoyed quiet time in the bush, from which she gained great strength. Walking was her salve. It freed her mind. It was through our mother that we caught a glimpse of our own proximate freedom.

*

Molly threw the blanket off her body and angled her legs from the bed to the floor.

She prized the window open and stared into the bleak winter day, the pressing sky. Outside noises filtered into the house. Kids played in the park up the hill. She heard the thump-thump of a ball across the road at the sports stadium. A motorbike. A highway truck. She jammed her finger down on the boombox by the bed, closed her eyes and inhaled, nodding to the tempo, inviting the music in.

Molly ambled to the kitchen and guided firewood into the belly of the stove. The tune she heard made her feel alive, adventurous, spontaneous. She lit the kindling, listened for the burst of flames, the crackle. Watched for the first curl of smoke. She breathed in, waiting as the fire caught and held. All the while humming to a song about 'Precious Memories'.

She felt the heat moving over her face and through her body.

Molly leaned closer to the stove and ever so gently blew the embers to coax the fire.

It was time to wake the children.

Bob

Michael Winkler

It is customary to write about the extraordinary: remarkable people, unforgettable situations. But I want to do the opposite. I want
to tell you about someone extra-ordinary. In a world that cele-
brates the exceptional and the elite, Bob Weems was the antithesis.
He was like a stock character in a computer game. Forever overlooked, even when he was right in front of you. Which is why it is
surprising that at four o'clock on each of the past three mornings
I have woken up with his story filling my head.

I contacted a couple of people from my hometown for their
memories of Bob. Neither could recall him, or even his name.
I had to excavate some old school photos just to verify that I hadn't
invented him. Country towns are full of kids like Bob Weems – or
at least, they used to be – but their stories don't usually get told,
because they are just there, existing.

One of the persistent myths of Australia is egalitarianism. In
my country town, everyone knew their place. The kids from neighbouring farms were the overdogs. Their parents typically had land
and money, which translated into status and purpose. The farm
kids had motorbikes, horses and decent guns – not like the townies' bent-barrelled .22s and air rifles. In town the lower rungs were
occupied by people like the Weems who had no money or connections. We also picked on anyone whose family was conspicuously
religious, or who had been skittled by suspicious misfortune.
Lowest status of all were the kids who lived in houses without
electricity on marginal land outside town limits. One family had
just reached fifteen kids when the father died, which elicited as

much sniggering as sympathy. Their neighbours had an unlucky thirteen children. Not much food, no new clothes. No-hopers, we called them. That's not a proud thing to recall.

Of course, if there had been any immigrant families we would have happily picked on them, but there weren't. In the whole town at that time, the 'multicultural' element was a bloke who worked on the roads who was reputed to be 'half-Asian'. Which country in Asia? Don't know, didn't matter.

I have no doubt that if there had been any Aboriginal kids we would have ensured they were the true underclass, but they didn't exist. I went through my entire schooling and left the town without ever knowing whose Country we were living on. There were ugly, racist jokes, but they were abstract because we had never met a First Nations person. For example, the standard response when you thanked someone for a favour was, 'No worries, I'd do the same for a blackfella.'

Except. When I finally locate my Form One school photo to prove Bob Weems existed, I see in the front row an adopted girl who, a decade or more later, discovered she was Palawa. In the middle of the frame is a tall teenager who left our school soon after; she looks a bit like some First Nations people I know, and she has the same surname as a prominent Yorta Yorta family. And there is one tiny fella I do not recall at all, who presumably was just passing through town, who could plausibly be First Nations as well. They were there alright, hiding in plain sight. Did they not know? Were they, or perhaps their parents, consciously choosing not to identify? 'I'd do the same for a blackfella.' Well, maybe there's a clue.

*

Four a.m., and Bob Weems won't budge from my thoughts. Last week I would have struggled to recall his face or name. Now he has taken up lodging in my brain. Tiny trivial details are dredged up. I cannot imagine a more improbable focus for the work of memory. It is like spending three night-mornings obsessing about a stone you saw on a hillside when you were a small child.

I was eight years old when I moved to Bob's town from another town several hours down the river. We were in the same class at school. Bob's father died a year or two after we arrived in town. Bob's mother was grey-faced, miserable, as skinny as a rollie. His older sisters were fat as suet and trudged the town looking down, as if they weren't worthy of meeting anyone's eye. They knew their social standing.

Bob was of nondescript height, non-descript build. He had shaggy, dirty hair, disproportionately tiny eyes, a beaky nose. There was no-one who particularly liked him and no-one who cared enough to dislike him. He was unintelligent, but so were plenty of others. In high school he was part of the group cut from the herd during English classes and led away by the Remedial teacher, but his learning wasn't much remediated.

We were never friendly – he was probably smart enough to know that I was less popular than even he was – and I remember us punching each other, on a couple of occasions. Neither of us were fighters; perhaps we saw safe options in each other when all-ins developed in the schoolyard, as they occasionally did. Boys used to punch each other for a lot of different reasons. It didn't have to mean much. Or anything.

Memory's next station is high school. Form One Religious Instruction. It was usually taken by a doddery, dull Anglican, but on this occasion the instructor was the younger of the town's two Catholic priests. He was asked by a student if swearing was wrong. A strange, shiny smile appeared on his face and he answered that everyday swearing was not sinful, but saying 'Damn you' or any-thing blasphemous was wrong.

'But there is nothing very wrong,' he said, with that odd glow-ing grin, leaning towards Bob who was sitting in front of him, 'in everyday swearing. Like if I said "Bobby Weems, you little shit."' He was leaning so close to him now. 'Well, that is no big deal at all.'

I was sitting behind Bob, so I'm not sure how I know what his face registered, but I do. He was bewildered. That priest was popular in our small town, and we whooped at his improbable words and Bob's discomfort. Why pick on Bob, the least fortunate kid in that not-very-fortunate classroom? Because the universe picked on Bob, I guess.

I never heard any rumours about the young priest at that time, and people I trusted thought highly of him. But at his next town or the one after, he was convicted of sexually assaulting a boy, given a non-custodial sentence, and the Catholic Church moved him to a different state. I don't think that is part of Bob's story; it is just another unhappy thread of some sort.

Our town had a footy team and tennis teams but no cricket team. When I was fifteen they decided to create a team to play in an Under-16s cricket competition with three other far-flung towns. I joined the team. So did Bob. So did most town lads our age. Bob was the wicketkeeper, and he was hopeless at catching, but our whole team was hopeless. Utterly, dispiritingly hopeless. Not one of us had cricket clothes and, once or twice, adults from the other towns' teams sniffed that we were disrespecting the sport by turning out in footy shorts and grubby once-white t-shirts. We didn't look any good, play any good, feel much good.

As wicky, Bob used his body as a sort of mattress to stop the ball when his hands failed to do the job, which was usually. This meant a lot of pain for him, taking the leather ball on his unprotected body, and you could hear him squealing. No-one hated Bob enough to be happy he was getting hurt, and we weren't insensible to what he copped, but it had no effect on us. I know that he dropped every catch that came his way off my bowling, and everyone would abuse him, and I was glad it wasn't me being abused, and I hated that he dropped those catches, and I can't remember specifics but I probably abused him too. Who ever heard of a wicketkeeper who can't catch? Who ever thought to give Bob Weems a role with that much status?

I guess he left school at the end of that year – Form Four – because all of the academic stragglers did. I guess I saw him around after that. It was a small town. It would have been of no consequence to either of us.

The town cop for most of my childhood was not a confrontational man, but he was replaced by an overbearing bully. One night, according to people who claimed to have been there, the cop grabbed Bob's head and smashed his face into the windscreen of the police car. Bob would not have made any smart remarks to the officer because Bob didn't know any smart remarks. A day or two later, I remember standing in the street and looking at the crack snaking across the bottom of the cop-car windscreen. The policeman took a different job not long afterwards.

I can't remember when Bob died. I think he was eighteen, but he may have been nineteen. He drove into a tree.

Existential crises come and go. They are big in the teenage years, and then fade, and then rear up again at inopportune times in a life. I remember wondering what Bob's time on earth had been about. What was it for? It seemed a pointless life, and then it had a pointless death, and that was that. Did he kill himself? Did he just drive badly? Would it have been different if his father never died? If his mother had any resources: financial, social, emotional? If he hadn't been picked on by the popular priest in Religious Instruction? If I hadn't punched him? If he hadn't had his head smashed into a police-car windscreen? If we didn't yell at him for dropping all those catches?

*

The internet doesn't care that it is four a.m. I start searching the names of other members of that defeated, defeatist cricket team. I am shocked to find one fella alive; he went to jail young, and I'd imagined an early demise, but I can see him on my computer screen looking cheery, drinking beer with a woman in a different small town. When he was fifteen he had something happening at home, I don't know what, so we would usually collect him before cricket at the back of the bakery, where he slept a lot of nights on old flour bags.

The main point of cricket practice seemed to be to hurt people. Bowling short and fast at unprotected parts of the body. Throwing cricket balls hard at each other from close range. The casual viciousness of unthinking teenage boys, and the culture of the town at that time. That desultory team of unhappy teens who only wanted to inflict pain.

The only person I recall being seriously hurt at practice was the younger brother of another kid my age. He was hit flush in the face with a cricket ball. It broke his nose, split it open as well, the shock of the colour red splashed everywhere. I don't know what we did to help. I suppose he just walked home. He also died in a single car crash before he reached twenty. When I heard the news I thought about the agony of his smashed nose, and if he was going to die early anyway, why had he needed to go through that additional pain. It seemed unnecessary.

One of our better players was cut out of a car crash aged eighteen. His brain was messed up, and I think I heard he died. A few years later in a big city in a different state, his brother, who sometimes played in our team, was murdered. The nets where we practised, if that's what we were doing, were over the road from where another of our players hanged himself. A couple of the lads in the team who went to prison straight out of school are probably also dead now. A lot of corpses.

Our worst game of cricket in that listless losing season before the town abandoned the sport was played at our home ground, one block from the top pub. I remember the team gathering early and staring at the roof of the hotel, and no-one felt like playing cricket or doing much else at all. You couldn't see anything – it was just a red roof – but the night before, a bloke had climbed up there with a gun and fired at this and that. He was an uncle of two of our players. The last gunshot of the man on the pub roof was directed at himself. Our town was page one of the city papers.

The cricket team was thrashed again, and we were half glad, and even gladder when we could slink off to our homes.

Guns and boys and pain and meaningless deaths. That's what I am dragging up through the pre-dawn gloom, matted and grotesque and unwanted. There were good people in that town: unfussy churchgoers who provided welfare on the quiet and without show; rough diamonds who looked out for elderly neighbours; battlers who would never do you down. But I was young and my eyes were big and my skin was horribly thin, and I took no account of them.

*

My last memory of Bob Weems might be an injustice. I really don't know if he was there or not. I think people said he was, but I could easily be wrong. One day the school corridors were aflame with salacious news: a girl in the year above mine had six or seven lads from the cricket team on a picnic table near the caravan park. It made no sense to me. It did not match what I knew of her, although it matched what I knew of my teammates. I thought about it a lot. I thought it was possible it was something she wanted to happen, and maybe I was right, and I thought it more likely that it was something that just happened, and she didn't want it to happen exactly, but maybe didn't completely not want it to happen, or she wanted it to happen at the start but not later, and that may have been right. I thought how ugly my cricket teammates were. I thought how strange it would be to be the young woman, on the picnic table, their ugly cocks dripping under the streetlights, their ugly breathing, and so many of them. No-one said it was rape, but it certainly could have been. I didn't know then and I can't know now. It was just hard to process, and it made me miserable. A different sort of pain. I wanted to live somewhere else. My sensibilities were all wrong for that place, that time.

As I said, I think Bob was one of the group, but perhaps he wasn't. The girl had a distinctive name, but I can't find her on the internet. Maybe she has changed it, or maybe she isn't part of the mass contagion that is social media, or maybe she is no longer alive either. Maybe she and Bob are both somewhere else now. Somewhere better. Somewhere where you are not treated differently based on the colour of your skin, or who you love, or how much money you have. Somewhere out of my sleep-starved brain. Somewhere where the past can be the past, and Bob can hold some catches, and no-one is too ordinary to be special.

Bindoon

Sam Elkin

Over the din of my classmates playing Uno and talking shit at school one morning, I caught an announcement about a rural exchange program. Students could leave home for a term to learn about farming and the challenge of Western Australia's increasingly salty earth. As a fifteen-year-old who dreamed of one day getting out of the suburbs and into a big city, I'd never even thought about moving to the country. But things were shit at home and anywhere sounded better.

My stepbrother, Daniel, had recently suicided and my blended family, never that functional, was now disintegrating. My stepmother was deep in grief, and I'd go days without seeing her or Dad as they cocooned themselves at the other end of the house. My stepsister spent her time partying, shoplifting strappy dresses and getting high for days on end. My own teenage brother had moved out altogether to get away from us all. My dad – never a particularly attentive father – had checked out of parenting me altogether, and treated me more like an unwanted house guest who occasionally annoyed him by asking to use the home phone.

After daydreaming about a life of freedom in a swag under the stars, I got up the courage to speak to the academic counsellor about the program. I'd been scared of her since she'd ripped shreds off me for being drunk in class one morning and had deemed me a lost cause. As I sat down, Mrs Waller looked down at me from her high-backed chair. 'Well, Sam, I'm really not sure you'll fit in too well in the country, given your lifestyle choices.'

I stiffened. Was she referring to the drinking or the somewhat correct rumours that I was queer?

'If you let me go, I'll be good. I promise,' I said, picking at the frayed edges of my army surplus jacket.

'Well, I doubt that we'll be able to place you at a family home, as it's usually boys who do these kinds of farm programs,' Mrs Waller replied.

'Wouldn't that be discrimination, though?' I asked. 'Like, you can't just not let me go because I'm a girl.'

Mrs Waller looked at me like I was a boring joke she'd heard one too many times. 'No-one is discriminating against you, Sam. I'm just trying to be realistic.' She sighed and flicked through some pamphlets. 'There is a Catholic co-educational farm school in Bindoon that you could possibly go to.' She handed me the booklet. I looked through the pictures of old-fashioned stone buildings, golden hills and sunny orange orchards. Smiling kids sheered sheep, fed piglets and rode tractors. It was like nowhere I'd ever been before.

When I asked Dad if I could go, he initially said no when he heard about the $500 contribution he'd need to make. But after talking it over with my exhausted stepmother, they decided it was a good idea.

A month later, I left my high school in the suburbs for Bindoon. My dad drove us up the Tonkin Highway, passing newly cleared suburbs and giant signs offering cheap house-and-land packages. Once we hit the Great Northern Highway things started to look a bit more like the country, with smooth, grey gum trees and paddocks as far as the eye could see.

Bindoon itself was barely a town at all: just a bakery, a petrol station and a cream-coloured town hall. I wanted to get out and explore but Dad didn't want to stop. We kept going up the highway and turned off onto a gravel road. Two stone pillars with stark white crosses on top marked our arrival. We drove in slowly along the dusty road, past olive orchards and more dry paddocks. It was a beautiful day and I was feeling upbeat about my new life in the country until we passed a terrifying white cross painted with a grim scene of Jesus being condemned to death. I looked over at Dad, a lifelong atheist, to see if he wasn't having second thoughts about leaving me here, but his attention was back on the bumpy road ahead. I kept quiet as we drove past more eery scenes of Jesus's final moments as we continued down the long driveway towards the college.

Eventually a spooky, double-storey stone building and well-reticulated, rich green lawns emerged from the middle of the dry farmland. Its vast terracotta roof and rows of thick white pillars were partially obscured by a trio of improbable-looking palm trees that flapped around comically in the light breeze, making the whole place seem like it had been magically transported from a faraway land.

I had a map of the school and instructions to head straight to the girls' dormitory, and so we kept driving past scrubby bush-land. When we spotted the girls' dorm, I was relieved to find that it was a bit less scary-looking than the rest of the school – just like a country pub but with more crosses on it.

A woman in a polo fleece emerged from a side room to greet us. 'I'm Kayleen, the house mother,' she said. 'The girls who have arrived are all out and about, but they'll be back before long. I'll show you to your room.' She gestured for us to follow her up the wooden staircase and as we climbed the creaky stairs she explained the house rules. 'This isn't a hotel; all girls are expected to strictly adhere to the cleaning roster. Girls must be out of the dorms by 8.15 a.m. for breakfast, and lights out is at nine p.m. Strictly no exceptions. Any questions?' I shook my head.

Dad stood around for a minute while I unpacked but he soon decided it was time to go. We had a stiff hug and then I watched as his Nissan Pulsar kicked up a small storm of red dirt as he took off. I went back to my large, empty room. The furnishings were minimal, with only a small, rickety wooden cupboard and a wire-framed single bed alongside expansive views of bushy hills. It felt absurdly spacious in comparison to my small bedroom.

I unpacked my CD player and turned the radio on, relieved to find that I could still pick up Triple J out here. I hummed along to a new You Am I song before the midday news bulletin came on, full of news about the waterfront dispute and rise of One Nation.

I turned the sound down as I heard footsteps on the front verandah and then the staircase as a group of girls came upstairs. I was fretting about whether I was meant to say hello or not when one of them knocked on my door and asked to come in. The three of them plopped themselves down on my bed and started chatting with me, asking me about where I was from and what bands I liked. It was a much warmer reception than newcomers got at my own school back in Perth.

Vanessa was from Cunderdin, where her family grew wheat, and Amy was from a cattle station near Mount Magnet. Kylie's family lived in Pinjarra, where they looked after rich people's horses. I had only been 'down south' to Margaret River and 'up north' to Kalbarri and had no idea where any of these places were, but nodded along. Vanessa said she'd originally been at a boarding school in Perth, but had been expelled for smoking pot in the toilets. 'So, I ended up here with all these deros!' she said, laughing.

To flex my delinquent credentials, I told them about how I usually spent my weekends with my friends drinking vodka mixed in with frozen Cokes out the front of the Whitford shopping centre and trying to bum cigarettes off passers-by.

'Well, there's definitely no booze here: only the Brothers are allowed to get tanked on all their Church wine,' said Vanessa. They then ranked each Brother according to how much each of them looked like an alcoholic. Brother Frank was the clear winner, with his bulbous red nose and burst veins.

'So, have you heard about all the ghosts here at Bindoon?' Vanessa asked. I shook my head.

'Oh yeah, there's heaps of ghosts here,' said Amy. 'Seriously, there's lots of little dead boys who came here as slaves from England to build the school and then got raped by the Christian Brothers. There are bones under all the buildings. If you don't want the ghosts to haunt you, you've got to show them that you're on their side.'

'How do I do that?' I asked, nervous now. I knew it couldn't be true, but they all seemed convinced.

'You have to steal the rosary beads from Brother Keaney's grave – he was the worst paedophile of them all – and throw them in the river.'

'I can't do that,' I laughed. 'I'd get expelled!'

'You have to or the ghosts will fuck you up,' Vanessa said.

'Where's the grave?' I asked, feeling the weight of peer pressure bearing down on me.

'At the front of the main administration building,' Kylie said. 'That's why you have to sneak out at night to do it, otherwise you'll get caught.'

'But I don't even have a torch. Can I borrow one of yours?' I asked.

Amy broke into giggles, and they all collapsed about laughing at me.

'Is that all bullshit then?' I asked.

'Nah, it's all totally true. But you'd be fucked if they caught you. I can't believe you were almost going to do it.'

I laughed along with them, relieved that I wasn't really going to be pressured into vandalising a grave on my first day.

They left to get ready for dinner. The temperature dropped markedly as evening set in, and I had to put on both of my jumpers before we walked down to the dining hall. The four of us kept warm by sliding along the gravel and throwing twigs at each other along the way.

When we arrived in the quad outside the dining hall, the girls pointed out the statue of Brother Keaney; a huge bronze figure with his hand resting proprietarily on a small boy's shoulder. 'That's him, that's the pedo. It used to be out the front of the school, but the old men who got abused here kept complaining, so they moved it back here,' Amy whispered to me.

I looked up at the huge statue. The little boy looked terrified.

The dining room was full of retro dining tables and cheap plastic chairs. Metal strip wall heaters turned on full blast to take the chill out of the air. There was a steaming bain-marie next to a huge stack of white plates and cutlery. A few of the boys had arrived for the start of term as well, and they were laughing and loudly boasting about what they'd each done on the school holidays. I eavesdropped on their tales of hooning around on quad bikes and family trips to rodeos. I didn't even know there were rodeos in Australia.

One of the Brothers sat at the head of our table to supervise. He was younger than the others, with big, wavy brown hair and a cropped beard, like someone from The Bee Gees. He introduced himself as Brother Byrne and asked us how our days had been. They all rushed to answer, smitten with him. A much older man with a bulbous nose, who I assumed must be Brother Frank, clinked a fork against a glass and started to say a prayer. Everyone put their heads down, closed their eyes and followed along. I looked around, expecting at least one of the girls to roll their eyes at me, but they all did as they were told. It dawned on me that most of the students were actually Catholic; as an atheist, I was in the minority.

There was a cacophony of chairs scraping as the three front tables were permitted to go over to the bain-marie to receive their dinner of lamb with mashed potatoes and mint sauce. When it was our turn, I followed along and got the lamb, despite having recently become a vegetarian. I got the feeling this wouldn't go down well among these farming kids so I ate the lamb. It was delicious.

The next day, the rest of the boarders arrived from all over the state, and the place started to feel full. A group of Aboriginal girls from Broome arrived on a minibus late on Sunday after a long journey. They received a frosty reception from Kayleen, the house mother who directed them to two rooms at the furthest end of the corridor. My new friends who had been so welcoming to me barely said hello to them.

We started school the next day. The classes were basic – it was more like the stuff we learnt in Year 7 than what I'd been learning in Year 10. Many of my classmates couldn't write more than a few sentences, and their spelling was terrible. At lunchtime, I saw heaps of kids lining up out the front of the principal's office. I asked Amy what they were doing. 'They're all waiting for their dexies. Half the school is on them,' she said. 'Heaps of the boys here were expelled from other schools and then got diagnosed as ADHD and came here.'

'We should break in one night and steal the bottle and have a party!' said Vanessa, before getting in line herself for her daily dose.

At the end of the school day, we had to get changed out of our school uniforms and into our farm gear. I emerged from the change room in blue jeans, a broad-brimmed hat and a blue canvas work shirt. I felt like I was playacting in a western. One of the teachers read out a list of which area of the farm we were assigned to for practical agriculture duty. I was assigned to sheep duty with Brother Gorton. Six of us reported to his banged-up Toyota Hilux. He was a tall man in his late sixties, with a big belly and wild white hair. I went up to pat his ancient-looking kelpie who rolled over for a tummy rub. 'Jump in the back, kids,' said Brother Gorton. I followed the others as they climbed up in the tray of the ute.

He drove us round to a grain bin, where one of the boys arranged for the grain to be poured into the back of the ute. From there, we drove off towards a sheep paddock to feed the flock.

'Don't sheep just eat grass?' I asked one of the kids.

'Yeah, but look around you. Can't see much grass, can ya?' I had to agree.

I laughed in delight as we went over various bumps in the road with the wind in our hair. When we got to the edge of a paddock, Brother Gorton told me to jump out and open the fence, a job I could actually do. I leapt back in and we took off, grain trailing onto the ground behind us for the sheep to eat. I felt a massive sense of achievement for the tiny part I'd played in providing care to the flock.

Over the next few weeks, I did the rounds of the farm, working in the cattle sheds with Brother Kelly, the chicken sheds with Brother Byrne and stacking hay bales for Brother O'Malley. Hay baling turned out to be brutally difficult; my feet stung, as the hay managed to find its way through my socks and poke into my ankles.

On the weekends, we attended Saturday night Mass, given by an aggressive and inarticulate priest, who even the Brothers seemed unimpressed with. After that, Brother Turney opened the Saturday night tuckshop: the sole opportunity for us to buy lollies and Cokes for the week.

I settled into the rhythm of life on the farm. I never felt the presence of ghosts, but sometimes on the weekends older men would turn up unannounced and wander around the school grounds like they were visiting a graveyard. A group of us were playing basketball one day when one of the strangers wandered over to the far edge of the court to watch us. I suddenly didn't feel like playing anymore, and so I sat down next to Kylie who was braiding another girl's hair.

'Are they the ghosts you were talking about?' I asked her, trying to make a joke.

'They're the abuse victims,' said Kylie under her breath. 'They come here all the time because they can't get over what happened to them. One of them calls in a bomb threat at least once a year, and we get to sit on the lawn all day.'

Like clockwork, the school received a bomb threat the following week and we were all marched outside while the emergency services did a thorough sweep of the buildings. I felt anxious when I thought of the many places that could've been used to plant an explosive device. There was random mechanical stuff everywhere, how could anyone know what was meant to be there and what wasn't? As we sat on the grass, gossiping and playing cards, I eventually forgot about the bomb threat until an orange-clad firefighter turned up to tell us that we were safe. None of the teachers talked with us about why some former students wanted to blow up the school; it was just an accepted part of life.

Towards the end of term, my teacher remembered that I was meant to be learning about Western Australia's salinity crisis, so I was given a handbook and some worksheets to complete. I copied out a diagram of a salt interception scheme and wrote out the physical indicators of agricultural-induced dryland salinity from the book; including 'mid-slope seepage', 'bare soil', 'surface soil salt stains' and 'soil blackening'. I didn't understand a word of it and my teacher didn't seem to know either. Saplings were ordered, and my classmates and I planted them alongside a couple of people from the education department while a local photographer took pictures. With thirty saplings planted, my salinity project was complete.

On my last night, my new friends and I stayed up late listening to music and chatting about what we were all going to do next year. Some of them were coming back to Bindoon for Year 11 and 12, but most were planning on dropping out and working on their parents' farms. 'You should come back next term' Kylie said to me, and they all smiled and nodded. It felt so nice to feel wanted that I started to wonder if I should stay after all.

The next day, I sat on the front verandah with my bags watching my friends get picked up by their parents to take them home for the holidays. They all greeted their parents with a hug. As I sat waiting for my dad, I thought about my time here. It was quite weird in some ways – especially the bomb threats, scary statues and all the other reminders of the starving little barefoot boys who'd been forced to build the school. I hated going to Mass and I didn't dare tell anyone about my sexuality. But I loved picking oranges in the orchards and working on the farm. I liked my classmates and even some of the Brothers. I did miss going to the movies and going to CD stores, but I didn't miss my own unhappy home at all.

When Dad finally arrived, I was one of the last to leave. As we got on the road, driving past the scenes of Jesus's death in reverse,

Dad told me that my stepfamily had moved out and that his new girlfriend, Stacey, and her two teenage sons were about to move in. I stared out the window at the rich sunlight shining across the green hills as I tried to process this news. I felt gutted that I wouldn't be seeing them again, and exhausted by the prospect of having to play happy families with a whole bunch of new people.

When we stopped at the local servo to get petrol, I was surprised to see a full-colour picture of myself in the local paper holding up a sapling. I looked like someone else; someone happy. When I got back into the car, I told Dad that I didn't really want to live with his new girlfriend and her kids and would prefer to stay in Bindoon. He said that that would be fine, since they were going to be short on space at home again anyway.

Inside Those Leafy Walls

Jo Gardiner

It was in the pale limestone country of the south-east of Australia that I was born. Later though, when I was a girl of about ten, we moved even further south to the bottom of Australia, near the Prom. So, I fancied I came from a direction, like a breeze might, wafting in and picking up the strong scents of the Mallee and drifting them on across the border.

I loved everything about our one-teacher school in Buffalo, a long bus ride from our farm: the smell of chalk, the books that stood on a shelf and could be borrowed, the alphabet cards, the maps. I loved the dimpling of the left-hand page of an exercise book nearly filled, and the softness of its bulk.

Bending down beside me, as he wrote corrections, the teacher's hand paused then swooped, hovered, then swooped again, pen strokes flying across the page – spells conjured by the strange arrangement of letters. Within *hearth* I discovered *heart* and *earth*; within the world lay a word that was itself a shadow of the world. I loved to dip my nib into the dusky pond of the inkwell and lift it out carefully, musky scent filling the air. I smoothed out a page of my exercise book and looped letters in the way the teacher showed us on the blackboard. The sound of the nib scratching on paper, the shape of dripped ink on my blotter, gave me pleasure of a particular sort, for in that ink I smelled a home, a small room that existed within me. Soon I discovered that writing things down meant I could store experiences like honey in a jar, and in that way, at any time I pleased, I could travel back along memory's thread.

*

One morning, when I was a few years older, I got up before light, saddled up and launched out across the back paddock without intelligence of map or guide. I set out on a journey with the easy, natural feeling of wearing jeans and riding boots. I rode my pony across the spinning world, my mind and his feet such close companions in open, breezy fields of solitude. Moving my pony along tracks across the country was like following lines on a page.

Slowly the sky bloomed the same colour as the lavender in the far-off Bald Hills, as I watched the track unroll before me. Wildflowers appeared in white and blue clusters and purple patches. I kept an eye out for the tiny native orchids in the shade of acacias, and for pink and orange native peas out in the first patches of sun.

At our approach, a foal cantered off across the paddock, tail and mane nothing more than light flickering in and out of haze and dry grass, hair the same texture and colour of that grass. Alone out there, I got hold of ideas so full of possibilities, daydreamed in the thickening light. Out there, I eluded time and slipped from that dimension entirely.

I rode for hours, and soon the afternoon hummed about me and the faint, earthy perfume of dried cow pats was in the air. I jumped the pony over a log and trotted through sun dripping liquid gold across the paddocks, scattering quail as I went.

As it grew warmer, I turned down to the creek, jumped off the pony, took my bits and pieces from the saddlebags, made a little fire and set the billy full of water on it. Soon, as my pony cropped at the grass, I sat drinking sweet, milky tea and eating hastily buttered scones as fish slept in the brown stream that ran along the boundary of the place. Insects droned and a breeze lifted through the rye. I closed my eyes as another riff of warm air drew through the pasture and over my skin, bringing the scent from a thick stand of tea tree beyond the river.

I climbed on the pony's back and we continued south towards the wildest part of our place – the untouched wilderness we called the Basin. The pony's hooves kicked up dust, and galahs, startled, flew up from tussocks in a pink-and-grey panic. Ragged black cattle lifted their heads and silently observed. Further along, red Herefords strolled languorously in a mob, their white faces bobbing above the long waves of pale-yellow grass. I tipped back my head, felt the sun hot on my face. I turned onto the track to the river and cantered for a while beneath the few lavender-bellied clouds that hung motionless above us.

It was so quiet out there, different from the day before when I helped out in the woolshed. It had been a scorching December day. Breakers of cloud rolled over the chaos around the woolshed, the light heavy with dust and the rich, musky odour of circling sheep. My father sat back in the saddle on his big, lanky piebald, calling directions to the sheep dogs, hat pulled low.

Excited, the dogs panted and yelped as they nipped at the heels of the flock, gathering them into the yards. As the sheep mobbed, their tiny hooves clattered on the ramp up out of the heat through timber posts. In the glare of the hatchway, a damp hessian sack hung, cooling the air that streamed inside. The sudden dimness inside the stone-walled shed stunned the sheep as they were snatched up and rolled onto their backs by shearers in blue singlets who dripped sweat and ran their big shears close along woolly backs.

I threw my arms wide and gathered fleece up to my chin, carried it to the classer's table. Wrinkled, creamy wool brushed my nose. Delicately ruffled at the edges like a seashell's scalloped rim, it was soft at its rippled centre. The classer tossed clouds of wool in the air and they fell with a soft hiss. In long strokes he combed out the fleece while I looked around for my father to see what I should do next.

It was my father's habit to say, *Listen*. And I did. Because I hung on his every word, I would spend a life listening so carefully to the world, trying to hear the soft pish as birds landed on the river teeming with wood duck, and underneath, the fish slipping between wading feet. Trying to hear even the spider's thread spinning, even rats sleeping between the rafters, the soft turning of their heads in dream. Out in the paddock he'd stop in his tracks, raise up a hand. And I learned to be still and listen as song flowed from the butcher bird.

In this way, I soon learned that everything sang of itself. My father's words connected me to the world, so that all my life I would remain in its thrall.

*

As I drew near the Basin, small clouds followed me along; the air trembled, some sort of mysterious music glowed from the brightly painted forest vibrating with birdsong on that yellow ochre afternoon. The day's heat swam around me. Grass parrots flew up from low branches, sudden spots of vivid green that lurched up and away.

As I entered the darkness of the forest, the unfamiliar smell of wet leaves hung heavy in the air. I picked a way through the trees and cut across a gully. It seemed to me the forest spoke in complex sentences. Birds' voices suddenly disappeared, and I heard only the sound of a swift-flowing stream. Each step on thick leaf litter resonated softly along the joints in my body. Then something made me draw the pony to a standstill.

After some moments passed, I sensed a presence, and watched a deer step lightly from tree-filtered dimness into a column of light near a creek. The forest surrendered her up like the form of grace that arrives only when unsought. She lowered her long, slender neck to the stream and drew her soft lips back to drink. As light wandered across her flank, thickly freckled and smudged amber, shivers of delight washed through me. She paused, raised her head high and looked directly at me, unafraid. So self-contained, so filled with quiet knowledge of her own wildness, she considered me as one might a strange light.

Then the creature caught my scent and was alarmed. I blinked, and in one lovely, singing movement, she flowed away. And as the deer dissolved into the trees, the grace of it moved me, though I knew that was not its purpose. When she was gone, the forest quivered with her absence.

*

On the way back, skirts of dry, orange grass flared out from the fence posts. Further along, the grass was yellow and then white with lack of rain. As we drew closer to home, the pony's ears pricked up as he anticipated the feed at the end of the journey. I pressed him into a canter and his eager hooves struck the dirt road with their clean rhythm, crisply formed as heartbeats, legs flying like fingers scattering across the keyboard of a piano.

This motion was like the rhythm of chopping kindling for the fire, which I did often. At first I was wild in my blows but then I would settle into a slow *thwack, thwack*. The head of the axe would pull me back on its pendulum path. I would prop my boot up on the stump to hold steady and split piece after piece. The sound would ring across the clearing behind the house. As each lump of wood split away and dropped, I'd pick it up, line it up on the stump and split it more finely again, pausing only long enough to bury my forehead in a bent elbow, sopping up sweat like gravy before swinging the axe again, its weight dropping me securely to my task and releasing a resinous fragrance from the wood.

*

By the time we reached the last stretch, the sun had dropped low behind the tops of the trees and the overexposed paddocks were dotted with merinos, backs turned to the west, long shadows blue on the yellow pasture. Further back, the hills turned purple and the cattle mauve against a white plain. The track we'd come on was a ribbon of velvet flung out behind us. And, as the Earth turned away from its sun and grew colder, just in that moment when shadows receded to indigo and the paddocks turned violet in the evening, I felt at peace, gave myself up to the star-blown sky, became a part of the turning universe moving in a steady hum, revolving around me. I knew myself to be part all the things I'd seen that day: the grass parrots, the branch that bore them, the sky that longed for them. From between those gullies and creeks, from across the solitude of the land's wide expanses, my life was drawing its shape.

As my pony drew to a halt at the home gate, I looked back. Soon I would be in my room dreaming with a pen on a scrap of paper, tracking ink across the page, spinning songs from air, recalling the quiet beauty of the deer standing in that column of light and how she moved something within me, turned something over. And I suddenly knew that in the moment she disappeared inside those leafy walls, she took with her some part of me that would never be returned.

The Bridge

Frances Olive

The Warialda Bridge was built across a gully, hinging the town like the dusty body of a bee between two brittle wings. A muddy streak lay at the bottom of the gully. It didn't look like much, but you had to admire the persistence of the creek that had gnawed away at the plains until a bridge was necessary – a bridge that let you walk across the sky.

Walking home from school, the violin bumping against my thigh was heavy with memories of squeaking on street corners at the Honey Festival, heavy with being the only child called out of class to take music lessons. But I was strong enough to carry it all that day: my big brother was back from boarding school, and he was walking by my side.

The sky was white-blue. It was one of those days when you're always squinting, like most of the days I can remember. That town was a patchwork of squinted glimpses woven together by the smudgy fingerprints of heat. Never a complete picture. You can't see the whole picture when your nose only reaches the hips of everyone who matters. You only know that something isn't right. You don't belong here, and the afternoon doesn't bring any cool relief. It brings monsters.

The boys – there were three or four of them. I wasn't sure. They seemed to fold in on each other, multiplying and dividing like the apples and bananas I drew at school. Slicing them neatly with my pencil. A fruit salad of boys in the middle of the bridge.

They stood with their fists in the pockets of their brown school uniforms. My uniform was blue, marking me out as one of the kids from St Joseph's. There were only forty of us. There were only two thousand people in the town. There were only three or four boys standing on the bridge. But three or four is sometimes enough.

I'm not sure how they got hold of my violin. I just remember seeing the familiar case, suddenly small, in strange pink hands. The handle was flaking at the edges. It was a battered hand-me-down that only caused me trouble. Now it was causing me trouble again.

He held my violin out over the railing. It swayed there in its black coffin, and I thought about the hollow, golden wood. How light the violin was when I squashed it under my chin. How it nestled uncomfortably against my neck, a creature made of elbows, needing me to help it sing.

The boys stared over my head at my big brother. That's who this was all for. I didn't matter. I was just another violin.

I didn't look at my brother. This shame was worse than playing 'Silent Night' for loose change on street corners. My big brother. Just standing there, red hands by his sides, mouth dry and empty.

My face was sticky with melting dignity. The bridge was longer than it had ever been, and emptier than the yawning gully. If only somebody would come, I cried silently. Any one of the two thousand people who hadn't yet been lost to the relentless erosion of the town. Any one of them would do.

These boys would not inherit the lives of their grandparents. Back then there was a place for them that was decent and dignified like the song of a violin. They knew we didn't belong. We still stank of the city, with our violins and our Catholicism and our boarding schools. It was rubbish, all of it. It was what had gone wrong, had to be. And it was going in the gully. It was going to soar and crash. They were taking back control.

They picked me up by the waist of my dress and held me over the edge.

Did the bridge know that there was no water down there anymore? Did it sit around chatting to the other bridges about how pointless it all was? It didn't provide safe passage across perilous torrents, connecting lives and loves that had been severed by the flow. No. It tied together a broken patch of land using a white-hot patch of sky. The trolls didn't hide under the bridge anymore. They walked in the sky with everyone else, untethered, the soil slipping from their shoes like so many violins, like so many little girls, tumbling from the empty sky into the empty gully. The town had dried up years ago.

They held me over the edge, and I dangled there lumpily beside my violin. My sweaty tears rained into the gully. When I finally remembered to pray, I swore I would practise every day if the two of us just got home safe. I would play 'Silent Night' and 'Go Tell Aunt Rhody' and 'Bound for Botany Bay'. I would play like an angel on my golden violin, and I wouldn't complain.

Warialda means 'place of wild honey'. A sweet name. But then you get to thinking, so you went and built a town over a bees' nest – and then you wonder why you get stung? The bees are just waiting for the creek to disappear, the footpath to crack, the bridge to let go of the sky. They will come home, humming like violins. And the river will flow with honey.

The boys didn't drop me into the gully. It got embarrassing after a while, and they just put me down and swaggered off, trying to decide whether they were victorious, and what exactly they had won.

They didn't drop me, but I fell anyway, through that drying town, through violin lessons, through boarding school, all the way back to the city those boys tried to throw off the bridge.

I soared. I crashed.

Meat

Claire Baker

I have a confession to make: I don't eat meat.

Fairly pedestrian as far as dark confessions go, but for a farm girl who grew up a willing aide to regular slaughter, I still cringe when I say the words out loud. Death, the brutal bloody meaty reality of it, was an everyday part of growing up on the farm. Whether for sustenance or sport, we killed. We killed our own animals, dressed and froze them. And ate them. The sweet, poddy lambs were named 'Lamb Chop' in unending succession because that's what their final fate was. Familiarity with blood and the consumption of flesh runs so deep in me it drives a curious inversion that makes abstaining feel like the transgression. Indeed, refusing meat was only something I considered after the death of my father, who passed when I was thirty years old. I think of him every time I choose the fish, and hope he's not too disappointed in me.

My relationship with my father was pretty special. Growing up on the farm I was his eager helper. One of the many blessings of having Fred for a dad was that it made little difference whether I was a girl or a boy, so I happily sat at his feet in the tractor, followed him to milk the cow in the morning, and held countless bits of wood steady while he sawed or nailed them into place. I learnt to drive our Toyota Troopy at the age of nine because it meant I could go and pick up Dad from the tractor – a feat I only managed by sliding under the steering wheel to reach the clutch pedal. This was possible because on the wide-open paddocks of a wheat farm in the Liverpool Plains there's not much to hit.

Shadowing Dad on the farm meant also shadowing him when

he slaughtered the sheep and chickens, stalked and shot the deer, and made a dent in the local rabbit, kangaroo and even cockatoo populations. In my young mind, I was determined to prove my bravery and grit by participating in all three of these domains of killing. In fact, each of these was an opportunity to spend time together as a family, which still stand out as happy memories. Each type of slaughter had its own conventions and reward – a chance for the family to come together and work alongside each other to achieve a common goal. These were good times that wove together notions of killing and eating animals with ideas of self and family that run deep, not just in my own psyche, but right through rural Australia.

*

I am now a social researcher and often work with farmers. A recent trip to the Central West of New South Wales included an overnight stay on an organic Wagyu cattle farm. This meant an awkward and jarring conversation about a non-steak dinner option. *Will they think I'm an idiot? Some tree-hugging, cow-loving lefty from the city? But I'm a farm girl, I swear!* The unease I felt at confessing my pescatarian ways was physical, emotional and social. The odd one out in a cultural practice that was foundational to my identity in rural Australia, which even now has the power to mark 'us' and 'them'.

As we lived relatively remotely – about 50 kilometres from the closest small town on what were then gravel roads – being self-sufficient was important. We grew our own veggies, and a few times a year we would kill and butcher our meat to fill up the big chest freezer. The chooks were the most fun – the saying 'running around like a chook with its head cut off' doesn't come from nowhere. Dad would slice the head off with an axe and we'd wait for the body to stop its jerking, bloody dance enough to grab it by the legs. Then, stoking the fire under 44-gallon drums full of boiling water, we'd dunk the feathered bodies and more easily strip the carcass. We killed ducks and chickens in this way, and I'm not sure at what point they transformed from clucking companions that would follow me around the yard, to dead flesh. I remember my younger sister being affected by these killing days, but my instinct to swallow the feeling and prove myself was so strong that I don't remember it as a conscious decision I made, or ever thinking I had a choice.

The days we killed sheep and pigs for meat starred my father. My memories of walking the animals into the small yard at the back of the shearing shed, and helping catch each one, are sensuous: the smell and greasiness of lanolin; the dusty, dry yard; the musty darkness of the underfloor space as we raced from watching the knife slice the sheep's neck in the shed to the yards underneath where the hot red blood would drip through the grating to form dark wet pools in the dust. Too young to help with the load, I'd watch Dad shoulder the dead sheep onto a hook by the back leg, and watch as he carefully slit the skin, slicing the sharp knife along the line of fat as he separated the sheepskin from its body, peeling it off like a coat. Careful not to nick the bag of guts, he'd skilfully turn them out to spill onto the ground. Then he'd separate off the pieces of the carcass, right down to splitting the skull with an axe and scooping out the brain. I remember kneeling to look at the small cavity the organs came from, wondering at the complexity of this simple sheep body. Family legend sits slick and hot in my hands, as I vividly remember cupping my open hands for Dad to place the brain and liver in my palms and poke kidneys onto my fingertips so that I could deliver the yield to Mum back at the house. Once the carcass was divvied up enough to fit, we'd stand in line at a table next to the bandsaw as Dad passed us chops and chumps to group into freezer bags and tie up.

The value of self-sufficiency and the ethics of this type of killing are clear: the animals were very well cared for and had relatively low-stress deaths – no crowded transport or inescapable scent of death in an abattoir. Not to mention that the food miles were low. These memories don't concern me, and actually inform my choice to not eat meat, because it is very rare that these conditions of life and death can be met within our largely industrialised meat industry. Mum and Dad used every part of the animal, and only killed what was necessary for our family and friends. What troubles me is that our relationship to killing has become so estranged that it rarely factors into decisions about what we eat. The 'civilisation' of food procurement separates us from this process as meat gleams behind plastic film in the bright white light of supermarkets. My basic test is: if I am willing to slit its throat myself, I'll eat it. These days I'm not, so I don't. But I once was the girl who was and did.

*

My father's sport of choice, beyond cricket and tennis, was deer hunting. Our living room was adorned with various taxidermy, including a couple of stag heads with antlers of sixteen-points or more. One of these now sits in my garage as it quietly falls to pieces because I just don't know what to do with it. Our family holiday was, more often than not, a trip to a remote hunting property where we would stay in small single-room wooden huts, with a campfire for a kitchen and a drop toilet at the end of a winding path. Dad and I would leave under moonlight and track the deer via their love-heart-shaped tracks and rubbings on trees. We'd be downwind and silent, Dad communicating with his hands and eyes. I still find myself slipping into the old habit of strictly stepping only into the footfall of the person in front of me when I'm walking in the bush with the kids or with friends. If I was really, really lucky, he'd give me the honour of being the one to take the shot. But never when it was a stag, and he'd never kill a young one, instead leaving it to grow its points. These animals were also used for meat, and Dad would butcher the carcass out in the field. My favourite food may still be the most incongruent of delicacies: fine strips of venison and garlic, seared in a smoking hot wok over a campfire in outback Australia.

Alongside this sport was the great Australian (settler) tradition of 'roo shooting, rabbit shooting, feral pig shooting and even, to my continued shame, cockatoo shooting. As a farmer, anything that jeopardised the crop was fair game. The long-term and wide-ranging impacts of industrialised agriculture on the landscape are still being played out, but the devastating impacts on biodiversity and the perversion of natural food chains through the introduction of feral species remain blights on our natural environment. Humans have set up the perfect conditions for imbalance, having sequestered and cleared country for our purposes, provided a concentrated food source of crops and reliable water sources of troughs and dams, and then struggled to control the very impacts this created. This often took the form of violence, whether through shooting, poison or disease. When we went hunting for deer, you paid for the privilege of shooting a deer. Kangaroos, on the other hand, were worthless.

Out at the hunting ground, there were great mobs of eastern greys and towering groups of big Reds. Each one was a thing of beauty: deep, lashed eyes, proud human-like chest and shoulders, the instant power of their legs. But together they seemed limitless and never-ending. One morning, as the sun came up around Dad and I camped on the ground, the dawn slowly burnt the mist off and I was surprised to see the dark shapes around our perimeter reveal themselves as a line of kangaroos surrounding us. That season was dry and hard and at times you could walk through mobs of kangaroos, many of which were sick and slow, paralysed by ticks, and they'd only half-heartedly limp away. Seeing this was hard. Kangaroos are beautiful creatures and witnessing these black-eyed animals suffering seemed to back up everything I had been told: there are too many, we need to shoot them for their own good.

But this killing hurt. Out spotlighting at night or when out with Dad in the paddocks, the pride I felt knowing how to use the scope, being able to take the kickback from the rifle, and being a good shot never quite erased the pang of guilt and regret. But it was what I did to find my place in my family, and that place was right next to my proud dad. Needless to say, it was a bit of a shock when I'd stay over at schoolfriends' houses in town and marvel that their family outing involved a walk to the town pool and spare change spent on ice cream from the corner store on the way home. The culture shock of playing with pink My Little Pony toys, not to mention feeding the pet rabbit, was real.

*

Even now, as I write this, I don't know if I'm confessing my murderous sins or begging forgiveness for not eating meat, so deep is the tie between the two. The simple act of refusing to eat meat has become a sliding scale with which I can measure how much I belong in any particular setting, and in rural Australia – bound so tightly to the socio-cultural practice of eating meat and to the economic process of its production – it places me on the outer. Growing up, meat consumption symbolised a strength and robustness that you'd have to be a special kind of fool not to partake in. This symbolism and the deep socialisation of this throughout my childhood means I still feel a wave of embarrassment when I refuse meat, even as an adult. Even though I doubt anyone cares very much about my particular eating habits, I think it says a lot about our meat-centric culture in Australia, particularly in rural Australia, that this is an outcome.

Industrialised meat production is problematic on many levels, including the ethics of breeding technologies; the quality of life for animals in feedlots and other intensive farming arrangements; the environmental impacts of producing feed, such as increased land use and mono-cropped pastures; dealing with animal waste; the costs and impacts of transporting live animals; the emotional impacts on abattoir workers; the ongoing use of plastics in meat-packaging for supermarkets, and more.

While I'm not opposed to meat consumption, I do think these profound challenges need to be addressed in a way that means that choosing the steak doesn't come with a side of ecological and moral degradation. And I think this is difficult in a country so steeped in the money and markets of agricultural production in ways that determine many people's way of life and their choices in farming. This tension is played out every day in rural Australia, because while our culture supports industrial agriculture in very deep ways, the national myth of the rise of modern Australia as 'riding on the sheep's back', driven by the virtuous farmer, is coming up against the limits of endless growth. Just as we need to reassess our reliance on the wealth of underground mineral resources, so too we need to reconfigure the ways in which the soil and biota that agriculture relies upon are managed for the future. These are moral questions, not just economic and scientific ones.

In a globally connected world, the current generation growing up in rural Australia will be aware of the climate crisis and the need to better manage our use of land and water. How are young people growing up on farms thinking through these questions? Farms account for more than half of Australia's land mass, so in many ways our collective future is in the hands of our future farmers. And if, decades later, a dyed-in-the-wool carnivorous farm girl like me can break with tradition, what is happening for those growing up in rural Australia today?

A Montage of Memories
from the Country School Bus

Adelaide Greig

Every year, I dreaded the golden orb spiders.

Our long dirt driveway was lined with fir trees and in early spring, on cue, the spiders would emerge to weave their web palaces, full of egg sacs, strung between those green pillars. The morning sun would hit the drops of dew gathered by the lace strings before dawn, and make them glow like minuscule fairy lights, illuminating them, making them easier to avoid but also more corporeal, more of a threat.

Golden orb spiders, although grotesque with their bulbous yellow bottoms and hairless, spindly black legs, are not venomous to humans and posed no danger, except to my imagination. Nonetheless, my heart would race as I faced the first tribulation of the day, those hanging fields of my eight-legged foes, and moved through them as if imitating an art thief sliding through the laser beams protecting a masterpiece. It was a careful walk in which those little arachnids and I scuttled from each other's footsteps with a perceptible squeak.

Once, after a miscalculation on both our parts, one announced itself about an inch away from my face, dangling on a single thread. After the expected moment of horror as my two eyes met all her eight and the adrenaline skyrocketed through our systems, we tore ourselves away, hoping to never meet each other again. She scurried upwards in a panic to be rid of me, and I lost all spider-related trepidation as I recognised a deep rumble coming from the now near road. A new fear overcame me. I needed to get to the end of the driveway. I started running towards the promise of the metal gate, which marked my finish line.

The bus was coming.

*

I spent my teenage years and about half my childhood on a medium-sized acreage near an insignificant town in New South Wales, and for most of that time I went to school in Canberra, the nearest city. To get to school, and to get home, I would catch a Deane's Buslines school bus that would pick us up at the end of our driveways and return us there ten hours later. The system was rather simple – one bus would service a certain area and pick up the kids from a group of towns, then we would drive to a depot where we'd get off and change to the bus that correlated to our school. In total, I spent about three hours a day on that bus.

If you hit the seats, a plume of dust would erupt up into the air; there was no air-con or heating, and the jolt of driving over every pothole or roadkill kangaroo echoed up through your spine. But a yearly ticket was only $50, and besides, there wasn't any other choice.

Unlike public transport, with its constantly shifting hordes of patrons made of up strangers of all ages and attitudes, all avoiding eye contact, there would be roughly the same kids every day on both halves of the bus ride, and inevitably it became a microcosm of the schoolyard politics that governed the rest of our day once we were dropped off. The older you were, the further up the back of the bus you sat; the cooler you were, the more chance you would ever get to sit on the long, raised seat that spread the entire length of the back row. From there, the queens and kings of Deane's surveyed their territory – their rows of straight-backed, exceedingly uncomfortable chairs upholstered in garish geometric prints.

Throughout my high-school years, there was a pair of especially long-legged sisters who always took their place up the back.

They would stroll past, surrounded by a cloud of Impulse spray and confidence, where I sat in the middle rows. One time, the older sister's phone came clamouring down the aisle beside me, evidently thrown there with force. When I picked it up and handed it back, she said with a coy smile, 'There's a new iPhone out, I need to break this one so Dad will buy it for me.' I clutched my copy of the fourth *A Song of Ice and Fire* book to my soft tummy of stubborn baby fat and willed something erudite to come forth from my mouth to condemn her vapid wastefulness, to use this one chance to assert my intelligence, to let them know that while they sat above me, I had the true high ground.

I said nothing, and she returned to her dusty throne.

The first time a boy asked me out was on the bus. I said no because he was a nice boy who deserved a skinny girlfriend, and I wasn't that. He was upset and we didn't talk for a while, but after a few thousand rotations of the steady wheels below us, he returned to giving me an earbud to his iPod so we could listen to pirate metal. I found him on Facebook recently – he's in the navy and engaged to be married. I wonder if those moments crushed up on a bus seat together are as brightly illuminated by the afternoon sun in his memory as they are in mine.

*

The stakes of catching the bus on time were high – there was only one, and it waited for nobody. Many afternoons, after dawdling at a daydreamer's pace back to my locker or having an ill-timed bathroom urge, I found myself sprinting at break-neck speed through campus, pushing through groups of city kids who gathered to chat after class had ended, with the freedom of knowing they had many paths, at many times, home.

If I ever got to the stop just in time to witness my metallic steed riding off without me, hot tears would well with the realisation that I would have to face the frustration of my mother, who now had to drive over an hour just to pick me up. I would chastise myself for being too fat and too slow, poor at time management and disorganised – unable to walk or drive myself home, missing the bus became a symbol of all I wasn't but should be. Only once, full to the brim with rebellious spite, did I storm back up into school and triumphantly join a group of my friends as they wandered to the local shops to buy chocolate milk and sit in a park. I called my mother and, with all the gall of a defensive teenager who knew they were in the wrong, announced that I was walking to Grandma's and would stay there for the night.

Most of the time, however, as I walked back up to school after missing the bus, back through those groups of city kids oblivious to my plight, I would imagine I had made it and was sitting with the steady thrumming of the engine below me, taking me home. Taking me out on the highway, crossing the border. Past the petrol stations and dead grass and empty dams aching with thirst. Around the paddock with the horses who didn't have enough shade to sit under on hot days and who always looked sad. Next to the tulip farm and the alpaca farm, and through the tiny roadside village with the post office and my old primary school.

There was one bridge out of the village towards where I lived, where the larger properties were, and rumour had it that if the creek underneath flooded, the bus wouldn't come and you wouldn't have to go to school. It never did flood, so I never found out if it was true.

I was a different person on either side of that bus ride. While Canberra is far from a buzzing metropolis, any city has a substance to it that the country does not. The country is defined by its absences. By the silence that greeted me when I stepped back onto my dirt driveway. No businesses or gossip or double-storey buildings or cars driving by or takeaway coffee cups or ATMs or cinemas or playgrounds or bits of old chewing gum stuck to the ground.

There were fruit trees and grasses and cow pats and golden orb spiders. Sometimes, the cows would be grazing or chewing cud near our boundary fence nearest the road, and I would reach over to pat their giant heads, before once again making my driveway expedition. People who have not seen a cow in person do not realise how big they are, or how loudly their bellows reverberate across the yellow expanse of a paddock.

I didn't need to be erudite or informed or switched on when I came home to the farm. During the rare times it rained, I would splash in every muddy puddle up the driveway, ruining my school stockings. I picked up the turtles that would get lost and take them back to the dam so they wouldn't be eaten by birds. The birds sometimes lost their own battles, like the poor, lonely goose who incurred the wrath of the cows and was consequently squashed to death against one of the same fences over which those cows would moo at me. I floated through endless imaginary worlds, always alone but never lonely, with my cast of fantastical friends conjured in my mind. I tried to fish for yabbies. I kept an eye out for brown snakes. The vastness welcomed me with open arms every afternoon, and I would willingly leave it every morning, when the bus took me back to the rest of the world. It was a mutual understanding between the three of us.

*

The bus carried me through these worlds and the years with a predictability that was both depressing and comforting. I was incredibly innocent. So little of the outside world penetrated those steel beasts, which made the shock of when I was eighteen and moved to Melbourne all the greater. I began sitting in trams full of nobody you know and everyone you don't. I would stare at the route maps printed on the walls and be overwhelmed by how many places there were to go. I would spend whole mornings hopping from one tram to another, ending up in suburbs unknown, marvelling at how even if I rode to the end of the line, another tram would rumble along to whisk me back. No-one knew my name. The tram was terrifying, and it was freedom.

But I left my childhood on that bus, and, as with all childhoods, it is difficult to look back and avoid nostalgia altogether.

Some part of me is still flying along the highway, trying not to make eye contact with truck drivers, avoiding the nasty kid who bragged about shooting cockatoos through the head, feeling first love, first loss, eating a Paddle Pop that the driver would stop and get for us from the little village shop on the last day of term. And that part of me will always be there, on the road in-between my worlds, somewhere on the bus ride home.

The Drain

Meg Sattler

The drain was a direct line between school and home. The water had long dried up, and now there were bottles and cans everywhere. Our snap-pants dragged in the red dust, dirtying our hems. Mine were fake. Everyone else's were real, proper Adidas – that's what I thought, anyway. Maybe theirs were fake too. Maybe they also went to bed dreaming of finding fifty bucks on the ground outside Foodworks, so they could get some new clothes on the next family trip to Alice. Ones with three stripes, not two or four. But I don't think so.

When we walked along the drain we sometimes stepped around people, sometimes right over them. If there were babies, my sister would play with them and give them juice. She was ten and not quite so bothered by how many stripes she wore.

But I was twelve and my friends were all bigger than me. Not in age but in size. They towered over me like giants and had real breasts and defined calves from playing netball. I was a twig from the city who they'd taken in. Was it because I was cool or because I was some kind of project, the outback equivalent of Tai from *Clueless*? I didn't know. Here, the cool girls wore flannel shirts – and not ironically.

It's a lot of pressure, existing on the margins of the popular group. I was always on my toes, perpetually ready to be exposed as an imposter and booted out. My bookish, animal-obsessed existence was okay in the city. I was the quiet kid in a loud family. Non-offensive, unexceptional. Nobody expected much of me. But here, that wouldn't work. I was an empty jar, ready to be filled with the quirks and characteristics of others in the group to invent a new, cooler, bigger, more teenage me. A throwaway slang word here, a lie about my mysterious city life there.

When we moved, I'd packed my favourite top: a lime-green striped and stretchy number that I'd bought from Just Jeans with my Christmas money. It was the one that had appeared in the TV ad campaign that year. But after my first day of school in the Territory, it was relegated to the back of the wardrobe where I hoped it'd be swiftly eaten by moths. By day two I'd become a new person, dressed in the one item of branded clothing we had in the house: a huge white t-shirt emblazoned with a Nike 'swoosh' that I had fished out of my dad's tennis kit.

'You look different today,' one of my new friends had said with a smirk. 'Where's your little green top?'

'Oh, I just wore that because everything else was in the wash.'

That started a year-long project of saving every ounce of my lunch money, so that once a fortnight I could buy a new item of oversized sportswear. I'd slip each piece into my collection and, when I met my friends at their various entry points to the drain, casually make remarks about having just unpacked it from a forgotten box. My tiny frame swam in Mambo shirts that got covered in sticky flies, Adidas shorts, and big cotton pants we called 'baggies' that made me feel like Aladdin. When Dad went on work trips to Darwin I'd ask him to buy me extra clothes and he would happily comply – parental guilt easily assuaged by a $20 t-shirt.

By May of Year 7, all of my friends had their periods, and proudly stated at lunchtime and recess that they *had* to go to the toilet, taking with them little blue boxes of Libra Fleur. When we sat in a circle on the dusty oval and they asked me if I was the last one left, I said 'Oh God no, of course I have mine. I just don't need to talk about it as much as you all do, it's so *gross*.' I didn't menstruate for the first time until two years later.

*

The drain was where my friend told me she'd taught her baby brother his first nursery rhyme: *nigger nigger pull the trigger.* She laughed, and I opened my mouth to laugh too but nothing came out. Afterwards, I thought about how the only time I'd ever seen that word in my twelve years of life was in *To Kill a Mockingbird.* My family swore a lot, but I knew the N-word was so far out of bounds I could barely even say it when telling the story to my dad later that night. We were sitting out the front, as we did most dinnertimes because it was too hot inside, eating sausages and cold supermarket pasta salad. He was furious when I repeated the rhyme.

'Get out of my sight,' he said.

I went sulking into my room and slammed the door. *I* wasn't the one who'd said it. That girl wasn't even cool – she was only on the periphery of the cool group. I didn't ever walk home with her again after that.

The drain was also where we first met the boys. My two girlfriends and I were walking back to school in the evening to practise netball – if you were good at netball you got to go to Katherine for the interschool comp. They had been telling me about West Coast Coolers, which they had tried when their dads were away on trips.

Then three boys approached us, all fresh from footy, stinking of sweat and the faintest remnant of Samboy Atomic Tomato chips.

The tallest spoke first. 'Where you goin'? School's over, eh.' He had big eyes that looked wetter than most.

The other two pushed him around, egged him on. 'She doesn't like you, brother.'

He was interested in my friend, the tallest of the three of us, whose dad was a truck driver. She had friendly dogs from fighting breeds, a mum who always gave us good snacks (like whole-packets-of-lollies good) and occasionally a road-train engine parked in her driveway.

'We're going to practise netball. We're gonna go to Katherine.'

'That's gammon, eh.'

'Isn't. Anyway, why do you care where we're going?'

The boy's friends pushed him again. He nearly toppled into the drain and they burst into maniacal laughter.

'You like me or something?' my tall friend said.

The three of them were all muscle. One wore a Chicago Bulls singlet, one a Bob Marley t-shirt and the third no top at all. I noticed sweat drip down his chest in a way I'd never seen before – not up close, anyway.

The next day at school, the tall boy invited my tall friend on a date. He just marched straight up and asked her. I didn't think people dated until they were at least sixteen. The two of them went out after school that same day to buy chips and gravy from the Ampol and watch footy practice. She phoned me afterwards to tell me that the shirtless boy wanted to go out with me.

'Me?' I was filled with fear. I'd dragged the phone from the hallway into my room, and had covered both the phone and my head with a jumper.

'No, your mum, eh,' she laughed. 'Anyway, you'll say yes, right? It'll be fun. Then we can all have boyfriends together. I told him you said he was hot.'

I felt sick. I did say that, but it was a lie. I did not think he was hot. I just knew that was the right thing to say because I liked his muscles.

*

The shirtless boy and I met at the drain. His house was at the very end, near the school, but he came to the part near my back gate, fully dressed this time. We walked past the school to the civic centre. There was a movie on, a special event put on by the council.

'This movie's gonna be alright, I reckon. Bit scary but. It came out last year in the city. My cousin's already seen it.'

As he spoke, I counted the bits of rubbish in the drain. Six juice bottles. Three wine casks.

The movie was called *The Glimmer Man* and from the poster it had indeed looked scary. I'd told Mum I was going with my tall girlfriend. She'd given me $10. Five for the ticket and five for a Coke and chips. I intended to add the snack cash to the vegemite jar in my room where I hid my money. I was saving for a new pair of Vans, and was only $28 short.

During the movie he held my hand. I turned around to see if anyone was watching but it was pretty dark. I wondered if I should do something with my fingers, like stroke his hand a bit. I'd seen other people do that. But we both just kept our hands there, not moving, as though they were glued together. As soon as the movie finished we unlocked them and put them back where they were meant to be. I tried to be subtle as I wiped the sweat onto my jeans.

I wasn't allowed to walk on the drain at night. I'd promised I wouldn't. But it didn't feel much different to during the day, except you had to be a bit more careful in case someone was sleeping and you didn't see them. A dog walked behind us, slowing down or speeding up when we did.

'They said your dad's a nigger lover,' the boy said.

'Are you allowed to say that word?'

'What do you care, you're white. I think you're the one who's not meant to say it.'

'True.'

'You don't say much, eh.' He laughed, kicking a bottle top.

'What do you want me to say?' I laughed too, thankful that it was night-time because I was sure my face had turned beetroot red.

'I dunno. Say something smart from Melbourne. Do you think we're all weird up here?'

'Nah. I kinda like it here.'

'Yeah. Bet you've never been in a school full of blackfellas before though.'

'True, I haven't.'

'You ever kissed one?'

I'd never kissed anyone. Black, white or other. The thought filled me with fear and I felt like I was going to be sick. Worse than when I'd come off the Zipper at the show.

'Not really.'

He laughed again. He and his mates were always laughing, like they were in on some secret joke.

'What's so funny?'

'You gotta work out who you are, girl.'

Even though I didn't really know what he meant, I was offended. 'Well, what about you? Do you know who *you* are?'

'Nah, not really. But I wouldn't come here by choice. You people, all the doctors and social workers and stuff, you come then you go, like a holiday. But it's just our normal life.'

That was how Mum and Dad had described it to us, too. *It's a working holiday, it's not forever.* My primary school class had even done an assignment about where I was going – this little town with goldmines and sacred places that always had two names.

'Well, it is kind of like a holiday. I mean, it's cool here.' I felt like I was missing a point, but I didn't know what it was. 'Is that okay?'

'As long as you're not one of those church ones. Come up here, wanna help us or whatever. Are you?'

'We're not allowed to go to church.'

'Good. 'Cause we don't need it. Same people who caused the problems in the first place.'

I thought about my Grade 6 project on the First Fleet and how I'd drawn little British flags in the margins. I got an A+.

He bent down and suddenly his mouth was on mine. It tasted like blue Powerade. I pushed my lips forward, not sure what else to do. It made him stumble backwards.

'Do you wanna stop?' he asked.

But I hadn't hated it as much as I'd expected. 'Nah,' I said. We tried again. He opened his mouth, so I opened mine and my tongue started doing its own thing, like it was trying to get a bit of skittle off his teeth.

'We'd better get home, eh. Your nigger-lover dad will be wondering where you are.'

'Don't call him that, he doesn't like that word.' I thought about my parents inside, waiting for me. Thinking I was out with my girlfriend and her mum. I felt a bit sad.

'Sorry,' he said. Then he laughed. He laughed so hard he bent over and kicked a rock into the air.

'What?' I asked.

'I guess now you're a nigger lover too.'

I laughed then, and it wasn't the fake laugh that I'd been perfecting for half the year. 'I don't *love* you, okay? I'm only twelve.'

'Chill out, eh. You're so uptight.' He let out a long whistle and threw his head back.

I sank into the comfort of finding my real laugh again. It seemed to fill up my big t-shirt and make it fit better. We walked and kicked rocks and cans, the sky lighting the way to my Colorbond fence.

They say the stars here shine like nowhere else. I think that's true.

Sweet and Sour

Lily Chan

Every year in July, the small farming community of Mareeba in Far North Queensland would be whipped into a state of excitement as the biggest social event on the calendar drew near: the Mareeba Rodeo. People would come from far and wide to see the majestic beauty and ferocity of the bulls, and to witness the skills of the cowboys in their attempts to tame and conquer them.

The Rodeo also doubles up as the township's annual show, where the convoy of thrilling rides, mechanical laughing clowns, and trailers filled to the brim with showbags and trinkets galore strategically surround the rodeo stands to capture the crowds as they come and go. Pocket money is enthusiastically handed over by the fistful in exchange for five minutes of excitement.

A Rodeo must also have its Queen, and thus a bevy of young ladies enter the pageant each year for the chance to adorn a shiny tiara and attain some local fame. The traditional ballgowns are swapped out for cowgirl attire but the showy colours, sequins and tassels still feature, with embellishments of leather fringes and feathers. In place of dainty heels, pointy leather boots that have been polished to reflect moonlight are worn, though there is no concession to height.

On the eve of the Rodeo, a grand procession around the town's main street takes place. Each entrant sits demurely in the back of a trailer or ute that has been garishly decorated with masses of crepe paper, streamers, balloons and hay bales. As the procession slowly makes its way down the street, the entrants toss lollies into the excited crowd in a blatant attempt to win votes. In my final year of school, one of my friends dared to enter the pageant. To our delight, she won the runner-up position of Rodeo Princess. I remember being in awe of her effervescence and spunk.

In all, this is a weekend earmarked for fun. The kids immerse themselves in the joy of rides, dagwood dogs and jumbo slides; the teens and their older counterparts embrace the social gatherings, smoothly lubricated with wine, beer and spirits. Friendships are formed, romances bloom and the occasional scuffle breaks out. On this glorious Rodeo weekend, the high expectations of many are met.

My feelings towards this event depart somewhat from the majority. In fact, I have always approached it with much trepidation. You see, while my friends were happily making Rodeo weekend plans – where and when to meet, what to spend their allowance on, which special outfits to wear – I could not partake in this fun because I would be busy working.

My parents operated a Chinese takeaway store in the township and, in a rare flash of entrepreneurial spirit, they also rented a food stall at the Rodeo showgrounds. The stall was nothing more than a small tin shed with a concrete base, but it was of sturdy construction with its own electricity and gas supply. The top half of the front and back walls could be opened up to serve customers and enable them to see the food being freshly cooked in the four huge woks within. My mother hung a blackboard at the front which listed the compact selection of dishes on offer: fried rice; sweet and sour chicken, pork or fish; spring rolls and dim sims.

Though I knew the stall was an important income supplement – the takings from that one weekend equated to about a month of trading at our shop – I couldn't help but resent having to work there. Twelve hours on my feet all day taking customer orders, stuffing steaming hot food into plastic containers and constantly replenishing ingredients from the freezer and fridge. My little sister, who was four years younger than me, did not escape either. By the time we shut the stall at around ten p.m., we ached all over, covered in oil and dust with tiny burns all over our hands and, most embarrassing of all, smelling like deep-fried chicken.

What I really hated, though, was how it made me stand out. As one of only two Chinese families in the area I was already sensitive to looking different, and I did my best to keep quiet and not bring attention to myself. But working here, I felt like a big beacon was placed on my head. There was no blending into the crowd, no opportunity to be like the normal white kids who could spend their pocket money on the laughing clowns or hold their parents' hands as they boarded their first scary ride. This is not entirely true, of course. When there was a lull in the mid-afternoon, my mother took two $20 notes from the till and give these to me and my sister, together with permission to go out for a roam while it was quiet.

I spent most of my time and money on one particular ride. I can't recall the name anymore, but it was one of those typical in-the-air spinning rides that was fast enough to give you a thrill but not too scary to induce the expelling of liquid from either end of the body. Once the safety barrier was in place, the seat lifted, and I was spun around faster and faster, until I felt my body being pulled slightly against gravity, my long black ponytail whipping into a tangled mess. With my eyes closed, I embraced the wind and imagined I was flying away from the loneliness, and just enjoyed the sensation of moving through air.

After spending my last few dollars on the fourth turn of that ride, I took a deep breath to gather my courage and started trudging back towards my family's stall. Suddenly, I heard someone call out, 'Hey, Girl!'

I turned my head and saw a tall lady with a mop of brown ringlets leaning out of a beige trailer and looking straight at me with a smile. The large sign affixed above her head at the top of the trailer read *Dutch Pancakes* in bold cursive script.

I walked over towards her, feeling a little nervous and subconsciously checked my clothes to see if anything was out of place. 'Are you calling for me?' I asked uncertainly.

'Yes,' she smiled, small creases forming near her eyes. 'I have seen you working hard at your parents' stall.' She gestured towards my family's stall which was diagonally opposite, several metres away. 'It is always very busy, the food must be good.'

'Thank you,' I replied, and not wanting to be rude, said, 'Your pancakes smell delicious as well.'

The crinkles in her eyes deepened. 'Maple syrup is magical.' Then she quickly ducked her head back in to reach for something. Before I could turn away she had popped out again, her lean, tanned hands holding out a paper plate piled with three fat, steaming pancakes generously slathered with syrup. 'On the house, for you.'

'Oh, thank you ...' I stammered as I awkwardly took the plate. I wasn't quite sure what to think of it, but before I could say anything a customer had approached her trailer and she waved me away with another grin.

I went back to our stall bearing this precious gift. My father's eyes lit up when he saw it. He'd always had a massive sweet tooth. Ever the honest daughter, I told them how I obtained it.

'Then you must return the favour,' declared my mother, and she started to fill a container to the brim with food. She handed the hot parcel over to me. 'Here. Take this to her.'

So off I trotted back to the pancake trailer. The lady welcomed me again and, seeing what was in my hands, rewarded me with another smile. As there were currently no customers to divert her attention, I was able to linger and we had a little chat. I found out that her name was Karin, and she was from Belgium. Both she and her boyfriend had come to backpack around Australia and they decided that working on the show circuit would be a good way to see the countryside. I looked inside the trailer but did not see anyone else. I asked if her boyfriend worked in this trailer with her.

'Yes, but he just went out during the quiet period to see the Rodeo. This is our first one, it is very exciting! I will have a look later when he comes back.'

As she was speaking, she picked up a fork, speared a piece of food from my offering and took a big bite.

'This is delicious! The batter is fragrant and crunchy and this sauce is so tangy – a little sweet but also sour. What is it called?'

I grinned at her. 'Sweet and sour pork.'

She chuckled. 'Makes sense.'

I asked her to tell me some more about her travels. Although I was a quiet and shy person by nature, I had learnt how to converse with customers through working at the shop. For the next ten minutes I was wholly absorbed in Karin's retelling of her adventure in Australia. Before joining the show circuit, they had spent a month in Sydney. She described to me how the white sails of the Opera House glistened like diamonds in the sun, how the golden, sandy beaches and gentle waves washed all her little worries away, and how the city felt so new and fresh in stark contrast to her home that was steeped in antiquity and tradition. Oh, how I yearned to visit that place!

Karin then asked me what was worth seeing here. I fell silent for a moment. I'd never thought too much about the place, apart from pondering how soon I could leave it. I hadn't really considered it from a visitor's perspective before. At the end of the day, it was still my home, so I put on my best smile and told her, 'This is a place of nature. The name Mareeba means "meeting of the waters". Though it may not appear as dazzling as those places you have just visited, it has its own hidden charms. Kangaroos come out at night to feed on the grass, sometimes they even bound along the main street! The big mud-shaped monuments on the side of the road are giant anthills – those ants are a hardworking lot.'

I racked my brain to think of more positive points and recalled my last school excursion to the local farms. 'Mareeba was originally well-known for growing tobacco, but smoking is no longer cool so the farmers have had to switch to other crops. Now it's famous for growing mangoes. They are the biggest, juiciest and sweetest ones you'll find. It's a pity they're not currently in season, but if you're still in Australia over summer, look out for them in the fruit shops. A lot of travellers actually come here during picking season to find work.' I was rambling a bit now, and I think Karin could see it.

'And how do you like living here?' she asked gently.

I was quiet for awhile before answering. 'It's character-building,' I confessed, before hastily adding, 'but there are nice people here, too.' I originally said this to soften my disdain for the place, but, when these words came out, I realised it was true. Nice people like Mr and Mrs Soda, our elderly Italian landlords who lived above our shop and would watch out for me and my sister while we played in the backyard. Like Christina, my best friend at school – her crazy ideas and wicked sense of humour lightened the dreariness of my daily life. And like Karen, the young lady whose parents owned the Shell service station next door – perhaps she saw me hanging around near the servo by myself a lot and was worried I'd get hit by a car, so she often took me in behind the counter and looked after me.

My thoughts were interrupted by a hungry kid who was clutching a scrunched up $10 note in her hand. Karin put down her almost-empty food container to serve the girl. Reflexively, I glanced towards my family's stall and saw that a few customers had also started to gather. I sighed and thought I had better head back. Mum's English was not so good, it was better for me to take the orders. I bid Karin a quick farewell and promised that I would try to visit her again tomorrow. She flashed me a now familiar wide smile and gave me a wave with her spatula-wielding hand.

As I threaded my way through the crowd to return to our stall, I realised I felt a little happier and my mood was lighter than before. Unexpectedly, a chance encounter with a stranger from a faraway place had helped me realise the silver lining of the small country town I call home.

The Old Bushblock

Dorothea Pfaff

Dawn, Saturday. My bedroom door opened abruptly, and my father's one-word command was rudely shunted in.

'Bushblock!'

Then the door slammed shut again.

Greyish light was seeping in around the edges of the blind. Beyond the window, I could hear the scuffing of tyres on concrete and then a clank as the trailer was hitched. I groaned and turned over under my bedsheets.

Muffled scraping, murmuring voices and shuffling continued, permeating the room, and I knew, without looking outside, that my brother and father were loading the trailer with rakes and scythes and shovels, industrial-sized plastic buckets and leather work gloves.

I staggered out of bed and moped off to the kitchen, where Mum, dressed in Bushblock drab, was stacking cold lemon drinks into the esky. With barely time to down a piece of toast, Dad had us all piled into the Kingswood and we were off.

On the front bench seat, Mum was squeezed between my brother and Dad's elbow as he wrangled the stick-shift, and us four girls were in the back. It would be a day of hard graft and sunburn for the lot of us. To my father, however, it was a day in the countryside. He'd grown up in a Bavarian village, surrounded by undulating sweeps of pristine forest. He'd named our house after an endemic oak tree from his neck of the woods. Back then, I had no notion of his love of trees. I was just a surly adolescent, grumbling from the rear seat about another hot day and child labour.

The Bushblock was a rectangular three-acre lot beyond the fringes of suburbia, surrounded by market gardens, chook farms and undeveloped crown land. Dad's block sat on a hill, and rose in a steep gradient from the road. He had hewn a rough track, which wound its way up through bushland to a ramshackle shed in the middle of the block. The shed's corrugated iron roof was used to harvest water, which was funnelled into an adjacent metal tank. Dad had cleared scrub from the top half of the block and planted pine trees, with the perverse idea of creating his own small forest paradise. Did he really think he could recapture the cool gloom of those walls of dark green from his youth? The dank smell of rotting leaves underfoot? Rambles on meandering forest paths in the depths of winter, walking stick in hand? This was Western Australia, the state of glare.

He must have known that his dream of a verdant countryside was not translatable to this land, and yet, he persisted in battling it out with the brutal summers and the Bushblock's sandy soil, through which water ran like a sieve. Dad had taken care to choose pine species *Pinus pinaster* and *Pinus radiata*, which could withstand intense heat and sparse winter rain and were proven performers in our climate. He started out with trials of small batches of seedlings and, as the years progressed, he established rows and rows of pine trees, eventually covering half the block. By the time I was a teenager, he'd planted several hundred pine trees. The first rows of trees were already a few metres tall. Their roots had tapped into the water table and they could fend for themselves, but as you traversed further up the block, trees planted in successive years were not yet established. Near the top of the block were rows of spindly saplings that relied wholly on regular watering.

*

Dad swerved the car sharply right onto the bumpy Bushblock track and we were jolted out of our sleepy complacency. As the car wheels sought traction on the soft sand and the trailer rattled along behind, us four sisters, shoulder to shoulder in the back seat, lurched from side to side and bounced up and down. When we came to a stop at the shed, Dad jumped out of the car and surveyed his domain. Somehow, he grew a little taller as he breathed in the fresh air. Then he strode across to the metal tank and knocked on each corrugation, listening for a dull thud that marked the water-line. This elicited an exclamation of joy (because there *was* water in the tank) and then a mutter of disappointment (because there was never enough of it). In any case, work started with alacrity. An order went out for one of us kids to take the buckets off the back of the trailer. Someone else was sent to retrieve the tap fittings from under the shed steps, where they were kept out of sight in case of would-be water thieves or vandals. Dad attached the fittings onto the tank outlet and turned on the tap, and all our ears tuned in to the marvel of clean water drumming into a bucket.

Dad took charge of dispensing the limited supply. His tried-and-true method was to fill the buckets one after the other without turning off the tap, minimising spillage by deftly shifting through an empty bucket once another was filled. Meanwhile, us kids schlepped uphill, following his exacting instructions to give each thirsty pine sapling half a bucket only, and to make sure the water did not drain over the sides of the shallow depressions he had moulded around each tree.

I rued my father's lack of foresight in planting the pine trees on the upper half of the block, which meant we had the heavy work going uphill, full buckets of water just about tearing our arms out of their sockets as we staggered forward headfirst, then running helter-skelter downhill with the empty buckets jangling, so that Dad had a ready supply for the constant stream of water.

We were wet with sweat and covered in grime by midmorning, and the sun was already high in the sky. To me, the idea of creating a micro forest was ridiculous. Wasted energy. And anyway, we were too late for some of the younger saplings, which hadn't survived the harsh conditions and the long interval between drinks. They were merely brittle sticks poking out of the ground. I wanted to shout, *Get over it. You're not in the Spessart Wald now.* It all felt so un-Australian.

One summer day, when we were all working hard at the Bush-block, some good friends of my parents turned up. They were just passing by on a Sunday drive, they said, and saw the car parked. They must have looked pretty hard, because it was parked a good distance off the road with scrubby bush screening the view up the track. Mum was mortified to be seen in her work gear with leather-gloved hands and dirt caked in the creases of her face, but Dad was in his element, despite his mended workpants and tattered cap. Always the charming host, he greeted the interlopers cheerfully, led a tour of his beloved trees and offered around plastic cups of homemade lemonade.

I may have whinged mightily, but for us kids, at least, there was always some free time. When we were younger, we built a cubby under the low-hanging branches of a tree and sipped on thimbles of water poured from a teapot. As teenagers, we turned cartwheels on sand cleared of twigs and rocks and competed for the straightest and longest handstands. Every now and then, Dad stopped work to rip a prickly pear from a wild tangle of cacti that grew along the fence line. With a gloved hand holding the fruit, he peeled away the spiky skin and pared off slices of soft orange flesh for us to pick from the blade of his penknife.

But mostly, Dad was hard at it scything down knee-high weeds and grasses, with my brother and mother hard at it beside him, and together they cut a swath from one side of the block to the other. He sent us girls off to get rakes and showed us where to build up piles of dry grass and pulled weeds. These small piles were then mounded together into one wide bundle and set alight in a clearing. Dad's rule was that the fire could only be started from one spot, so that any lizards or other bugs hiding under the heap would have time to scurry out before the flames took hold.

When the dry grass bristled and crackled with flames, Dad threw on a few logs of dead wood and we watched the lot burn. Then he whipped out the camera for a classic family snap. He commanded us all to bunch together next to the fire while he took a shot. His idea of happy families.

I have a photograph of the five of us kids – a ragtag bunch in our shorts and t-shirts – standing beside a blazing fire. My eyes are half-closed against the smoke. I can't recall if it was an insect bite or a splinter or an ember spat from the fire, but I had the sudden urge to scratch an itch on my knee, just as Dad pressed the shutter button. In the photo I look rather petulant, face turned away from the fire and standing on one leg, with my opposite hand on my raised knee. The rest of the crew is standing stock-upright, staring straight at the camera. My older sister was on me for weeks afterwards. *Think you're a model or something?* she accused. *What a poser*. She didn't buy the insect story.

When the flames died down, Dad raked out some hot coals with a stick and laid out the potatoes, some wrapped in foil but most in their bare skins. When they were cooked, we scraped off the blackened crust and ate the delicious creamy flesh. Charcoaled hands for a few bites of spud. It was a flimsy reward for the hard labour of tending to that land, which, for all I could see, was only work for work's sake. It would all have to be done a few more times before the hot season was over.

After Dad kicked the last of the embers thoroughly into the dirt and poured over half a bucket of precious water, he reloaded the trailer. Only he could do this job, because it required precision to ensure everything was tied down properly and that there was enough extra space for the firewood he'd collected and roughly chopped to bring back home. And last thing before we all piled into the car in our filthy rags, Mum scouted around for velvet-soft kangaroo paws, and these would grace the coffee table in our lounge room for the next week.

*

140

Every spring, Dad hired a man with a tractor plough to clear a fire-break around the perimeter of the Bushblock, as required by the shire. Even when they were tall and fending for themselves, the pines had an innate weakness compared to the eucalypts, banksias and grass trees, which had survived on the property for hundreds of years. The pine trees could not regenerate after fire. They could be jeopardised by something as simple as a cast-off piece of glass catching the sun's rays and setting the undergrowth alight – us kids were regularly sent to remove bottles and broken glass from the verge.

The risk of fire never diminished. I imagine my father spent many stifling summer nights lying awake, worrying about his trees. Many times, in extreme heat conditions, Dad drove out to the block by himself to water the more desperate trees and check all was well.

Sure enough, despite all his efforts, a fire tore through the Bushblock one afternoon. The culprit was a weld spark from a neighbouring shed that flew across the wire fence and set dry grass alight. As a post-mortem later revealed, the grassfire spread up the hill towards the pine trees and devoured the pine needles that lay thick on the ground. Flames licked their way up the tree trunks, and a raging blaze cut through the middle of the pine grove.

Many of the mature trees were burnt out to black husks. Dad was stoic, but the calamity hit him in the jaw. You could see it in the way he shrugged and wandered aimlessly around the lounge room and up and down the hallway, when he was usually out in the yard fixing something. For a few days he grieved the loss, but he was fatalistic. Despite all he had done to mitigate the fire risk, in his heart he'd always known there were no guarantees. The neighbour didn't apologise, and Dad never put him up to it. Instead, he pulled down the burnt wrecks and counted himself lucky he still had some good stands of trees. Nothing was irredeemable, he rationalised. Nature had taken and would replenish. He simply planted more pine trees.

The lost trees and the extra work of re-establishing his little forest did not dampen my father's enthusiasm for weekend jaunts to the Bushblock. He cherished that plot of land. He loved turning up every time with a sense of anticipation to see what had changed and what needed doing. There were always jobs to be done – collecting firewood; cleaning out the shed gutters; removing trees that had become infested by termites; and at Christmas time, selecting a symmetrically formed pine branch that would serve as a Christmas tree.

For many years, long after us kids had left home, my parents continued to make regular pilgrimages to the Bushblock, especially during spring and summer. Once, in my late thirties and seven months pregnant, I flew home for a visit. The long-absent daughter returns. Never mind – I'd clashed with a Bushblock day. There we were, Mum and I, on our hands and knees pulling lupins – a useless task, as they had already set seed and would be sprouting again with a vengeance next year. Mum, wheezing with hay fever she had surely acquired from years of Bushblock work, kept reminding me to have a drink. Dad was down the hill, out of sight, working the scythe on rampant grasses and weeds. He was already over seventy by then, but there was no question of packing it in.

When the Bushblock was put on the market after Dad's terminal diagnosis, he was reluctant to sell. I was angry at his reticence and told him so. The land was a millstone. Mum couldn't manage the upkeep. She couldn't pay the rates or afford to have a firebreak ploughed each spring. He was mortally ill when he relented and signed away his plot of land. It was a great consolation to my father, before he died, to know that the buyer loved the pine trees.

*

Last week I was back in the area, to visit a nursery specialising in camelias. I took Mum with me, because she's a keen gardener and has a talent for picking the best plants. On the drive home, we detoured a few kilometres to see the old Bushblock. We meandered along back roads from the opposite direction to that which she knew, and took a wrong turn here and there, so we saw something of the district. Not much had changed. The roadside stall where Mum bought farm eggs was still there. The fibro shack on stumps where friends of my parents raised their six kids still stood starkly on the corner of a cleared block looking out over a lake. In the distance, concrete works poked out above the tree line, surrounded by a buffer of bushland.

We pulled up in front of the Bushblock. Majestic grass trees graced the front verge, as they had for centuries, but the property had been transformed by the new owners. An imposing brick and wrought-iron fence dominated the street frontage. A plaque on the automatic gate announced the property as *Pine Forest Estate*. Behind the fence was the Australian bush, just as Dad had left it, except now it was sparser, more like a native garden. Beyond, many of the pine trees still stood. They were giants now. We drove around the corner to get a better view of the upper section. At the top of the block, a two-storey house with a large balcony looked out across the canopy of the pine trees.

I drove Mum back home on a highway bulldozed through bush and market gardens, to make space for encroaching suburbia. Slung in a valley below the road, brick houses on small blocks baked under a torrid sun, and there was only the zigzag line of corrugated-iron roofs poking out above the bitumen. Mum commented that Dad would never have built a house in a ditch with no trees, no interruption of green.

It was then that I really understood why my father had not wanted to sell his Bushblock. The years of work. Dirt-smeared faces and calloused hands. All that careful attention to planting and tending and watering and watching and hoping against fire. He wanted us to enjoy the full grandeur of the trees in their prime, which he knew might be beyond his own lifetime. We threw away that inheritance.

*

I have a favourite photograph of my father, taken by me on one of many trips to the Bushblock when I was a teenager. Told to hurry and get the camera from the car, and not being sure how to use it, I huffed about irritably. In the photo, Dad is standing in front of his pine trees, with his arms outstretched, holding a bobtail in each hand. Their mouths are agape in protest and their blue tongues lolling. Dad's cap is lopsided, and he has a relaxed, boyish grin from ear to ear – nothing like the stern, dominant figure I remembered from my youth.

The picture is out of focus. As he was for much of my life.

Bad Dreams and a Trusty Shovel

Angus Thompson

My first memory is of searing pain coupled with a supreme sense of isolation. I was standing at the swings, facing the front door of the house, waiting for my mother to burst through the fly-screen door. In between was the no-man's-land of the barren front lawn, which seemed to expand infinitely like in a bad dream.

I lifted my foot off the stubbly grass to reveal a quivering bee, hoisted off the ground by its entrails that were still hooked into my clenched arch. The wailing began without my say-so, but I brought it to full force so it would cross the distance between myself and home. I didn't want it to be carried out into the paddock, where the sound of my distress would diffuse in the wind, and no-one would come to my rescue.

I spent the first few years of my life on a sheep station near the clifftops of the Fleurieu Peninsula, in South Australia. It was a tongue of land poking out towards Kangaroo Island, which on clear days I could see across the ocean from the property. The homestead was owned by some cattle baron, and it was up the hill from the shearing shed where Dad worked. My father's lineage included some of country New South Wales' wealthier landowners, but he survived by working on the land of others.

The fence line around the house and yard created an island in a sea of paddocks, which abutted a strait that Mum told me more than once was filled with great white sharks. As to their numbers, I can't say, but oceanic explorer Jacques Cousteau had been drawn to the area to study them. To me, looking out to the sea from those windswept paddocks felt so elemental, like we were living at an outpost at the edge of the known world. Who knows, maybe Cousteau viewed it in similar terms.

It was the same awareness I felt when Dad drove along the steep ridgelines of the far-reaching paddocks, where the spines of hills almost touched the darkening clouds above. On one occasion, he pulled over to slice part of the flank off a dead kangaroo while I watched from the back seat. I can't remember whether we ate it for dinner or if it went to the working dogs.

Even at an age when I delighted in climbing trees, and brushed off the pain from scaling barbed wire fences, the sparseness of the area in which we lived terrified me. The adventure my siblings and I experienced running through paddocks where the bulls roamed, stepping over cattle grates or traipsing through the forested area behind the house, was often tinged with the feeling that real peril wasn't that far away. Mum, who had absorbed her own trauma as the child of country doctors, may have passed on this fear by osmosis. Though it was most likely transmitted through the tenor of her voice as she dealt with everything with no immediate help at hand. Visitors were infrequent and the other properties were either invisible or tiny in the distance, much too far away for a five-year-old to fathom. In my dreams I became stuck in some forgotten pocket of our garden while monsters approached me with sinister intent.

I keenly remember Dad raining blow upon blow of his shovel on a rearing snake that had invaded our backyard. I have a mental image of it poised in an S-bend before moving to strike, as I watched from behind the flyscreen door, where my mother had gathered me and my siblings. Death by shovel was Dad's preferred method of disposing of the most biblical of foes, I came to learn. But it was never tidy, and the pieces didn't stop wriggling for some time.

Dad had a gang of kelpies housed in a run out the back, but we got a corgi for the family. We called her Tessa, and on her first few nights she cried and cried outside our bedroom doors because she was alone, so my parents gave her a Paddington Bear soft toy as a friend. While Tessa was still young, Mum would have to put her in an esky so she wouldn't chase the car down the long driveway when she took us to school. She was also our guard dog from snakes, her barks prompting Dad to return to the arena with his trusty shovel.

You can bet I dreamed about snakes.

Our house, in which I often scared myself watching *The Simpsons* Halloween episodes and lay on sheepskin rugs next to black house spiders, was the setting for some of the scariest dreams I've ever experienced. It had a long hallway with high windows, and I imagined ghosts wafting through it at night. In one dream I ran down that hallway after my brother. He was playing and laughing, but I was behind him and scared. He disappeared and I suddenly crossed a doorway of bright, white light, and it was just me in the middle of an arid landscape scattered with animal bones. I was calling out for him, and I was lonely and frightened.

A couple of times I left the property in the back of an ambulance, woken in the middle of the night by a team of paramedics after I'd apparently had trouble breathing. I wonder what I had been dreaming about before then, and whether it was of being choked.

Our time in the country ended one day when a pair of electric shears plunged into the back of Dad's left hand. Mum piled us into the car, with Dad in the front seat, holding his limb in a crumple of rags. In Adelaide, my father underwent surgery, while my aunt and uncle distracted us at their place with *Jurassic Park* toys. Dad retained the use of his hand after a metal plate and screws – which he could feel on cold days – were placed into the back of it. He was let go from his job and we moved to Sydney soon after, into the suburban home of my grandparents, who were severe but benevolent.

*

For me, nostalgia – and possibly childhood itself – began at the age of six. I took to the suburbs instantly – the house-lined streets with children just down the road, the next-door neighbour with a pool that I learned to swim in, the summer evening walks where we admired the front gardens of others. I believe that Mum felt it too: the ability to breathe a bit easier when you are no longer contemplating daily life in such rigid terms.

When we were grown up, my parents agreed that Dad would go back to the country for work. I think that made it easier for *him* to breathe, returning to a world that made sense. When I first visited him, it was to a wintry homestead in the south-west corner of New South Wales during the desperate last years of the millennium drought. Driving his quad bike around the deadwood landscape, I saw sheep separated from their flock and struggling to stand, and that uneasiness, that knowledge of mortality I carried with me as a child, returned. Some sheep that didn't survive went straight to his kitchen table. One night we ate a simple dinner together and I tried to find commonality in the fact that, as a result of a sporting injury, I too now had metal in my hand. After leaving, I did not return to that place. I didn't want to. And I have only briefly visited one other farm he worked at since then.

My father is a man who spoke of getting kicked by hooved animals as though it was like receiving a papercut. His wiry, though battered, physique has always been younger than its years. But, in the end, even he tired of the hard labour of his country existence, swapping paddocks for a hardware store's garden nursery in a coastal town.

With the passing of time, I'm able to view the bush with a little more romance, a place of songbirds and earthy palettes far away from the urban cacophony where I now live. It's a place of meditation through exploration, with elements of beauty and drama in the way the land unfurls.

Recently, I saw a snake sunning itself on a patch of lush grass and I didn't quake, just watched it slither to the safety of a mound of rocks upon my approach. I stood at a termite mound and marvelled at the ugly claws of a goanna with its head buried in the underground city as it had its fill. I still see monsters, though they're no longer of my dreams. The fear is still there too, tucked away in a part of me I actually hope I never shed, because these days it looks a little bit more like respect and wonder for the place from which I've come.

Pah Paw Pa

Youssef Saudie

'Oi, sand nigga, this way,' says a mate as we move towards the classroom door for recess. Two other friends laugh. Another friend says, 'Yeah, dune coon, we're hungry, let's sit over there.' He points to the blue table under the sun. I look at their pale faces and peach-fuzzed upper lips and move to join them. They are my friends. I just wish my brown skin wasn't the centre of every discussion.

High school in Alice Springs is a racism hotspot. But I have learnt to be proud of my Egyptian culture and shake off the most racist remarks, which started when I was in Grade 2.

*

I can feel the sweat on the back of my knees as we sit cross-legged in class. This always happens in the summer in Alice. It feels like at any moment your skin could just melt right off you.

Our teacher is about to tell us something. I gaze up at her pale white skin as she says, 'We have a new student today.'

The newcomer is standing next to her. She has dark brown hair and caramel skin. The new student commands the classroom, speaking with great confidence. Everyone looks up at her. 'I'm from Pah Paw Pa,' she says, before enthusing about the place she has come from. But I start to tune out when I hear 'Pah Paw Pa'. She's talking gibberish.

Pah paw pa. It occurred to me later that I haven't taken in her name. She's just *Pah paw pa* to me. She swings on the swings at

150

lunchtime as if the playground is already hers. I think about asking her about *Pah paw pa*. I just think about it.

When the school day ends, Mum picks me up in her dusty Toyota Camry.

Sitting in the back seat as we drive home, I tell her about the new student. I say with a chuckle, 'She's from *Pah paw pa*.'

In the rear-view mirror, I see my mum's eyebrows furrow ever so slightly. 'Where?' she asks.

I slowly move my lips: '*Pah paw pa*.'

Mum says, 'You mean Pa-pu-a: Papua New Guinea. That's where you were born.'

For a moment, I wonder if I need to get my ears tested. And then my head floods with questions.

I don't remember Mum ever telling me where I was born … but I thought I was born in Egypt? Or Australia? One of those two. Papua New Guinea? What Egyptian is born in Papua New Guinea? The idea that I was born anywhere but Egypt or Australia is inconceivable to me. It is just weird. I'm already the only Arab in my school. They always pronounce my name, Youssef, as 'Yosef' or 'Joseph'. But how can I blame them if I didn't even know the name of my own birthplace until today?

Mum takes a right instead of a left, and I realise we must be stopping by the grocery store before heading home. As we hop out of the car, Mum continues talking about how she and the rest of the family lived in Papua New Guinea for over five years before settling down in outback Australia. Apparently, my sister was the only one out of the three of us born in Egypt.

'You were born in Lae and your older brother was born in Port Moresby,' she says.

Mum explained that when I was two, in 2002, my parents' qualifications were finally recognised by the Australian government and they were able to work here. So, they moved to Alice Springs, the first place they got offered a job.

Walking into the grocery store, my mum receives glares from a room of white faces. We're used to it. She's always the only person in a room wearing a hijab. But she rocks it with different colours and jewellery. There are some brown and bla(c)k faces around, but usually they aren't acknowledged at all. You can see people turn their heads away from them or even walk in a different direction.

In the fresh produce section, Mum sees someone she knows. This often happens, because she's a doctor. The lady has dark brown skin and tight curly black hair. My mum's face glows. Her eyes bulge and her mouth opens in surprise. She isn't usually this excited. They start speaking. Not English. Not Arabic. But Pidgin, a common language in Papua New Guinea, which she picked up while living there to communicate with her patients. The lady smiles while talking with her. She seems so excited: it's like she hasn't spoken a word of Pidgin in years and she can finally speak to someone. People stare at them, speaking a foreign language in the grocery store, but they don't care.

There's a girl behind her. It's Pah Paw Pa. I stare at her in shock, still processing everything in my mind. She laughs at me. Grinning, my mum finishes her conversation, and we move away.

At home, Mum sits me down on the living room couch. She starts to explain Papua New Guinea to me. She shows me a black and gold bird of paradise painting in the living room and explains that this is the bird on the PNG flag. And that the reason why her rice is always so delicious is because she adds coconut milk. In Papua New Guinea they used fresh coconut.

*

It had taken my family seven years to tell me where I was born.

*

The next day at school, I find Pah Paw Pa, on the swing set.

'Are you from Pah Paw Pa?' I ask. I know I'm saying it wrong.

'Yes, I am. Papua,' she says. She keeps swinging as she speaks to me.

'I was born in Papua New Guinea,' I say. 'In Lae.'

She smiles and says she was born in Port Moresby. 'I'm Papuan and proud,' she says, as if someone had questioned it.

So there we are. Two Proud Papuans. Smack-bang in the middle of Australia.

Territory

Holden Sheppard

Nine

I don't belong on a backyard cricket pitch, but for my cousin Lockie, it's his home turf. Sure, it's literally his yard: a quarter-acre in Mahomets Flats, backing onto broccoli-headed bushland so close to the Indian Ocean you can hear waves crash and smell rank seaweed. But it's more than that. From Lockie's relaxed shoulders and his confidence as he smacks the ball into the cracked Super Six fence for a four, you can tell this is his territory.

I'm a visitor.

Backyard cricket should be fun, but my shoulders are always tensed because I'm crap at it. Every dropped catch is further proof I am as unco as my older siblings say I am; more proof I don't belong in my hometown. And cricket is hardly the roughest, toughest sport – I mean, the guys on TV run around in white linen and break for tea. If I can't even do this, footy is right out.

My aunty always sends me and Lockie out here after school for fresh air, but I can never cram much of it into my lungs. Instead, I bat and bowl with Lockie for a breathless hour. I laugh when I fuck up, but beneath the self-deprecation is fear. I'm not carefree, effortlessly rough like other country boys. Something is wrong with me. It's in the corner of my eye, but when I try to look at it, it glides just out of sight, taunting me. I can't grip onto it. But my bones know it, and I'm scared everyone will soon find out I'm defective.

*

When the sun sinks behind the fence, Lockie and I join forces with my sister Gabi and his sister Julia, who, while we played cricket, were busy drowning their Barbies in the backyard mud. Like our heroes Captain Planet and the Planeteers, by our powers combined we pressure our mothers into letting us stay for tea. This is the pinnacle of pre-teen after-school entertainment. The pressuring works. When our fathers rock up – my dad is an earthmover, Lockie's dad is a bricklayer – they agree to ordering greasy Eagle Boys' pizza for tea.

Our mothers push us through the shower in double time: first our sisters, then me and Lockie. Two nine-year-old boys fit easily together in the brown glass of the 1980s-built shower recess.

I'm soaping up when Lockie starts pissing down the drain hole.

'What are you doing?' I ask. It's not like I don't know how to pee standing up, but it's usually in a toilet.

'You didn't know? We can do this.'

I didn't know we could pee in the shower. Maybe it's something he picked up from his footy mates. Maybe it's another thing I'm meant to be doing but I'm not.

A few days later, I'm in my bunk bed reading a new *Animorphs* book. The main character, Jake, morphs into a wolf and starts pissing to mark his territory. The character is mocked – and feels embarrassed – but he says he can't stop. There's an alpha wolf drive to mark his turf by peeing. What was unusual from my cousin is cool from Jake. In fact, the idea of marking your territory as a man is exciting, especially when I don't feel I have any territory of my own.

The next time I shower, I decide I want to be like Jake. I want to be a man. So, I start peeing in the shower. Straight down the drain hole. It's the first time I feel anything like a wolf.

But it is an omen. Unlike Lockie or Jake, who take up space in the outside world, my territory will be marked in secret.

Eleven

The principal of my Catholic primary school is an enigma wrapped in a nun's habit. Sister Margaret is progressive enough to have the whole school undertake daily guided meditations, but she bans pop-culture fads with the ferocity of King Herod. She has taken it upon herself to protect our idyllic country childhoods from the demons of the city, and technology, and America. Nothing is beyond prohibition: first she takes our Tazos, then our Tamagotchis, our Furbies, even our marbles. By the time she outlaws Pokémon cards, we have no approved hobbies left, so we start to turn on each other during lunchtimes.

When one of the other boys starts shoving me, I see red. I'm not violent, but that doesn't mean I can't be destructive. This guy has a huge shock of blond ringlets, so I go to call him Goldilocks when I realise I could twist the knife deeper.

'Gaydilocks,' I taunt. 'Gaydilocks. Gaydilocks.'

I don't fully understand what 'gay' means. Or why it's made everyone laugh so hard. Or why he's crying and running to the toilets. But I now know the power of that word. I just dropped Fat Man on Nagasaki. I ended the war, but I used a weapon I should never have touched.

And I am decidedly *not* gay myself, because at the tender age of eleven, I have a girlfriend. Emmaline and I don't do much except talk at recess and play our chunky grey-brick Game Boys together at her house. But things ramp up at the school disco. It starts with squeals of pre-teen delight when 'Everybody (Backstreet's Back)' – a total banger – tapers off into the first notes of a Savage Garden ballad, playing over the stereo in Bluff Point's Fitzgerald Hall.

Before we know it, all the 'couples' of Year 7 are being pushed together to dance. Emmaline drapes her hands over my shoulders, and I glance sideways to see where I'm supposed to put my hands. The other boys with girlfriends have their hands on the girls' lower backs. Those guys are much more popular than me – in fact, how I even have a girlfriend is beyond me – so I'm sure they must know what they're doing.

I perch my hands on Emmaline's lower back and start to sway.

'Lower,' says a voice, but it's not hers. We are surrounded by envious eleven-year-old spinsters and bachelors. For some reason they've zeroed in on us. 'Lower.'

Am I doing this wrong? Is this not how guys dance with girls? Should my hands be lower? Do I look like a massive virgin? I bet Emmaline is waiting for this song to finish so she can detach. I bet they all think I'm not a real man. I don't think I've ever received this much attention. It's horrible. I can't stand being looked at, especially not in what should have been an intimate moment.

'Lower!'

I make a face at Emmaline like, 'Okay, this is what we're meant to do, right?' and my hands slide down to the top of her buttocks.

Shrieks of laughter now. The rabble just landed the biggest dhufish ever on the end of their baited hooks. I don't understand. Did they want us to do this, or not? I've never been more confused or embarrassed. The laughter gets the attention of one of the nuns, who notices the inappropriate PDA.

'Two feet apart!' she bellows, forming her thick arms into a steeple and tunnelling through the whole row of couples to physically separate us all.

Emmaline goes to the toilets with her friends. We never dance again. I am relieved.

Thirteen

The dunny is a site of unexpected threats. We live in Strathalbyn, a semi-rural estate by the Chapman River, and always lift the toilet seat before we do number twos, especially in summer. One time, I sit down on a redback spider and narrowly avoid a bite on the butt cheek. Another time, a frog crawls through the pipes and bounds up out of the toilet bowl covered in shit.

One day, the dunny throws up a threat I never saw coming: Hugh Jackman. I blame him for everything. *X-Men 2* is coming out next year. One of my siblings has left the latest *Empire* magazine on the melamine toilet shelf that usually only hosts Archie Comics and empty toilet rolls. I can't take a dump without being faced with a glossy image of Wolverine. And there is no mistaking the rush of excitement each time I glance at Hugh Jackman's bronzed muscles pulsing out the sleeves of his skimpy, white singlet. A tingle of curiosity at what could be underneath that tank top, those denim jeans, that belt buckle. This must be how my mate Bruce felt when he showed me his collection of Sarah Michelle Gellar JPEGs. This is how I'm supposed to feel when I see Holly Valance and Carmen Electra on the cover of *FHM* or *Ralph*.

Unbeknownst to him, Hugh Jackman teaches me how to masturbate. Every time the wave of orgasm builds, I anticipate surfing it, riding the crest with my arms out like a hero, the way the surf rats of Geraldton do in Champion Bay. But once the wave breaks, nothing is left but cold seafoam fizzing guiltily on my skin.

*

After that, AFL games are tainted too. I love watching footy with the other men of our family, all swearing and shouting at the TV together. But now, while everyone else yells 'Holding the ball!', my pupils are dilating at the sight of so many hot men on one screen. They run, tackle, fight, wrestle. Guernseys stretch tight across their pecs. Sweat-licked biceps flex as they mark the Sherrin.

I don't want to act on this. Hugh Jackman is a movie star, but footy players walk on hallowed terrain. If I enjoy them for anything other than their sporting prowess, I will breach the man code. But I can't stop my mind disobeying me in my sleep. I have recurring dreams of being in the Collingwood Football Club locker room, where I stand pissing at a urinal beside one of the players while his teammates shower and soap up around us. I wake up with sticky boxer shorts every time.

I am out of bounds on the full.

*

Even at thirteen, me and Lockie still get excited when we rope our parents into turning an after-school hang out into tea. We muck around in Lockie's backyard kicking soccer balls around until they go over the fence, or sometimes we have a go on his skateboard. This is the era of Tony Hawk and Blink-182 and skate parks. The alternative boys my age have found their place in this small footy-and-surfing-obsessed town, but after falling off Lockie's skateboard repeatedly, I realise it's not for me. I'll never fit in with the footy jocks or the surfers, and apparently being a Sk8er Boi is out, too.

At dusk, Lockie and I head inside and play *Brute Force* on his new Xbox. Our little sisters are in the same room, playing *The Sims* on the PC. They drown their characters by throwing them in swimming pools and removing the ladders, or setting the house on fire and then removing all the exits, leaving their Sims doomed to catch fire and die. We all laugh at the macabre absurdity, and move on to illegally downloading songs off LimeWire.

But at night when I try to get to sleep, those pixelated Sims haunt me. I imagine them racing around sealed houses, hands clutching their burning hair, desperately looking for a way out that doesn't exist.

Fifteen

At fifteen, I encounter a confirmed homosexual. His name is Jeff. He's a checkout supervisor at the locally owned Supa Valu Central supermarket on Marine Terrace. I work there as a storeman, though everyone calls us floor boys.

One day, me and my fellow floor boy Bill are talking with Jeff when singer-songwriter Shannon Noll is mentioned. Bill and I reckon he would have been a better *Australian Idol* winner than Guy Sebastian. Jeff agrees, but not for the same reason.

'Shannon's kind of nice to look at, ay,' he says.

Bill and I laugh nervously and disperse. It was presumed Jeff was gay – the way he speaks, the way he laughs with the checkout

chicks sans flirtation – but this is confirmation. I don't think about
what I might have in common with Jeff, or how he could help me.
I think about getting the hell away from him.

When Bill and I cross paths in the warehouse later, we are in
agreement. Jeff is weird, a poofter. As I load cardboard into the box
crusher, Bill tells me about the singers he thinks are hot, like Avril
Lavigne. Outwardly I agree Avril is hot, but privately I like her
music more than I like her body. But I'm not going to make myself
a weirdo like Jeff, and definitely not in a place like the warehouse.
I love working here. Being a floor boy is a low-level shitkicker job,
but when I'm here I'm like any other teenage boy at his first job.
I lift heavy shit and move it around. I enjoy feeling normal. No way
I'd screw that up by being a homo.

But I can't control my body. My eyes can't help but notice the
hot guys who walk in, from customers to other floor boys. Stacking shelves and moving pallets around a warehouse leaves plenty
of time for thoughts to roam. I daydream about what I'd do with
Mark, the cute floor boy with dark eyes and a darker expression,
and Dave, a big burly surfer who frequently fucks up, but you
forgive him because he's so hot.

Some guys I'm not attracted to at all, like Shanksy, who's a
couple years older than me. When I sit in the warehouse to eat
my lunchtime chicken and mayo roll, Shanksy's in charge of the
fruit and veg department, talking absolute shit. He's a douche:
cocky, but without the looks or talent to back it up. He speaks with
unrestrained volume, like he's never doubted himself a single day
of his life. He blasts punk rock, like The Offspring's new album
Splinter, until a supervisor tells him to turn it down. If a supervisor
told me off like that I'd be horrified and never play music again.
But Shanksy shrugs it off, and next week he'll do it all over again,
without once giving a shit. This is his home turf and 'Hit That'
is his territorial pissing. I'm not sure if I hate him or admire him.

On Sunday afternoons, I take over from Shanksy as fruit and
veg boy. I put the radio on low volume and tune into *American Top 40* with Ryan Seacrest, while I guillotine pumpkins and

watermelons into quarters and suffocate them in plastic wrap. I prefer rock-and-roll to pop, but I'm only half tuning in for the songs. The American-based countdown show lets me imagine a world so different to mine. A United States of Ryan Seacrest: Hollywood and skate punk and Venice Beach and 7-Eleven Slurpees and Californian heat. When Kelly Clarkson's 'Break-away' hits the charts – a song written by Avril Lavigne, no less – I understand those small-town lyrics and wish I could make them come true. I imagine a United States of Holden Sheppard awaits me somewhere beyond the confines of my hometown.

*

One Sunday, we're short on checkout chicks, so they import a checkout dude from our sister supermarket on Durlacher Street. Chad is a year older than me. Hunky. Dark skin. Incredible smile. Top button undone to reveal his chest. Hotter than the floor boys I usually perve on. He is sex on legs. I keep finding reasons to go to his checkout so I can smell the intoxicating mix of his cologne and his sweat. My body wants him more badly than it's ever wanted anything. I need him.

But it's a non-starter in this town. Even on the off-chance he wanted it too, my father knows his father from karate. We'd never get away with it. I can never do this here. Ever. By the end of that shift, I want to die.

I go for the supermarket equivalent of a cold shower: a trolley run on the foreshore. In Geraldton, the railway line runs along the shore, divorcing the town from the ocean. The foreshore area is just potholey bitumen behind dilapidated and abandoned businesses. This town has a beautiful, powder-fine beach facing onto the turquoise Indian Ocean, but the rail line and its grey, cage-like metal fence separate me from the natural beauty beyond.

I find a trolley abandoned behind the surveyors' building. I wonder what would happen if I didn't collect it. Would anyone notice it was gone? Would anyone ever find it again? I entertain the thought for a minute, listening to the waves breaking on Town Beach, then come to my senses. Of course someone would notice. You can't hide anything in this town.

Seventeen

Catholic high school is different to Catholic primary school in that, instead of banning Japanese pop-culture crazes, the teachers are terrified of sex. Sex is *verboten*. Mentions of sex. Sex-based swear words. Drawings of dicks on school diaries. Sex scenes in movies that are mysteriously fast-forwarded through. The philosophy seems to be that as long as students can't see or hear about sex at school, it can't possibly manifest.

It's not until Year 12 that the teachers decide we are old enough to hear about the most taboo and X-rated of human acts: homosexuality.

In fourth-period Religious Education class, a textbook tells me being homosexual is okay with God – as long as you don't act on it. The words sizzle on the grey matter of my brain, where they remain imprinted for life. *Homosexuals are called by God to lead chaste lives*. The teacher confirms it: 'Just the idea of homosexuality makes me sick to my stomach.' If the Grim Reaper had a face, it would look like her grimace.

That night at home, I ask my parents where my baptismal crucifix ended up. They dig out a brown plastic box gifted to me by my godparents from a Sicilian *gioielleria* (jewellery shop) called Schepi's. I unfurl the golden thread and drape it around my neck. The cold, metal Jesus settles on my black sprouts of chest hair. Maybe God can lead me to the good land.

I take the Good News Bible from the shelf in our shed and place it next to my bedside with Catholic pride. I study it every night. One bible verse trips me up. More than Leviticus, which is unequivocal in its assertion that a man laying with a man must be put to death for the abomination. More than the Second Book of Samuel, whose story of David and Jonathan, I am sure, is one of two male lovers, and not just 'close friends'. My stumbling block is Romans 1:27: 'In the same way the men give up natural sexual relations with women and burn with passion for each other. Men do shameful things with each other, and as a result they bring upon themselves the punishment they deserve for their wrongdoing.'

I don't want to, but every time I read that passage, I get turned on. Men burning with passion for each other sounds so fucking hot. Despite months of reading the bible, and never taking my crucifix off, none of it takes. I can't stop burning with lust for men.

I want so badly to like chicks: to belong in this town the way Lockie and Bruce and Bill do. My desire to be straight coincides with my teenage puppy fat melting away and my acne clearing. Suddenly, girls are flirting with me, sending me letters and passing notes to me, calling me at home during dinner. But when I end up drunk at a house party with a girl sprawled on my lap, all I can do is half-heartedly touch her breasts. To get the engine from second gear into third requires some level of thrust I don't possess. I don't burn with passion for women.

*

On Thursday nights, I tell my family I'm heading to my room to watch *Alias* on my hand-me-down TV, a tiny analogue box from the '80s. Once my bedroom door is locked, my index finger curls around the volume dial, rolls it back to zero. I turn to SBS and crouch inches from the screen to watch *Queer as Folk* in total darkness and total silence. I never learn the characters' names, nor hear their dialogue. All I do is gape at these gay men on my screen living openly, and kissing, and going to gay nightclubs in New York. I wish I could join them on their foreign terrain. I lay in bed and imagine what my life could have been like if I had been born in New York, London or Sydney.

Every night that year, I fall asleep dreaming of being in a faraway land where I can be myself. Ryan Seacrest presents: the

United States of Holden Sheppard. The dream becomes an obsession, even more so than my nightly bible readings and guilt-filled wanks. The idea of breaking away becomes the main reason I keep living.

If I don't get out of this town, I will die.

Eighteen

In June 2006, I become a man. My mate Joseph and I have our eighteenth birthdays four days apart, so we throw a combined party at my place. Our mates and families gather under the patio on our half-acre block for stubbies of Toohey's Extra Dry and shots of Wild Turkey, and hot beef and gravy rolls.

A week later, I flee the country.

Four years of collecting trolleys and cutting pumpkins, on a starting rate of $6.12 an hour, gave me enough cash for a flight to Heathrow and a hostel booking. I'll work the rest out as I go. I call it a gap year, but I am determined never to return.

*

I land in London in the middle of a July heatwave. I expected England to be cold and rainy, but this new land is all warm sun and welcoming breeze. Within hours, I find my way to Covent Garden, the gay quarter, where I can barely believe my eyes. Bars and bookshops are teeming with guys like me. I find myself in a gay bathhouse on Tottenham Court Road. It is wet and dark, full of nude men, exposed muscles and armpit sweat. It's the football-club change room of my dreams. I strip off my clothes and remove my crucifix, abandoning them in a metal locker.

Naked, I step onto my home turf for the first time.

Mumma Bird

Jacinta Dietrich

Summer in my childhood is heavy with rain. Lush green rain-forests are thick with humidity and sweat. The creek floods and we sleep in our car and wait for the water to recede. In place of parched gum trees and cracked earth, we are overrun with rampant lantana and tea trees. In place of death by starvation, we have death by rot, by drowning; death by a trauma that was unusual and unknown in this country.

This is why I had never considered that I'd grown up in rural Australia. In the country, cattle died of starvation in wide, dry paddocks. The ground was scorched and the trees were set aflame. A kangaroo was shot at distance for being a pest. In the country, death came for you and its cause was specific. But my mum brought death into our home, and it smelled of burning sage.

It had never occurred to me to ask why she collected birds. Why birds instead of wallabies? Why birds instead of echidnas? It was just what Mum did. For as long as I could remember she had been collecting feathers. Most of them weren't anything special, just things she found on the ground. She would strap them together with old leather and use them for smudging. Sometimes she would bring them home just to look at them.

At one time, she had a handmade crow-beak necklace. It lived in a carved wooden box lined with red velvet. The box was beautiful, too beautiful for such a Gothic relic. But over time I have come to appreciate the macabre beauty of the necklace as well. The beak had been detached from the body (I never dared to think by what means), dried and strung on thin wire. It was oil-dark and glossy, bordered by beads of turquoise and onyx. Without the feathers, the nostrils could be seen – tiny specks where breath no longer stirred. My sisters and I were horrified the day Mum brought it home. She had bought it from a car boot market, and crows had followed the car the whole way home. She and I both saw it as an omen, but at vastly different ends of the scale.

Growing up, we tried plenty of variations of the same lifestyle – the zero-waste, self-sustainable, one-with-nature ecowarrior. We lived in a solar-panelled timber ... house is the wrong word for it, but no other dwelling fits either. I have since learned my extended family referred to it as 'the pioneer shack'. It was situated on a hill in the middle of a rainforest and coming across a snake while walking to and from the bus stop was a regular, and soon unexciting, experience. Bath time occurred in the tub outdoors and, depending on the day, we had just enough power to toast two slices of bread or watch an episode of *The Simpsons*.

After that we lived in a besser-block shed. I would press my hands against the cool brick, seeing how many palms I could fit across its width. I thought all bricks were that size for a long time. On the school bus every morning I would look out the window, waiting for this one paddock. In its centre, every morning and every afternoon, a kangaroo could be spotted as though waiting for the school bus to go by. It was the highlight of my ride. It was many years later when I discovered that the kangaroo was a statue, and my family has never forgotten the anecdote.

We had a small stint 'in town', where the population was less than 400. We had neighbours and a post office and, for the first time ever, I could walk to my friend's house. But small towns can be suffocating. It was time to go back to the bush.

Next, we lived on a commune, which I quickly learned was far more political than it was sustainable. We had a pit toilet, and at night – when we were too scared to make the trek out the front door and around the deck – we would wee in a bucket in the bathroom. Some mornings we'd wake up to the house reeking of piss. Instead of snakes, we had goannas that would climb all the way up onto our front deck, and possums that would tear open our rubbish bags and scatter our consumption and hypocrisy through the vegetable patch.

Memories of these places come and go, but the birds never leave. They were always there in some form or another, following us through. Mum would collect them when she found them – sometimes pulling over and stopping the car at the side of the road to claim the body. She would collect the bird gently, tucking it into the plastic bag that was always stashed in the car for this very occasion, and place it safely in the boot. She would manoeuvre it in-between the schoolbags or groceries. My sisters and I would dawdle getting out of the car, waiting for Mum to pull her bag out first. We never touched them.

Later that night, the smell of sage would seep its way through the house. Without going downstairs, we knew what that smell meant. Mum would have her smudge stick burning and would be slowly waving it over the bird's crumpled form. The smoke wound its way around and up away from the body, cleansing the bird of its past and its possibly traumatic end. On the few occasions we did come downstairs, Mum would explain that the sage was clearing the bird's aura, that it was cleansing away the negativity, that it was helping the bird to move on. Sage was, and still is, the smell of death and burial.

I now think that she wanted to bring peace to their end in a way she couldn't bring peace to her own life. Everyone wants to be a bird and fly off on a whim; to travel, to explore, to see the world. Mum just wanted to leave. But just like the sad and frail bodies she collected, she was stuck on the ground.

After the smudging, Mum would bury the body in the yard. Sometimes it was the front yard, sometimes the backyard and sometimes it was whatever garden bed we had spare space in. She would pour a little bit of herself into every bird before laying it in the dirt. I sometimes wonder how many bird cemeteries my mum created in our homes. I don't specifically remember her burying the frail bodies, but I know she must have. My growing up can be traced and mapped by small pockets of bird graves.

Prawn

Edie Mitsuda

Bus Number 7 was the north-bound bus, meaning that whenever I got on before and after school, I would ride in the company of teenagers whose parents owned farms in the genre of wheat, sheep or both. My parents didn't own a farm, not even an orchard, I lived along the highway and my stop wasn't a real stop, merely an area of gravel on the shoulder of the road where the bus driver could easily pull over. Next to the gravel was a block of vacant land filled with every kind of weed imaginable, ones that blew, twisted and spread their seeds in the wind. Beyond that was the ocean. I was the only person who got off there.

I caught the bus between the ages of fourteen and seventeen. This entire time the driver was a short man named Tony whose face seemed permanently tightened with the most severe frustration. He wore fitted sunglasses and a fitted button-up, which he tucked and belted into cargo shorts. He had a special microphone next to his chair that swung in the air like a pendulum, which he would talk into whenever he got angry at us. In fact, he was angry at us often, and had cause to be. We were disorderly passengers, always shouting or pushing, throwing things, inclined towards violence.

'You lot,' Tony would say, over the microphone. 'You lot, listen. Yesterday one of you threw a can of tuna out the window at the lights and it hit an old woman on the head. She had to go to hospital. She had to go to the *emergency room*, for Christ sakes. I could get the sack. Is that what you want? You want me to lose my job?'

168

Then somebody was bound to shout, 'Yes,' in reply, to the laughter of us all.

It was because of situations like this that I was scared of the bus. I was scared of the people on it and the way they would behave. Brutality and cruelty, these things were the first and most frequent responses to any circumstance. Both boys and girls would lash out with their fists if the moment felt right, they would shout insults with the intent to offend or cause harm. The erratic behaviour terrified me, and I wondered if there was no limit to what they would say or do. Did they fear no repercussion? Naturally, I never knew where to sit, so I sat somewhere in the middle, even though I was probably too old to be sitting anywhere other than the bench seat at the back. I tried not to let any part of my bare skin touch the carpeted chairs, sticky with miscellaneous liquid that everyone said was semen. Although no-one would say semen, they would say jizzm, or spoof.

*

My friends lived in town, so I rode alone for the most part, and by the time my stop came around there were very few people left on the bus: me, four boys who sat behind me, empty seats. Tony was friendlier to us then, once most of the rabble had departed, once the bus had descended into the strange, semi-quiet of the late afternoon, when the air above the road shimmered with glare and all of us settled back and crossed our arms, knowing there was still a while to go yet. This fugue state enveloped us every day except Thursday, when Tony would stop at a roadhouse so we could buy food from the bain-marie. Like any child who is suddenly able to do something their parents would never allow, I became frantic, gorging on deep fried items, potatoes, lasagnes, sticks of mashed corn. I ate aggressively, with an uncontrollable enthusiasm. I pushed things down my throat without tasting until I became physically incapacitated, until water leaked from the corners of my eyes and bile rose in the back of my throat.

'I've got a daughter,' Tony said to me one day, watching as I wiped my greasy hands on my legs. 'She's older than you. She's into all that stuff. Yoga, meditating, all that stuff.'

He'd surprised me with this conversation. He was standing in the doorway of the bus with his elbow resting on the frame. I was extremely confused – beyond pleasantries we'd never spoken. I was sixteen and in the habit of only saying half of what it was I wanted, all I could think about was getting back to my seat so I didn't have to speak to him, but he was blocking the entrance. Did I consider asking him to move? No. I was never forthright in this way. I lingered there, irritated. I thought this discomfort was something to be tolerated without complaint.

When I didn't reply he continued, 'I've never been into anything of the sort, although I do like to keep fit and healthy. I run, I go to Harriers on Sundays.'

'Right.'

'It doesn't matter, she doesn't live at home anymore, she moved out a while ago. She's in town. I don't think she'll ever leave town.'

'Good for her,' I said.

'It is,' he replied, and then we both stood in silence, although he still did not attempt to move. He must have known that I was trying to get in, but something prevented him from letting me past. Some fear or turn of mind. There was a look on his face that I had never noticed before, perhaps because I'd never been close enough to see it. He may have worn this expression all the time, like he was searching for something, or like he wanted something badly: an event, a colossal phenomenon that he could not put into words. Above all he looked as though he yearned for an energy to descend out of the sky and shake his life like a snow globe. *The audacity*, I thought. Because I wanted things too. I wanted things badly as well, but at least I tried not to make this so noticeable. Didn't he know that it was wrong to admit it? Worse to wear the wanting so plainly without even realising what it was he was doing. I couldn't abide what I saw, which I thought might have been desperateness.

*

I was saved by the return of the boys, who walked out the sliding doors of the roadhouse with cans of drink, their bare arms covered in permanent marker. The boys were taciturn, rarely spoke, and never to me. If I ever heard them talk to each other I would wonder how a person could get by using such basic faculties of communication. If I'd known any of their names at the time, I never used them. I do remember one of the boys being called Goat, because allegedly he'd had sex with a goat. This is what someone had told me, and I was disgusted by it, regardless of any exaggeration or falsehood.

'You lot rough and ready?' Tony asked them.

They replied yes. We filed back onto the bus. I ate and stared out the window. The vista passed by at an alarming rate, but I didn't take a lot of notice. I barely saw the occasional dead kangaroo or fox, and the accompanying crow that hopped away long before the bus ever reached its position on the road. Of course we never stopped to get out, to stretch our legs, because we were going somewhere. I thought I was going to art school, when I was old enough. I thought I had joy and misery inside me that would make good art, and I kept and held this purpose within myself in the uncompromised way that teenagers are able to. Apart from joy and misery what I felt most of all was beyond the sense of belonging, or not. Beyond the sense of feeling a stranger or a foreign body in the dry place where I was born.

I looked at the landscape without any attentiveness or intensity. Each time I saw a roly-poly tumble across the road I made a series of apathetic wishes. In winter these plants were green, tender-leafed and rooted in the ground. In summer they broke away and whirled. Behind me I could hear the boys speaking. They'd separated into two groups, one pair sitting on the back seat and the other slightly closer to me.

I heard Goat say, 'Going boat this weekend?'

And the other, 'Fucken ay. Dad said no but Mum reckons it's

fine. I'll just get up early and leave before he's awake.'

'My dad'd belt me if I took the boat without asking.'

'As if.'

'He would.'

'What d'you do, fish?'

'Yeah.'

'Get anything?'

'Heaps.'

They both sat quietly for a minute, then Goat said, 'You still talking to that chick?'

'Nah,' his friend replied. 'Over it.'

'True.'

'Yeah,' the boy said. 'She's rooting some other guy.'

'Serious?'

'Yeah, fucken footy bloke.'

'How d'you know that?'

'Everyone's going on about it. Said they were in a swag together on Saturday night.'

'Fucked,' Goat replied, then hesitated, and for a moment I truly thought he might have continued on and said something meaningful, like: I know, I'm sorry, I know how bad it can feel. At this realisation my fists pressed hard into the tops of my thighs. I couldn't stand the idea of him showing sympathy or concern. I thought, no, please, don't exhibit yourself in this way. I became frightened for him. Yet, he said nothing more, and I was relieved.

Then the other boy said, 'It's shit because we were gonna go to the ball together.'

'So what?'

'Now I have to find someone else.'

'True.'

'I can't be fucked.'

'What about her?'

'Who?'

'Her.'

'That girl?'

It took me a surprisingly long time to register that they were talking about me. I'd never considered that they were aware of my existence. On the bus I thought of myself as mainly invisible, helpful to no-one, and I didn't mind that. Better this than what was happening now: unwanted appraisal, unwanted scrutiny. There was nothing I desired less than an exchange of words with these boys, who I thought of as people to be avoided.

'She'd be up for one,' the friend said.

And Goat replied, 'Yeah,' laughing a little.

'Not my type, though.'

'What, Asian?'

'Nah. Prawn.'

'What?'

'Good body but an ugly head.'

'Right.'

'For you, though?'

'Nah, nah.'

But Goat's friend ignored him. 'Oi,' he said, loudly. 'You.'

'Fuck up,' said Goat.

'You, girl.'

I sat completely still.

'Girl. Girl with the hair.'

For some reason this struck me. Was I well known as a person with hair? Was my hair somehow a defining enough feature that it should be used as a method of identification? To me, it was brown, and normal.

I turned around and said, 'What?' I thought it was important to appear very disgruntled.

'Go out with him?' The boy used his thumb to point towards Goat, who shook his head.

'No,' I said, trying not to look too hard at them. Both were rangy and freckled and had the top buttons of their polos done up in an attempt to scorn the school uniform. Goat was wearing a faded cap ringed with salt stains and wispy hairs poked out of it near the base of his neck. His mouth was parted slightly, his lip curled, and you could tell that it was always curled like this. Always ready to say something should the need arise, to defend himself. Girls didn't like him, you could tell that. They didn't like him because he was skinny and he came up with stories, ones that made him seem better than what he thought he was. Yet, could you blame him? Always on the receiving end of the joke, somehow grateful for that position because there was no other way to get any attention. Imagine if his friends didn't make loud and hurtful statements about him, wouldn't he simply fade away? Lose all relevance? If any girl had the heart to accept him he would be good to her. He'd promised himself this. He wouldn't act the way his friends did, he wouldn't be mean. Presently, he looked down at his feet, and I knew he felt sorry for me, saw some essential part of himself in me. Sorry for shaking his head, even as he did it.

'Come on,' his friend said, clapping him on the shoulder. 'This is a good bloke.'

I stood and said harshly, 'Why would I want to do anything like that?'

Wobbling in the aisle, I tugged at my skirt that was riding up behind my backpack. I clung to the handles on the seats as I made my way forward. Tony was silent as I stood beside him, my whole body moving with the bus as it slowed, and eventually stopped. I said thank you to him before I got off.

He replied, 'Righto,' staring into the distance through his sunglasses.

*

My feet hit the gravel and the bus rolled away. A wave of air blasted me, hot from the road and the exhaust, and I squinted, fringe blowing back off my forehead. I could see Goat looking at me through the window while sweat started to show under the armpits of my school dress. I looked back at him. It seemed easy enough to do, when there was a pane of glass between us. When he was still enclosed in that transient, air-conditioned vessel

174

where things were both less and more real than anywhere else.

Thankfully I would have my chance again to do better, for them, and for me. I'd ride the bus tomorrow and the next day and the next, and so on. The same people there, the weight of their lives so obvious at such a density. Crowding, pushing up savagely against each other. Pushing up against me: strange and unlikeable girl, all my terrors, anxieties, forcing themselves out as annoyance and pretention. I watched the bus indicate and pull onto the road. I was humiliated, vengeful, yet I felt a wretched need to chase after the big green vehicle, bash my palm on the back window and tell everyone I was sorry. Even at that age, I believe I knew that all of us were trying our best. That we all had feral kinds of doubt plaguing us. That we were all, even me, good, honest, loudmouthed, foulmouthed countryfolk.

I shaded my eyes from the sun, watched for cars and jogged across the highway, starting up the hill towards home. A raptor bird circled above, looking for rabbits in the scrub. Sand blew from the neighbour's house in a swirl along the road. A roly-poly bounced from end to end, from right to left in front of me, and the way the wind rushed through its thatch of dry foliage, well, I thought it sounded like rain. I tugged again at my skirt, and felt the whole scene touch my heart. The clouds were moving slowly that day.

Move

Farz Edraki

I was always moving, even when I wasn't. Being in transit became a state of mind, beyond storage boxes and new school uniforms and Target Country stores. By the third school, I had learnt about friendship the hard way: that it was easier not to have it, especially if you are brown and wear glasses. By the fourth school, I had learnt how to field questions about where I was from, *really*. Did I grow up here? And my parents?

'It's complicated,' I'll now say, 'I was born in Iran, we moved to Brisbane when I was three, but I pretty much grew up in Deniliquin and Mildura – it's where I went to school.'

'Deniliquin. You mean Deni?'

'Yeah, like the ute muster.'

It's hard to picture how a young family from Shiraz, Iran, could wind up on the other side of the world in a town famous for a ute muster: a UDL-fuelled, Guinness World Record–winning assembly of utes and country musicians. But it was Australia in the 1990s, when permanent residency applications often favoured time spent in regional areas. John Howard was the first Australian politician I remember seeing on our TV, *The Genie from Down Under* was my favourite jingle to sing in the shower, and Australia was deciding whether or not to become a republic.

My parents never let me go to the ute muster (I wasn't old enough, nor was I interested in two-day dusty benders – at least not *yet*), but we went on many road trips. Deniliquin is in the Riverina region of New South Wales, not far from the Victorian border and many country towns we would gradually tick off our to-visit list: Echuca, Shepparton, Bendigo, Griffith. If it had a Sanity, Supré or Rivers – we were there.

For a daytrip to Echuca, Mum packed the boot with picnic rugs, flasks of hot water, black teabags, sugar cubes, dates, mandarins, naan and feta. Exploring a new town didn't mean dining out in new cafés. Unless you count the Driver Reviver pitstops along the highway: women in white polo shirts handing out Bushells tea in styrofoam cups. I was disappointed when we drove right past 'Australia's Best Pie' at Moama (and another pie shop making similar claims in Kyabram), embarrassed about lugging around two heavy cooler bags to roadside picnic tables. But now I see it for what it was: a sensible measure for a family living off one income. More than that, my parents always carried a part of their own culture with them in these cooler bags. There is nothing more Iranian than dunking sugar cubes in glass vials of black tea, just ask Googoosh.

They loved it all. The flat plains. The open road. The fifteen-minute commute home. Compared to Shiraz, with a population over one million, country towns like Deni were quiet, peaceful. To cross the road, you didn't have to close your eyes, put out one arm and hope the oncoming traffic stopped for you. There was no traffic. In Deni, at that time, there weren't even traffic *lights*. When we moved to Mildura, a town with 30,000 or so residents, I felt like I'd started high school in the big smoke. In reality, we had just moved from one country town to a slightly bigger one with a shopping centre instead of a street mall. My daily walk to school took me past a field of vines. It's the kind of town where everyone says hello to you on the street, and the shops promptly close their doors at five p.m., laying bare to an eerie kind of quiet.

But the relative peacefulness was something I derided as *boring* as an emo teen, losing more and more interest as my dad tried to drum up enthusiasm for country sightseeing.

'Come on,' he'd say, sticking his head through the car window. 'Don't you want to see Sovereign Hill?'

'Ronald is about to go to the Yule Ball, Dad.' Like other virgins of my generation, I always had my head stuck in a book.

Sitting in the backseat of our '86 Corolla, twisting the butterfly clips in my hair as I feverishly finished *Harry Potter and the Goblet of Fire*, I missed the tour of Ballarat's goldrush museum. Years later, when I went there on a school trip, the substitute teacher frowned at my packed lunch.

'We've got food coming,' she said, 'sandwiches.'

'Oh great,' I smiled, tucking a date into my pocket for later.

*

If my parents ever got lonely in Deni or Mildura, they never let on. Or at least, I was too self-absorbed to notice. In both towns, there was always an Afghani or Iranian family we came to know. Our family lunches inevitably ended in comments on my weight or swapping notes on the closest Persian grocer (Sydney, 700 kilometres away). They understood the same sense of isolation: the loss of food, language. Not that it was ever named.

We all found different ways to code-switch. Dad bought an akubra (which he promptly lost after accidentally leaving it on top of the car one day before getting in and driving off). I joined a netball team. I don't know why I chose netball; maybe it had something to do with the fact that I wasn't tall enough for basketball or fast enough for swimming. Because of netball, I had an excuse to get contact lenses. I was still brown and very much single, but maybe, just maybe, I'd look like less of a nerd.

Any hopes of new-found friendships with the blonde-girl cliques were quickly dashed when everyone realised I sucked at sport. The warning signs were there: several years earlier at the Grade 4 swimming carnival, I was asked to swim the width of the pool, not the length.

'You ... you can be WD,' was the command from Ashleigh, the netball captain. The tall girls with ribbons in their hair were assigned GA, GS, or even GD. But WD was the equivalent of having a big yellow Post-it on your back saying 'I'm Just Here To Make Up Numbers'.

By some miracle, or worker shortage, I ended up a netball umpire. I was terrified of both the players and their angry parents on the sidelines. When I missed contact offences, they'd yell 'DIDN'T YOU SEE THAT? C'MON REF!' like it was the Australian Open and they were John McEnroe. The fact that I can't even think of an appropriate netball analogy should convey my lack of knowledge on the topic. I wasn't skilled enough to play netball, let alone umpire it, but I kept my silver whistle in a safe spot in my bedroom drawer all the same.

One of my only happy memories from this time was one afternoon where, for some reason, we practised playing netball with a frozen chicken in lieu of a ball. In thirty-five-plus degree heat. As the afternoon languished on, sweat sticking to our white Edward Public School tees, the chicken slowly defrosted as it was passed around from student to student – eventually sitting in a crumpled, rotting pile of translucent pink-white flesh on the court. The sound of our childish laughter roused a teacher, but I didn't care. I was finally in on the joke, not worrying about being on the receiving end. On the unbearably hot walk home, trudging with my backpack past the eucalyptus-lined park and the fish and chip shop, I sucked down a blue Zooper Dooper. *Is this what belonging felt like?* My tongue was blue by the time I got home, and I stuck it out in a big, wet grin at *The Saddle Club* on TV.

When I wasn't reading *Harry Potter*, I tried to find solace in books set in Australia. But back then, I couldn't see myself in the pages.

In Tim Winton's Australia, childhood is all blonde kids, surfing and mystery. My version of growing up in the country had very little to do with family estate drama or tending to the land – or any of the other tropes portrayed in other country novels and plays like *Mallee Sky* and *Inheritance*.

We didn't know how to camp. We didn't have border collies. We didn't have a property – just a series of small houses and units my parents rented, planting new garden beds in each one.

*

After September 11, some things changed. Not overnight, these things never happen quite so quickly. But incrementally, over the space of days and months, I felt a gnawing distance between me and my white classmates.

That summer we went to Iran – the first time my parents had seen their family in almost nine years since stepping off the plane in Brisbane. At the airport in Shiraz, it felt like my entire extended family was there – holding flowers, clutching chests, their faces expectant. It was overwhelming, but not unwelcome. Visiting my grandparents' house, picking sweet lemons from the tree in their backyard, meeting my cousins for the first time, the smell of Ghormeh Sabzi in the kitchen, aunties on both sides taking me under their wing to show me family albums and insist on taking me shopping. Small details about my parents fell into place, too. It was all starting to make sense. Once we were back in Australia, those three months felt like a hazy dream – one I desperately clung on to.

'Did you meet Osama when you were away? Is that where you went?' the boys jeered from the back of the classroom, chewing gum.

'Yeah, we had a business meeting.' In on the joke, not the butt of it.

*

Almost a decade after that first visit back to Iran, my grandmother and my aunt visited Australia for the first time. Their trip coincided with a rare locust plague. Hundreds of locusts veered into our car's headlights as we drove around Wagga Wagga, where my parents briefly lived after I graduated school and left Mildura for an even bigger smoke: Canberra.

'It's so beautiful.' The locusts were amusing to my grand-mother, not an omen. My aunt commented on how lush and green the fields were, even when they seemed, to me, dry and arid. They asked after koalas and kangaroos. As we drove on dirt roads, kicking up dust in our wake, a Hayedeh song blared from the car's CD player.

When I got my own driver's licence at twenty-two, it took me a while to work up the courage to go over 100 km/hr on the highway. I annoyed everyone on the Federal by inching along the left lane at sixty, clammy hands gripping the steering wheel. But eventually, driving down the Hume, passing fields of canola stretching out yellow into the horizon, I felt at ease. I can't disentangle flat, open roads with my childhood – the two are so connected. The quiet space to think on long drives is now a luxury. Being in transit is a destination in itself, just like being neither entirely Iranian nor Australian is now my identity. I pack naan and dates for road trips – but when I pass a pie shop I always, *always* stop.

Seedpods

Benjamin Riley

At nineteen, I moved to Melbourne from the regional city of Wodonga in north-east Victoria and realised, for the first time in my life, that I'd grown up poor.

I remember the moment it happened. At one of the share houses I lived in through uni, my housemates and I looked up our high schools on 'My School', a government website showing, among other statistics, the percentage of students in a school who fall into each quartile of 'socio-educational advantage': a combined measure of socioeconomic and educational family background. My housemates' elite Melbourne private or selective-entry schools showed around 90 per cent in the top quartile. My school showed around 75 per cent in the bottom quartile. At the time of writing, the most recent stats, from 2019, are similar.

That brutal, restructuring shock arrived at the same I was learning other ways my experience of growing up in the country was different from most of the students at the sandstone university I had squeaked into. After I started my degree at the University of Melbourne, I wanted to write for *Farrago*, the uni's student magazine. As editorship was an elected position, this meant getting involved in student politics.

Little has shaped my politics more than the three years I was involved in the student union, where I encountered some of the worst people I have ever met. These young, ambitious activists and proto-politicians from across the political spectrum, several of whom have since been elected to higher office, came bursting out of high school with political fire and brimstone. They seemed to have emerged from their adolescence fully equipped with the language of organised political movements: queer, conservative, feminist, unionist, environmentalist – language providing some framework for thinking critically about the world.

I recall my own experience of high school very differently.

If you're unfamiliar with Wodonga, it sits on the Victorian side of the border with New South Wales, across the Murray River from Albury. If you're driving from Melbourne to Sydney, it's where you cross the state line. I used to say that you could always tell which side of the border someone was from because if you're from Wodonga, you say you're from Albury-Wodonga; if you're from Albury, you say you're from Albury. The other thing I used to say about my hometown is that, as a 'regional centre', Wodonga is too big to be a nice little country town, and too small and too far from Melbourne (the closest city at 300 kilometres away) to be interesting.

In place of the formal or informal education in politics, philosophy and social theory that I imagine my fellow student unionists had, an image of a typical Wodonga night with my high-school friends comes to mind.

I was sixteen years old, and along with my friends – a mix of nerds and stoners – we hung out in a kind of halfway house for teenagers who got kicked out of home but were too old to go into the foster-care system. One of my friends was living there with a group of other teenagers, under the apparent care of a 'lead tenant', a social worker in his twenties about whom I can remember two things: he was a devout Christian, and he picked up extra work as a party clown.

We drank, because someone always seemed to be around who could buy us booze, and passed around a joint, because my friend's mum's friend, who my friend moved in with after she too got kicked out of home, always had weed in the house. The lead tenant was often away at clown gigs on weekends, so there weren't any adults around; but then, there never seemed to be any adults around. Several kids in our friendship group were kicked out of home while they were still at school, so there were always places we could go to drink and get stoned without supervision.

Afternoons slowly melted into nights as we drank cheap, sweet cask wine, occasionally venturing out to the nearby Coles for snacks, running up and down the aisles laughing and shouting. Back at the house we talked about the social dynamics of our group, and what I realise now, looking back, were various traumas – social, familial, physical – which were flattened into the same haze of unending chat. Often, we talked about music; I remember some of my gothier friends were really into The Smiths, while I and others at the more cautious, mainstream end of the spectrum talked about bands that I now look back at and cringe.

We didn't, at least as far as I remember, talk about the world, about politics and the news. The idea that my friends and I could have an opinion on the upcoming federal election or the invasion of Iraq or asylum seekers at Woomera was totally unimaginable, let alone the idea of talking philosophy. The world extended as far as the neighbouring streets and ended, I suppose, in the hazy months that lay beyond our final exams. I can't remember us discussing what we wanted to do after we finished school, or any ambitions for the future. Our lives contracted in space and time to nights spent drinking and smoking and talking shit in parentless houses.

Despite the almost languid fog of these memories, I remember spending my teenage years barely able to suppress resentment and even rage. I resented being a closeted gay kid in a homophobic country town, I resented having no money, I resented feeling smarter than everyone else, I resented the sense that I was stuck in Wodonga and unable to access all that the world had to offer.

For much of high school, these feelings were unfocused and uncontained, but when I hit Year 12, existential dread set in that I would never escape Wodonga. So, I withdrew from my friends, chained myself to my desk to run endless practice exams, and scraped through graduation with a score just good enough to get into Melbourne Uni. Unlike the rich kids I met there, my own politics feel pieced together, painstakingly, over the course of my adult life.

These realisations in my early twenties weren't simply a reflection of a growing class consciousness; they helped solidify a narrative that growing up in the country had cut me off from the vast, complex world outside my hometown.

*

When I look back over the story so far, I have to admit it is discomfortingly cliched: smart, angry young gay man, stifled by suffocating small-town attitudes, escapes to the big city only to find himself rejected by the same snobbish elites he once sought to become.

Recently, my increasing distance from those years growing up in Wodonga has given me the space to wonder what might have been lost in the process of smoothing out my adolescence into that comprehensible narrative. In particular, when I think about the friends I spent those nights with, I worry that I have done a disservice to them and to our time together by instrumentalising their experience in service of my own hollow mantra of self-growth.

Looking for another perspective, I called Rhiannon, the only friend from high school I'm still regularly in touch with. It had been far too long since we'd last spoken; she's in Brisbane, and we haven't lived in the same place since we both moved away from Wodonga not long after graduation. I told her about what I was writing, and the memories of Wodonga I was trying to piece together. Confusingly, she seemed to remember a lot more than I did, and I wondered if that was because one unfortunate side-effect of being a closeted gay kid is a relentless self-focus and loathing.

Recalling the unsupervised evenings of our friendship group, Rhiannon laughed incredulously at some of the details I'd got wrong. For a start, I'd conflated two of my friends into one, assigning some of Rhi's own experiences to another friend I hadn't spoken to since my early twenties – a friend who had *not* in fact been kicked out of home. Rhiannon was the one living with a family friend, and hers was one of the houses where we'd spent long nights drinking and talking. It turns out Rhi also provided our supply of weed, not through the family friend but through her mum, who grew it in a backyard greenhouse so she could use it to barter for things like horse feed.

I'd also forgotten how hard life had been for Rhi after she'd left home; for example, on top of everything else, she'd had to pay for her own food and bills while still at school. Most shamefully, I had somehow forgotten that to afford that she'd worked part-time at the same supermarket where I'd worked (a Bi-Lo), a part of my life from which I had erased her entirely.

A few years after leaving Wodonga, the friend I'd cut-and-pasted into Rhiannon's life came to my twenty-first birthday party at my Melbourne share house. She gave a drunken, impromptu speech to the assembled figures of my new, post-Wodonga life, painting an unintentionally unflattering portrait of me, a figure I'd tried to escape from. She'd meant it playfully, but my new Melbourne friends were confused, unable to reconcile the angry, bitter teen with the man I had worked hard to become: someone who, I hoped, was kinder, who could better connect with his friends. Or perhaps my new friends didn't notice, and I was the only one left in shock at what felt like a violent incursion of Wodonga into my carefully constructed new life.

Talking to Rhiannon about all of this, I was startled by the depth of kindness in her response, not only towards the angry, bitter young man I had been, but to the people we were and the lives we lived. She still found moments of fun and joy in her memories of that time, those nights we all shared. Even the bad stuff, even when I expressed my deep, lingering shame about my self-absorption and the narrative steamroller I had run over our past. We were kids, she said, we were all doing our best.

*

We didn't have extended family in Wodonga; my family moved there in 1993 from the central-Victorian town of Woodend because my dad got a new job. I was six years old, the middle of three boys. My parents separated about a year after the move, so they were both left to navigate the strangeness of a new country town alone. At the same time as I was struggling to fit in at a new school (I remember inconsolably crying every day for months after we moved), my mum was doing the same thing in a new community, trying to build friendships and support networks from scratch.

Mum doesn't live in Wodonga anymore – a few years back she moved with her partner to a tiny little town called Stanley, about forty-five minutes south-west. When I called her to corroborate (or challenge) my recollections of growing up in Wodonga, Mum said it was true that, at least at home, we didn't talk about politics or the news. She had never had much faith in political institutions and became wary of discussing current events with my brothers and I; my older brother started to have nightmares about war and AIDS after his Grade 4 teacher began talking to her class about the news. Mum said, thinking about her relationship with her own parents, that when your interests are broader than what your parents can show you, your world can seem small.

It's not that Mum wasn't engaged in the world – she valued different ways of engaging, surrounding herself and us with the region's diverse arts community and the interesting angularity of its natural environment. I described my memories of aimless nights spent with my friends and long days in the flat, featureless expanses of Wodonga, and in response she recalled that when we first arrived she was confronted by the town's similarity to where she grew up: Traralgon in the La Trobe Valley. Her own hometown was a place from which, like me, she had yearned to escape. In contrast, the community in north-east Victoria presented her with something much more interesting than she had initially expected.

Despite my unappealing characterisation of Wodonga, the region as a whole has an interesting cultural scene, one I too

readily sand off when I think of the place. My mum has practised as a visual artist her whole life, so as kids my brothers and
I were around the arts a lot. Mum worked for years at the Albury
Regional Art Gallery (now the Murray Art Museum Albury), an
impressive space for a regional town.

An archetypal scene from my childhood: I am maybe nine or
ten, spending Friday nights at Mum's house, her lounge room
filled with people drinking red goon and playing instruments,
someone inevitably holding court with a djembe.

Moving into adolescence I violently rejected the embarrassing hippy culture of my childhood (we became mortified at the
thought of Mum being seen at school, for example), but now I
am grateful for it. We sang together those Friday nights, as far
back as I can remember, and still nothing brings me more joy
than singing with others.

Perhaps most relevant for me is that the causeway through the
floodplains separating Albury from Wodonga is home to Hothouse Theatre, one of Australia's best regional theatre companies.
The dad of my best friend from early childhood worked there
running the theatre's tech, so I spent a lot of time at the theatre
from a young age. (That same friend went to another famous local
arts institution, the Flying Fruit Fly Circus School – a full-time
school training young circus performers.) For my work experience in Year 10 I undertook a technical traineeship at Hothouse,
an experience that led to me working as an assistant stage manager
on professional theatre productions throughout my final years of
high school. This foundational experience is a big one to erase
in my bland characterisations of my hometown; Mum credited it
to her attempts to expose us to the arts, and presented it as evidence refuting my claim that growing up the country narrowed
my horizons.

*

My older brother, Nat, holds a less nostalgic view.

He told me a story about realising in his early teens he was in some way 'alternative', prompting him to search his immediate surroundings at school for a less mainstream interest with which he could identify. In the cultural wasteland of his adolescence, my brother's attempt to find an alternative scene led him to what seemed like the only available option: some of the other kids, the ones who weren't into sport, were into trucks.

Our school didn't really have any extracurricular activities, no theatre program and almost no music. In Year 9 I took the only available option and got my gun licence to try clay-target shooting. My brother Nat is a musical genius, but it wasn't until much later that he realised how much damage had been done by the fact that, as a teen, he could never have imagined pursuing music at university. In fact, despite being one of the smartest people I know, he never thought he could go to uni at all. He didn't think he was smart enough – no-one ever told him – and he couldn't remember any of his classmates leaving Wodonga for university in a city.

Nat reminded me of the trips we took as kids to visit family in Melbourne, where we stayed with my aunt and her three kids, who were a few years older than me and my brothers. I remember talking to my cousin Tim about staying up late to watch international soccer matches, wondering how he even knew something like that existed. Our cousin Kathryn gave Nat his first mixtape of cool music, and introduced him to Triple J, blowing his teenage mind. Years later, at nineteen, my cousin Kym was the first family member I ever came out to; she came out to me as gay in response. Our cousins seemed like aliens, Nat said, existing in a totally different world.

Prodding Mum a little further, she recalled conversations with a family friend, Sally, who had grown up in Melbourne. Mum had marvelled at Sally's apparent independence, catching the train after school to visit art galleries – an activity neither of us could imagine as a feature of our childhoods. Maybe, Mum thought, something as simple as having to navigate public transport in a city forced a degree of independence missing from life in a country town.

She also reflected on the overwhelming whiteness of the town and of our school. My own memory is of maybe three or four students of colour in my year level of around 150 students – naturalising our whiteness and further cutting us off from a sense of experience beyond our own.

*

My brother Tom, just two years younger than me, had a different experience of his teenage years to me and Nat – in part because during his final year of school, Wodonga's three public high schools amalgamated. Tom suddenly had access to a whole cohort of new people and to subjects that weren't on offer at our former school. That school had been a technical college some years before my brothers and I enrolled, and to its credit did at least have amazing facilities for subjects like metalworking and automotive. But at Tom's new, much bigger, school, he took courses in philosophy and international politics – experiences he credits with fostering a broader political consciousness.

Like Mum, Tom also commented on Wodonga's whiteness, saying that not being able to interact with all kinds of people inevitably constrains how you think about the world. Then he laughed and said that, in some ways, where he lives now (Northcote, in the inner-north of Melbourne) is even more homogenous than Wodonga – still white, but middle class and continuing to gentrify. Now, at least, he can leave his suburb.

If Tom's experience of Wodonga was less negative than his brothers', Mum too wondered whether some kids sought out things like metro daily newspapers and books of philosophy, while others just didn't. She said she had tried to present things to me and my brothers, ways of engaging with the world, but sometimes it seemed to her that her offers couldn't take hold. Following that thread with my younger brother, I asked Tom directly why he thought his views were so different from Nat's or my own. He agreed with Mum that while our different experiences of our teenage years mattered, much of it was down to personality.

Reading this account of our high school after I sent her an early draft to review, Rhiannon also interjected here with her own conflicting account, further highlighting the contingencies of my narrative. She took philosophy, learned the saxophone and sang in the school choir, even going on a tour around the state in Year 10. She recalled conversations with teachers about the impact on the region of the nearby post-war migrant processing centre at Bonegilla, and, after 9/11, Australia's involvement in the Middle East and our relationship with the United States. I may not have had these experiences at school, she acknowledged, but they were not altogether absent.

It's difficult for me not to think about these aspects, and my whole life story, through the lens of spending my teenage years as a closeted gay boy. I had always imagined my liberation could only come when I left for the gay bars of the big city, but what if access to a gay imagination was there all along?

I asked Mum whether she was aware of a gay community in Wodonga while we were growing up. She said she was always very conscious of wanting to be part of the community in all its diversity, and that being in the arts meant she had quite a few gay friends: her boss at work, a potter friend, another friend in her singing group. Most disconcertingly, I'd completely forgotten that my best friend in primary school – the circus kid – lived next door to a lesbian couple, and that we went to their house all the time. In my bemoaning an absence of gayness growing up in Wodonga, these women too had been erased. Mum told me she knew I was probably gay from a young age, and she hoped that her having gay friends might mean if I ever felt able to reach out, potential role models would have been within reach. But of course, I didn't.

This, I suppose, is the anxiety underneath all this: what if it's me? What if I was just so invested in my narrative of liberation from Wodonga's imagined, banal oppression that I had totally shut myself off to the possibilities of the world?

In response to this, Nat was much less equivocal: it was Wodonga. He argued that things would have been completely different if we'd stayed in Woodend. From there, Melbourne – and the world – was just an hour away on the train.

If you're from a poor family growing up in a fucked town, he said, you're pretty fucked. You've got to have at least one of those things sorted. For him, if (hypothetically) we had transplanted our family to Melbourne, it would have been completely different.

Nat described musician friends who had grown up poor in the city but had at least been able to find a critical mass of like-minded people to build a community with. Tom's experience of moving to the city was similar, but he said it wasn't a coincidence that in the community he did find, almost all his friends in Melbourne grew up in the country. I asked him why, and he said that people from the country who chose to leave for the city were more friendly and more open to meeting new people, because at some point they'd had to reinvent themselves and build a life somewhere completely new too.

What both of my brothers did acknowledge was that while we had, as Nat put it, come from a poor family growing up in a fucked town, the cultural capital we received in our upbringing gave us the leg-up we needed to get out. Because we spent our childhoods singing and going to art galleries, my brothers and I could 'pass' for middle-class white kids from the city.

*

When I began writing this, I had set out to examine, in short, whether I hadn't given Wodonga enough credit: if, in service of my personal narrative of escape from a country town, I'd scraped away the things that made that experience interesting and formative. It's true, of course, that our lives were and are always more complicated and contradictory than we might like to imagine. There were lovely things about growing up in Wodonga.

But in talking to my friends and family about the ways the

town and our experiences in it shaped the people we have become, I reach for different questions. What makes one person and not another able to escape the shitty predestination of growing up in a country town? And, more fundamentally, what makes one person and not another experience the oppressive banality I felt in Wodonga as constraining and deterministic?

In other words, in remembering Wodonga and its impact on my life, how can I pry apart my own personal agency from the limitations imposed on me by growing up in the country?

*

While Nat and I continue to feel the constrictive weight of our adolescences in the country, Tom has embraced, for himself, a liberating narrative of personal agency.

When I think back to my conversations with Rhiannon, I see her now as embodying, in a sense, both positions. She acknowledges she didn't have a lot of options, but has now made the astonishing choice, looking back at those often-difficult years, to embrace a kind and compassionate view of these young people, trying to make their way in the world.

For me, those things remain out of reach. I keep getting stuck on the idea that I have spent most of my adult life trapped between two halves of the same limiting narrative: that in the country I was constrained by the banality of a small town, and that in the city I was punished for the same wounds I had left Wodonga to escape. I'm still trying to break these stories apart to find something new. It feels trite to say, but I have to reckon with the fact that my hometown will always be a part of me.

While Mum and I were on the phone, she was startled by a popping sound behind her in the kitchen. Still on the line, she wandered to the windowsill to find that a row of seedpods she had collected on a walk the day before had cracked open in the afternoon sun, spilling small seeds. They were from a native called austral indigo, she said, delighted at the transformation.

Hearing Mum describe the scene as birds sang in the background, I smiled as a memory from childhood came to me, clear and bright. My brothers and I are kids, walking through Wodonga with Mum, at dusk, collecting leaves and sticks and seedpods to take home for art projects. When we got back, we would put the seedpods on a windowsill in the sun, excited to see what might happen the next day.

Driven

Jessica White

Sitting in a sun-warmed car, I look up from my book and watch light flickering through stands of gum trees. Along the ochre gravel road, the trees' shadows make stripes like a tiger's back. Mum and I are on our way to the audiologist's at Tamworth. Mum has the radio on, and although I can hear the ABC jingle clearly, I can't hear what the voices are saying. The trees give way to a wide expanse of paddocks. I lift my book to block them out and immerse myself in another world. I'm nine years old. We've been making this trip once or twice a year for the last five years.

We live in north-west New South Wales; from our farm it's a half-hour journey to the primary school in Boggabri (a Kamilaroi name meaning 'place of many creeks'), a small town of 1000 people. It's forty-five minutes to the supermarket and doctor in the nearest medium-sized town, Gunnedah, and an hour and a half to the city of Tamworth, which has a department store, a hospital and an audiologist.

A few years before, when I was four, I'd complained to Mum of an intense pain pooling in my neck and head. She led me to the trampoline beneath the shade of the apricot tree, thinking that the cooler air might do something for my fever. I lay on the taut plastic surface, a pillow beneath my head, and watched sunlight flickering through the bright green leaves above me. My neck still hurt, so I closed my eyes.

After a while, Mum checked on me. 'How are you feeling?'

I shook my head.

'Do you want to lie in the hammock?'

'Okay.'

She collected the pillow and led me across the grass to the hammock, strung between two poplars. I climbed in unsteadily, lay back and closed my eyes again.

The next time Mum stopped by to check on me, she somehow realised this was no ordinary dose of the flu. She bundled me into the car and we drove across the dusty gravel roads to the family doctor in Gunnedah. When he saw me, he told Mum to take me to the hospital in Tamworth immediately. This was another hour's drive away, but at least some of the road was sealed.

At the hospital, a doctor extracted fluid from my spine with a needle, and diagnosed me with meningitis.

The disease can kill in a matter of hours. That night I stopped breathing and, despite my parents being atheists, a minister administered the last rites. I was very lucky to somehow pull through, as considerable time had passed since Mum had driven all that way to the doctor and hospital.

A few weeks later, my parents noticed that although I had recovered from the illness, something wasn't right. I didn't respond when they called me, and I often said 'Pardon?'. So, there was another long drive – eight hours this time – to reach an audiologist in Sydney. After a series of tests, he announced to my parents that I had lost all of the hearing in my left ear and half in my right. I was severely-to-profoundly deaf.

*

I grew up on a property that housed four homesteads, one each belonging to my father, his two brothers and their parents. The brothers had grown up on the farm, then gone to boarding school and further education (my dad learned wool classing), then married and brought their wives back to the farm.

I became deaf towards the end of 1981. The telephone that my parents used at the time operated via a party line – a telephone line shared by a number of people and dialled using a pattern of long and short rings. Whenever the phone rang, my parents listened to the pattern to work out if the call was intended for them. A few years later, Telecom (as Telstra was then called) installed a line to our house. It often broke and would take them forever to fix. Years later, my sister, who is three years older than me, still spoke of Telstra with contempt; she remembered how little they seemed to care about their rural customers.

These days, a parent who learns that their child has a disability can jump online to educate themselves about their child's condition and access resources and support networks. But we were so far from anywhere that my parents had no guidance whatsoever about how to deal with my deafness. They had to rely on their wits.

I had learned to speak by the time I lost my hearing, and as I appeared to interact well with my brother and sister, Mum and Dad decided to send me to the local preschool with my brother one day a week. I detested being away from the farm. I much preferred being at home with my siblings and cousins than with strangers at preschool.

The next year I was enrolled in the local primary school. The other option was to send me to The Shepherd Centre for deaf children in Sydney, but it was too far away. I was too young to board and my father, a farmer and our family's breadwinner, couldn't leave the land. This meant that I was raised as what is known as an 'oral deaf' person – that is, a deaf person who relies on speech and lipreading to communicate.

*

At the audiologist, Mum sits in the waiting room with a magazine while I, in a sound-proofed room, listen to beeps and whistles through headphones. When I hear a sound, I have to press a button. The audiologist notes the pitch and volume of the beeps on a graph known as an 'audiogram'.

After the appointment, Mum takes me to Grace Bros, Tamworth's only department store. It's a double-storey complex with moving stairs, which is a massive novelty for a nine-year-old. At the top of the stairs is the furniture department and cafeteria. We line up with trays, and Mum buys me a milkshake and hot chips, and a sandwich and cup of tea for herself. We sit in silence as I suck the chocolate milk through a straw out of a tall, metal glass. Mum finishes off my chips. Then it's back in the car again, driving past paddocks tufted with wiregrass and clusters of houses nestled around wide intersections. When we pull into our driveway, bordered by a peppercorn tree, gum trees and Mum's carefully tended lawn, the dogs are barking madly.

'They can hear the motor, and they know it's us coming,' says Mum.

'That's incredible!'

'They have good hearing.'

*

There were seventeen of us altogether on the farm. Of the nine cousins, I was smack bang in the middle, with four born before me, and four after. We cousins rarely roamed as a group, but formed clusters depending on who was around when we met up. We made forts from fallen branches in the creeks, played hide-and-seek in our mothers' gardens, and helped our parents round up the sheep at shearing time. In spring we picked up lambs and handed them to our fathers for docking and castrating, checking their eyes for grass seeds so they wouldn't get cataracts. Most often, though, it was just my brother and I playing in the treehouse our grandfather had built, or whacking the purple heads off Scotch thistles with a stick. Once we picked a crop of wild mushrooms that sprang up in the paddocks after a rainy night.

My brother always stood at my right side so he could relay things into the ear that had some hearing. He knew what I needed based on what my body did: whether I turned my head towards him, or frowned, or raised my eyebrows to indicate confusion or that I had missed a section of a sentence. At times, he seemed an extension of my body; when he wasn't there, I felt the space where he should have been.

My siblings and cousins were loud, active, gregarious people, and I was assumed to be one of them too. Although I had lost a huge portion of my hearing, I could still hear enough to hear music, at least at higher pitches. I was expected, as were my siblings and cousins, to take music lessons or perform in plays arranged by our music teacher in the local small-town theatre.

We all attended the primary school at Boggabri. When we were all there at once – which was only for a year – we made up nearly 10 percent of the student population. I sat at the front of the class so I could hear, and while my teachers spoke clearly, I still had to lipread them, look down at my exercise book to write, then up again to read the next sentence.

As I grew up and moved through the school's four rooms (being such a small school, the classes were composite), the principal applied for funding to have navy blue carpets laid over the wooden floorboards, which otherwise magnified the sounds in the room – the clanging of metal tables and chair legs, rustling paper, kids sneezing or whispering, a lawnmower crossing the grounds outside. The background noise was unbearable and it made listening to the teacher more tiring than usual, as my brain had to try to filter out the background noise to find the teacher's voice.

*

A few weeks later, Mum and I return to the audiologist. He introduces us to a new piece of equipment.

'It's a frequency-modulation system,' he tells us, holding out two small rectangular boxes. 'Or "FM system" for short. Here, put this loop around your neck and put your hearing aid on the T-switch.' This is a setting on my hearing aid which enables me to hear on different frequencies. The loop is connected to one of the boxes. The audiologist takes the other box, with a small microphone plugged into it, into the next room. I sit in a chair next to Mum, swinging my feet, waiting.

'Hallo? Can you hear me?'

'Mum!' I shout. 'I can hear his voice!'

The audiologist strides back into the room, smiling.

When I give the FM to my teacher to wear, I no longer have to look at their face to read their lips all the time. I can simply listen and write in my exercise books. The teacher's voice is so clear that my body immediately feels lighter from the relief.

*

I turned twelve. The girls in my class started changing, forming tight impenetrable clusters in which they whispered about boys and buying bras. As someone who never watched TV, listened to the radio or read teen magazines, I didn't have a clue about how to negotiate these conversations. At lunchtimes I began to sit by myself, a book open in my lap, watching children kicking a soccer ball in the burr-infested grounds.

The next year, I started secondary school in Gunnedah, and my bafflement continued. Children learnt to talk to one another by listening to conversations, but I had never overheard a conversation in my life, and had no sense of their natural ebb and flow. My parents tried to coach me through role plays, but I couldn't see the point.

'Talk about the weather,' they suggested.

'Why? They could just look out the window and see if it's raining.'

I continued spending my lunchtimes alone, leaning up against a cold brick wall. Even at home there was no respite from my loneliness. My brother, sister and cousins were sent to boarding school. I would have gone too, but the principal at the time refused to take me because of my disability. A deaf girl had boarded at the school previously and she'd often had trouble with her hearing aids and wanted to go home. So I stayed on the farm with my parents. I was bored and I missed my brother and sister very much.

Each morning meant a six a.m. alarm to get to the bus on time. Some of my cousins still attended the same school as me, and my parents carpooled with my aunt and uncle and a neighbouring family. The bus arrived in a whirl of dust and I was often anxious, the long, lonely day stretching ahead of me.

There was so much driving, from home to the bus to school. From school to music lessons. From home to the audiologist's. The ribbons of gravel and asphalt roads, often empty of other cars, mirrored the sparseness of my days.

*

As a way of coping, I began to run. Just through a few paddocks to start with, then further, up into the hills on hot summer days. It was a relief to be completely on my own, with no-one demanding my attention or making me listen. The vast reserves of energy that I needed for hearing were released. They flushed my legs and arms, and I sprang over the sheeps' tracks through the wiregrass.

I gained a sense of strength in my body, and pushed myself further. I realised I could drive myself physically, the way I could with my schoolwork. Being hopeless at conversation, at school I focused on the things I enjoyed: stories, history, algebra, pleasing my teachers, getting high marks. From this I gathered a few crumbs of confidence, enough to chat to the girls I sat near at lunch. Just a few words about homework, here and there. At home, over dinner with my parents, I mentioned my forays into conversation.

'Well done, Jess! That's great work,' they exclaimed.

But beyond what I did at school, I had no topics to talk about. My coldness persisted.

*

The voices that I hear through the FM are intimate, as though the person is right next to my ear. They seem to eclipse the distance that I'm always feeling. It's like reading. All the times that I'm in the car or on the bus, I have a book open. Hours and hours, pages and pages. Reading means I can escape the awkwardness of trying to join in on conversations, and the boredom when I miss out on what's going on. It allows me to explore other worlds and times, and to forget the cold, clammy isolation that creeps back when I close the covers of a book.

As I can't hear on a phone, I write letters instead. I write to my relatives in New Zealand, and to penpals in Singapore. Opening and reading a letter is like listening to a person standing right beside me, their voices clear and engaging.

*

My father, although fit and hardworking, was always slender, and Mum deduced that his body wouldn't be able to keep up with farming life forever. When I was fifteen, we left the farm and moved to Armidale, the town where my brother and sister boarded, up in the tablelands where the winters were very cold.

Dad had painted watercolours since he was a teenager. In Sydney, working as a cab driver, he'd taken lessons. When he and Mum married and moved back to the farm, Mum encouraged him to keep painting. After working on the farm in the day, he would paint in his studio in the evenings. My brother and I sat at his feet, the camel-hair carpet prickling our knees, and drew on cardboard left over from cutting his mounts.

In Armidale, Dad taught Art at the boys' school that my brother attended. My brother stopped boarding and became a day boy, and I was a day girl at the girls' school (by then, our sister had left for university). Although my brother and I didn't share the same closeness that we'd had on the farm, I was relieved to be back with him again, the only person who properly understood the part of me that was missing.

Because in the country we lived so far from health services, and because the telephone was often broken, and because my parents had so little access to information about deafness, and because I was raised as oral deaf, it took me a long time to develop a Deaf identity.

People rarely understand the difference between being deaf and having a sense of self as a culturally Deaf person.

'What do you mean?' they ask.

'I knew I had severe hearing loss, but I didn't think of myself as Deaf.'

It wasn't until the beginning of my twenties, when I saw a counsellor, that I realised I was thinking of myself as a shoddy version of a hearing person, and placing demands upon myself to act like a hearing person – demands which were impossible to achieve.

All that distance surrounding us in the country meant that I was never exposed to other Deaf people, except through a few picture books or the newspaper. My parents, although they were doing the best they could, didn't know how important it was to have Deaf connections and role models.

My mother's family were New Zealanders, and on one visit my grandfather, an accountant who loved gin and cigarettes, brought with him a newspaper clipping.

'Deaf Olympians,' he explained, spraying gin on my face in his efforts to enunciate. 'All of the people competing are Deaf.'

I looked at the clipping. A huge man was lifting weights. I wondered if he kept his hearing aids in as he lifted. It didn't occur to me that he might be too deaf to need them; my only association with deafness was with someone who wore a hearing aid. I knew that many deaf people signed, but I figured I didn't need sign language because I had some hearing. I didn't understand, because I had no Deaf role models, that sign language was a way of forming a Deaf identity and becoming part of a Deaf community.

It wasn't until my early thirties that I made my first Deaf friend, Donna McDonald. Donna was writing a memoir about her experiences of deafness. She had initially attended a school for Deaf children in Yeronga, then was moved into a mainstream school and lost contact with her friends. She grew up surrounded by hearing people, but reconnected with her Deaf friends later in life. From reading her book, it seemed to me that she had found the pieces that completed herself.

Donna's book launch in 2014 was one of the first events I attended for Deaf people. The Bundjalung writer who launched the book observed that my friend 'grew up without Deaf elders'. Hearing this, tears began to seep from my eyes. Puzzled and sad, I hastily wiped them away with the back of my hand, hoping the people on either side of me hadn't noticed.

Five years later, I attended another book launch, this time with a friend who is the mother of a Deaf child. This launch celebrated a book of photographs and stories of Deaf people. I was tired and overwrought, working in a job that I loved but did not think I could sustain because it demanded so much hearing. I no longer had the energy, nor the support from my colleagues, to keep it up.

I watched my friend signing with her daughter. The girl's face was bright with attention, her confidence clear as she wheeled around, smiling, and signed with her friends, then turned back to her mother. To my horror, I began to cry uncontrollably. My friend, understanding and patient, waved away my apologies.

That night I told my partner of my embarrassment that I had burst into tears.

'Why were you sad?' he asked.

'Because I'm alone all the time, and the only time I realise it is when I see other Deaf people, and I notice what I'm missing.'

He didn't answer, nor did I expect him to. I had grown up. The distance in the country, the long car trips from town to town, the hours of sitting by myself, had become an indelible part of who I was.

Although it made me sad, I knew it wasn't a bad thing. Reading words was a means for me to connect with other people, and so I began to write them as well. Without those long car trips, without my desire to overcome my isolation and connect with other people, I would never have started to write. Growing up deaf in the country made me a writer.

Separate, Initiate, Burn

Carly Rawson

The windows were shut against the smoke. The beginning of our year of extraordinary escalations. The long, slow shuttering; the movement from within to without. We shut the windows and it started something. Doors, streets, cities and borders. Cloth on our faces, our bodies reined so tight we skittered around each other like nervous horses. Before a sickness commandeered our lives and left us as airless as pieces of meat in Cryovac bags. Brimstone brought in the year and I thought then that bad was bad enough. Lying on my bed in a pool of sweat as the Kmart fan curdled the air. My heart between my teeth as I listened to my baby fret in the thick dark of his room, waiting for him to call my body to his.

Days inside. The EPA issuing warnings in no uncertain terms. It was impossible not to watch the news. Glued to the TV in my sweltering Carlton cottage. My naked son bounced at my feet with a cardboard tube he imagined as a hose, pointing it at the screen and screaming 'FIRE! FIRE!' I knew I should have turned it off, but I couldn't. I couldn't move. I felt my dull bones blackening. My bones aflame. My bones glowing neon and combusting like cheap Chinatown fireworks. 'Mummy grew up there, baby,' I whispered. 'I grew up there.'

The fan didn't work. My husband slept soundly. I resented his radiant heat and the weight of his body on the mattress beside me. I resented the lightness of his load. His history was living, unambiguous and well maintained. It was neatly contained within a three-suburb radius. I couldn't sleep for grief. The future was being prematurely born and my mind spun like a bore. It pushed back, tunnelling beneath bluestone and suburban sprawl, below carcass-strewn highways and roadhouses, back to the old forest and its wandering ghosts.

*

Let's say her name was Jade. Let's leave the town unnamed. It's unrecognisable now anyway. This story belongs to another millennium but permission for heavy-handed excavation is not granted by distance alone. So, in a town that is no longer what it was, there lived a girl who wasn't Jade and a girl who is no longer me.

There were five of us in our gang. We imagined ourselves as a single unit: impenetrable, fortified by the fierce, semi-erotic love particular to fourteen-year-old girls. All of our fathers were millworkers except Jade's. Her family had money somehow, a big house on the hill, a pool. She was learning clarinet, a metronome on the shelf of her Laura Ashley bedroom while we played air guitar in front of *Rage*. Her body was long, strong and perfectly formed when we were tight with puppy fat, our hair and skin an oily mess. She'd arrived early and confidently to womanhood. It wasn't the money, it was grace. She wore white, crossed her legs and tossed her shining hair. She didn't have to try; she was. An elegant curiosity in our crude little town, she was the jewel in our toy-shop tiara.

Our town was too small for us. Two thousand closed minds with no-one coming and no-one going. A hole, we called it, repeating it devotedly like a mantra. *What a fucking hole. What a fucking hole*. A more accurate description might have been *tomb*, a chamber of re-enforced forest walls with a steely ocean door. Back then, though, it was simply a hole and we were buried alive. Its beauty was of no consequence. We thought traffic lights were beautiful, fast food outlets, big flat movie suburbs where everything was ordered and identifiable. Where the natural world was exiled and not breathing its dank breath all over you, not blocking your way.

The lock sprung once a year. A groaning, seismic shift as the town opened up on Boxing Day and the first of the dusty cavalcade of tourists snaked out of the bush and began moving through on their way north. Ours was the first town on the coastline and the last choice as a destination. Too rough around the edges to be easy, it lacked both amenities and friendliness. Still, we absorbed the overflow: those families who were more intrepid or less fiscal. The camping boating fishing types.

The locals responded to the influx as though they were under siege, but we lived for it. All long, empty year we'd been busy sketching out the details of our phantom romances. Our excitement was boundless. We wanted fresh blood – boys who didn't smell like bongwater or fishing trawlers, who wore Air Jordan sneakers instead of thongs and flannelette shirts. We wanted girls whose cosmopolitanism might rub off on us, no matter how outer-suburban it might be. The internet was years off; we needed news from the outside world, and they were our cultural ambassadors. All of our longing to this point had been speculative and embryonic. The previous summer we'd been too young and shy to bridge the divide, but we'd been readying ourselves. When they arrived, so would we.

The sudden death of Jade's father in November stymied us. The shock was so disorientating that for a month Jade turned quietly in slow circles. We did what we could but mainly we just shuffled around a breach we couldn't comprehend. Jade put herself together and came back to us for Christmas. You could see the effort it had taken. She was like a mosaic, beautiful but jagged, all her cracks and mortar showing. It made her reckless too, a naive hope that being broken once had made her immune.

*

Did it begin like this? We were at the beach, fat and greasy in our sunscreen. Not Jade though. She was leaning against the sun-splintered fence, cool as fuck. The surf was rubbish. They pulled up, the metallic finish on their car blinding, and beckoned her over. We called her back. *No, no, no.* A chorus of protestations lost to the wind.

Or was she waiting in her driveway? Behind her the house was a shrine. Her mother was Catholic again. She shuffled from room to room, keeping the curtains drawn and the candles lit. Blinkered with suffering, in a Valium stupor, her mother didn't see Jade wave the car down as it crested the hill. She wasn't watching as they pulled over, one of the boys getting out to make room for Jade in the back.

The former or the latter, it makes no difference. Whichever way, she was taken from us.

She was in the middle of the backseat and they were driving to the waterfall. She pointed out the turnoff sign but they sped past and although the music was loud, so loud, she could hear the absence of an indicator like a bomb exploding in her head. She turned to the boy on her right, her new friend, and saw that his teeth were gritted, his pulse jumping in his neck. She held her breath.

Off a fire trail too far out of town, in the thick of a state forest, they tied her to a tree. She was struggling as they stripped her, so they restrained her with a rope they'd bought with them in the boot of their car. A eucalypt, it's bark smooth and pale against her burning skin. They started to close in. She singled out the smallest one, the one with the soft eyes, and began to talk.

I remember this word for word. I can't forget the rhetoric of it, how she reduced herself first. Insignificance as a predicate for survival. I wondered, still wonder, how she'd figured it out so young.

'Don't do this,' she said. 'I'm not worth it. You are making a terrible mistake. Your future is big and this moment is small. It will ruin you. Your families. The shame. You can save yourselves. It's not too late. It's not too late. How well do you think you'll handle jail? Who will be there waiting for you when you get out? Who will forgive you for this? For doing this? I'm really not worth it. I'm nothing. Nothing.'

'FUCK THIS!' The small boy turned away, punching a tree as he walked off. The circle broke. Someone called her a slut, spitting on her as they gathered her clothes and headed back to the car. She was naked and tied to a tree. Did she cry then, piss running down her legs, or was she simply breathing hard, each breath an affirmation? *I'm okay, I'm okay, I'm okay.*

She told us she heard a twig snap. It was the boy with the wet brown eyes. He cut the rope with his pocketknife and threw her t-shirt at her feet before running back through the bush to the others. She didn't move until she was sure they were gone, until the dust cloud kicked up by their tyres settled like dirty talcum on her skin.

She got home. Showered and scrubbed and slept. She didn't tell her mother or the cops, only us. And this is the story she told, or the story I remember her having told – that she talked them down. She was quieter after, her wattage dimmed right down. What could we do or say? Our awe seemed inappropriate. We felt, more than ever, like children beside her. We made no new friends that summer but stuck to ourselves. I can't recall if any of us even found someone to kiss.

School started and we began our troublemaking, throwing in our lot with the local boys. Better the devil you know, as they say. Jade got packed off to boarding school and six months later I left home and moved to the city. For some country kids – too many that I have known – the city unleashes something feral in them. They go wild, become dangerous. And I was one of them. I continued my personal study in holes and when I finally came up for air I had no family left in that town and all the girls were gone. I heard second-hand that she was doing well at many different things, had a husband and a pair of photogenic children, but I didn't look her up. I didn't look anyone up, I was too ashamed to account for myself. The town had retreated further into the bush. It had become inaccessible to me, overgrown, the way an untended grave disappears over time.

Until a fire comes.

*

I was lying in bed and the eastern seaboard was burning. I was thinking about legacies, about what my son stood to inherit. I couldn't drive the images away, the unerasable newsreel of destruction. I kept coming back to the same shot, the familiar stretch of highway threading through a firestorm. I had always imagined the bush there to be the scene of Jade's story, although I cannot recall if she ever specified the exact location; if she did, I've since forgotten. There, or somewhere near there, it didn't matter: it was all ablaze. But it was then, as the forests of my childhood were reduced to ash, that it occurred to me how implausible her story was. For the first time, I considered that she might have lied. That she didn't, couldn't, talk them down. That she couldn't see her way through the shame to tell us the truth, had chosen instead to protect us from it.

The room was so hot. The alternative version came to rest upon my chest like a carrion bird. The truth then, as I imagined it, was blindingly obvious. The small, brown-eyed boy, as pretty as he was, had a lot to prove. He had gone first. She had described him so vividly, his appearance, his small act of mercy, that it could only have been an act of erasure. I saw then how ridiculous it was. That a young girl naked except for a t-shirt, wild with terror on the side of a highway, could get home without being abused again or taken to a police station. That a young girl was no Samson, no matter how long and luscious her hair, and even if she was, a pack of wild dogs is not a lion. I saw them finishing with her and dumping her back at the beach, just some holiday fun, the damage minor and impermanent, like sunburn.

So much has passed between the telling and retelling, so much has been consumed. Who can say what it is true and what isn't? Likelihood is no absolute and I'm told that miracles do happen. I've learnt the hard way that conviction is a mirage, and that we all fall by its wayside thirsty and lost. I do not know much and what I do know is chipped away, little by little, with each passing year.

But I can be almost certain of one thing: as the country burnt and a nation floundered in paroxysms of grief, one person did not. In an elegantly furnished house of ambient temperature, a woman sat before the news, twirling the stem of a wine glass between her long brown fingers. She sat and she drank and from time to time she refilled her glass and raised it to the screen, toasting the carnage.

Every Saturday in Summer

Samantha Leung

Every Saturday in summer, for the agonising five years we lived in Geraldton, my family spent at the Aquarena. The Aquarena had a fifty-metre outdoor pool, a twenty-five-metre indoor pool (both of which were deep enough for water polo, naturally), a wading pool with a proper slide that you climbed up stairs to access, and truly excellent chips. In Geraldton there were four water polo clubs: the Rats, the Demons, the Serpents and the B52's. My mother, father, sister and I all played for the B52's, named for both the band and the shot. It was a club tradition, at the Christmas party, to drink the shot and homebrewed tequila – a mistake if there ever was one – then drop to the ground, no matter how sticky, and pretend to be 'dead ants' every time 'Eagle Rock' came on.

If you've ever lived in a country town then you know the thing to do is play sport. Sport in the country means Country Week – for the uninitiated: a massive boozefest with various sporting matches thrown in – and congregating around the pool, field, pitch, whatever. It's like church, say twenty years ago. Sport in Geraldton means water polo. Now, water polo for most people means being drowned on-and-off for about an hour. But water polo for me means living. And in Geraldton, it was really the only thing I was getting out of bed for.

Geraldton: the windiest place in Western Australia, probably Australia, quite possibly the world. So windy the trees grow sideways and you know you're closing in on the town when everything starts tilting. Geraldton is a country town that lacks idyll.

Bordered by the Indian Ocean and edged by canola, it's a place where it's common to leave school after Year 10 for a trade, and everyone is either related or going to be, whether or not they know it yet.

In high school we used to joke that the neighbouring town Northampton was a hole. This is a classic slur for those living in a small town – there's always someone whose town is smaller and more of a hole than yours, however marginally so. But really, this moniker applied just as well to our windy stretch of the west. Geraldton was a place where you got stuck, and I, for one, couldn't wait to leave.

*

My family embraced water polo that first summer after we moved to Geraldton. We'd spend every weekend at the pool, where my athletic ten-year-old sister – who, despite being two years my junior, was considerably taller and stronger than me – and I played up to three games apiece. For years, I'd verse my enthusiastic, white Aussie mum in our opposing C-grade teams, as we played out a comic battle for Leung-family dominance. Dad – a short-sighted, five-foot-eleven, intimidatingly solid Chinese-Australian – would spend the game swimming up and down the pool, somehow never managing to hear when the ball landed near him, despite the screams of his entire team and whatever family member was sitting on the sidelines that day.

Before water polo, the newness of Geraldton had quickly soured. I'd arrived in Year 8 with the thrill of a new place, new uniforms and (fingers crossed!) new friends. It didn't take long to realise that I didn't fit into our new west-coast home as seamlessly as the rest of my family. Almost everyone in my year was white and, for the first time, I noticed.

My skin stretched in Geraldton and grew brittle atop the brownness. If my skin had a flavour it'd be the Zombie Chews we'd buy from the canteen: a thick, tough exterior and filled with sherbet that'd make your tongue buzz. Get through that outer layer and my skin is simmering, just waiting to make your mouth pop at the next reminder that I wasn't from here. Unknowingly starring in videos teachers would play in class (any video that featured an Asian person: 'Look! It's Sam Leung!'); my homeroom teacher's gag about kamikaze Asians; my classmate waving his sushi as he taunted, 'Better get back to your whaling boat, Sam. I'm running out.' It didn't help that in my year it was just me and Anup who weren't white. Tamika and Marika from Kununurra had left to board in Perth after Year 8. Four brown kids out of forty is like a bad joke at a party, and two out of twenty-five, well, you're the punchline. Every summer, I'd wait restlessly for the beginning of a new water polo season. Ready to be embraced by people who believed racing down the pool and tussling over the ball was the *best* thing you could have in common.

If you've never played water polo, you're missing out. There are six players from each team on the field, with a goalie at either end, egg-beating in their netted cages. When the whistle blows, both sides shoot down the pool with their fastest or least exhausted player, making the swim-up for the ball. People think it's violent. And they're right. You might haul yourself out of the pool with a fat lip, jarred fingers or ripped bathers – togs, if you're from Queensland. I even knew a girl who broke someone's nose (by accident!). But in Geraldton, its popularity is a peculiar phenomenon. There'll be a barbeque running; stands filled with people chanting 'Tits out for the boys!' whenever there's (a much hoped for) risk of bathers ripping in a women's match; and men's teams huddled in the Aquarena car park for a post-game beer, waving people over to join them as they walked past.

There was a small contingent of girls from school who played. (Ironically, despite living on the Indian Ocean, most of the boys in my year could barely swim.) Maddy, Tayla, Rosie, Shaunace and Tegan – who was two years above the rest of us – were all fellow converts, though none ever grew quite as fervent as me and Tegan. Maddy and Tayla had played for years in C- and B-grade, and Tayla's dad, 'Schoie', was a B52's staple. The family dynamic wasn't coincidental; water polo was generational in Geraldton. It was something that you were born into, bred for. But my love for the game wasn't instantaneous. I was tiny growing up, and it wasn't until the start of my second season that I knew I'd found it: my place, in this bitterly windy town.

*

At age thirteen, my family and I pull into the Aquarena car park. Mum locks eyes with me, trying to reassure me as we walk into the indoor pool. It's my second year of water polo and I'm about to play my first game of B-grade, after just one year in Juniors and with only one C-grade game behind me.

Mum, Dad and my sister head off for a good seat in the stands as I join my new team. 'What are you doing here?' Maddy and Tayla ask.

To be fair, I'm not known for my sporting prowess at school. I'm still instantly and self-righteously offended in the way that all teenagers manage with ease.

'I'm the new goalie,' I say.

I'm met with blank stares. Given I am small – one of the shortest in our year, at five-foot-four – and not built with the brawny wingspan of a traditional goalie. I focus on pulling on my cap and slipping my mouthguard in, trying not to appear as nervous as I feel.

I've been enlisted as their new goalie thanks to a terrifying decision in the last quarter of the Juniors' grand final. Our coach had placed all our best players on the field, which meant I'd ended up in goals. Facing down the formidable Alicia Brown who was sprinting towards me with the ball, sans defender, I'd instinctively sprinted out to meet her. She scored, but that little moment landed me an invitation to women's B-grade; *'Most Improved Juniors' Player'* at that year's awards; and the satisfying feeling of *finally* being good at one physical activity.

The whistle sounds and our six players sprint from the lane rope marking the field's edge. The game has begun.

I watch from inside the goalie's cage as we win the swim-up, waiting for the ball to make its way towards our goal.

We're losing but it doesn't matter. For once, everything feels effortless as I block goal after goal, pulling myself back with my left arm as I reach high with my right to stop a lob. Even taking a backhander straight to the face doesn't hurt as much as it should. I never feel this good.

I see Maddy and Tayla's faces as we rise from the pool. People are congratulating me.

'Great game,' Maddy says.

'Thanks,' I reply and smile, big.

At the water-polo social that night, people I've never spoken to are leaning over to tell me they saw the game. My family's there and my dad is so proud. He's grinning and going on about how fierce I was in the pool – Dad loves a bit (read: a lot) of aggression and plays every game of polo like he's still on the rugby field.

That Saturday, I am a success. Two days later, school's back and I can't wait to leave this place again.

*

Out of the pool, I'm a bloom that's late to bud in this place of wind-bent trees. My Geraldton life and teenagehood can be divided into 'before water polo' and 'after water polo'. All my school report cards, from my Townsville primary school to Geraldton high school, are stamped with solid Cs for PE and that classic consolation prize: 'Sam is an enthusiastic member of the class'. As a kid, I was thrilled if I wasn't left in the horrifying final three whenever my classmates picked their teams in PE. But in the lonely, white misery of high school, water polo saved me. I might have been terrible at all sports that mattered at school, and an olive-brown that never tinted to the much sought-after Australian gold – a shade so desirable that Maddy and Shaunace once basted themselves in olive oil in their pursuit of it, which ended exactly how you'd imagine (bright red and peeling like dandruff). But when I inhaled the chlorine stench of the Aquarena, I *belonged*.

My body lengthened. My arms stretched out like branches as my shoulders learnt to bend back, almost unnaturally, until I could fling a polo ball two-thirds down the pool. My legs grew thick and strong from their constant egg-beating. In goals, I learnt to leap waist-high from the water, my legs rapidly propelling me as I reached skyward.

*

In Geraldton, I learnt to bend. Moulded into my new watery form, I stretched out, away from the wind and my high-school melancholy. It was only five years, and whenever I'm asked where I'm from (which is often) I never name it.

'I'm from Queensland,' I like to say.

But really, it's been a long time since I was from Queensland. And there's not a place that defined me like Geraldton did. When I moved to Perth, and later to Sydney, I let the baking heat and tugging wind of Geraldton pass into my memory. If I didn't look behind me I wouldn't have to sit with my unhappiness or my horrible unease of being 'other'.

Twelve years after leaving, that feeling lingers. I don't go back there anymore and I have few friends from there that I've kept. My family loved Geraldton, and I think they would've stayed longer if they could have. They loved the ease of it, the community.

And yet, in Perth, water polo was never quite the same. It wasn't the messy congregation of families and friends, with those excellent chips and dirty chants. Perth was too large a city to have just one pool that generations of players could flock to every summer. Like its urban home, it sprawled outwards, far too wide to ever wind back into a community.

*

Five years leeched into my bones, skin, eyes. I can no longer remember the roads we would take to get from our house beneath the water tower to school, the Aquarena, the two shopping centres. But there are things I do remember: wading through the weed at Back Beach, always careful not to lift my foot lest a cobbler slide beneath; never wanting to leave the pool and the excitement of summer as another water-polo season rolled in; my unhappiness of always feeling wrong in a place that never came to feel right – too brittle, contrary and brown, always straining against the wind.

But now, in the city, I crave the ease and simplicity of it. The way we'd swap crayfish for bottles of wine over the fence, the time my visiting aunt and uncle forgot to pay their bill and the café phoned our house, the way everything in town takes fifteen minutes or less to reach. But, most of all, the way that everyone I want to see is already at the Aquarena, every Saturday in summer.

Looking Back, Looking Up

Jes Layton

'So, you're heading down then?' my brother, Ben, asks, voice tinny over the phone.

It's been almost a year since either of us have ventured out of Melbourne. It's 2020 after all, but the question still rankles.

'I mean, yeah, probably. I dunno.'

Ben huffs, and I imagine him: my bearded, balding twenty-seven-year-old brother trotting down the street at night, walking his tiny pug, Lando. It's a good time to get in the regular check-ups with Mum, Dad and me. Though it feels a bit special this time when he says: 'Y'know you can see Saturn, Mars and Jupiter tonight?'

I place my cup of tea aside and get up to kneel on my bed when he tells me to look outside my window. I do, and though it is a clear, moonless night, the stars are difficult to see.

'Do you see that yellow-looking one?' Ben directs me. 'That's Saturn.'

Between the blinking planes crossing the sky to and from Melbourne Airport, a cloudy, pervasive purple haze blots out any dots of light like spilled ink over words. If I squint hard I can make out one, maybe two stars out the window. Jupiter shines brightly – well, as brightly as it can here – and Saturn follows with its faint yellow hue. I know somewhere behind the smog there are thousands of stars – streaks of nebulous light traversing the sky – and my chest suddenly aches to not see them.

How long had it been since I'd seen a full sky?

Where we're from, one glance up can be filled with hundreds

of stars before you turn your head slightly and see another completely new hundred.

The regular calls of magpies, noisy miners and kookaburras were the soundtrack to our childhood. Looking up, with my brother on the phone, I'm suddenly consumed by nostalgia for the little girl who was me, who loved the sun-drenched paddocks boxed in by metres-high gums. Who spent afternoons pretending thistles and bat's wing ferns as tall as your shoulders were dragons that needed slaying, who spent weekends waging wars on bull-ant mounds that deserved a swifter death than three freckled kids armed with cricket bats and water bottles.

Where we're from, you can look up and see the actual band of the Milky Way.

*

I grew up around the Otway National Park, in a small township of Yeodene on Guildjan land – the coast less than an hour away, and Melbourne/Naarm closer to three.

My childhood was punctuated by moving between my divorced parents' houses each week. From my father's house in Yeodene to my mother's house first in Birregurra, then Colac. I would move back and forth across southwestern Victoria like a massive hermit crab, fitting into new houses for a little while, just long enough to discover the best climbing trees, see how long I could stretch the three-minute-shower rule on a new tank, or squeeze in a few whimsical adventures, before moving on again.

Honestly, I was a bit of a feral kid. Between my two front teeth was a gap about the size of a two-dollar coin. My hair was knotted, inconsistently brushed, until I got my first pixie cut at eleven and never looked back. Quintessentially the middle child, I had no problem hamster-wheeling a big corrugated-iron tank across the paddock with my siblings as huntsmans, millipedes and all manner of creepy-crawlies rained down on us. Throughout school, I bullied a girl by taping a safety pin to the end of a ruler and jabbing her whenever she came too close to me. Another I belittled mercilessly for being a 'lesbian' (she wasn't). I picked fistfights with the boys during lunch and, as you can imagine, more than once I found myself on the steps outside the principal's office for lunchtime detention.

I wasn't always a good person, when I lived down here before. There are parts of my girlhood here that I will probably never reconcile, that will always be hard to face. My early life was characterised by a lot of anger, jealousy, shame. By long stretches of near-solitude broken up by longer drives on pot-holed dirt roads in a sweaty, fart-filled bus to enter society and then exit again.

A lot of this anger, I've learnt, stemmed from there not being a single year in my life that my sexuality and gender wasn't questioned.

*

I grew up as a girl. I grew up loving stars. I was a queer girl for most of my teenage years. To say that I struggled with my identity growing up would be an understatement, but I became public, became *visible* very early. In the local newspaper, in front of news cameras, at school, my visibility as a queer person in a rural area was not within my own power – I was always just *that one*. Obvious to everyone, especially people I had never met.

The first time I remember my identity being questioned, I'm six, just starting Prep and utterly infatuated with my Grade 6 buddy, Kirsty. She seems to be loved by the world. I want to be her; I want to be near her. Freckly face, pulled-back ponytail, braces: she seems to be near-angelic. I want her to hold me, carry me, pick me up and be with me. Sometime into my first few weeks of school, Kirsty's friends ask her if I am a lesbian. I have been called this before, a small girl often gets that when she insists on being 'the daddy' in mummies and daddies, and prefers to go by Jack or Jake instead of Jes during play. My siblings had never minded, so it's a surprise when the kids at school do.

Atop Kirsty's lap, I can't understand what they mean. I don't know what a lesbian is yet, but I know it's bad. Kirsty doesn't let me sit on her lap or be with her and her friends during playtime after that. It may just be that it is uncool for a Grade 6er to coddle their Prep buddy so much – there could be a number of reasons why distance is suddenly placed between us. But my six-year-old heart clings to their mocking question. I retreat into my ill-fitting shell and mourn the sudden universe of space between us.

*

There's a magic to growing up in the country, under the stars, that I don't think others know how to appreciate.

It's night, about nine o'clock, and I'm lying on the trampoline outside along with my two siblings and my mum. I'm around twelve years old and we're in Birregurra now, in the first of a few rental homes we will have in this area over the next few years. Enough acres to explore for hours, manna gum trees for climbing, a near-empty dam that, in a couple of months from now, we'll roll my sister, Emily, down into with a bucket over her head and her hands tied behind her back. This will be a good memory. But for now, the night is quiet, the mozzies keeping their distance. There are no words, just the four of us lying down on the trampoline. The silence seems right.

I roll onto my side, lean my head against Mum's shoulder and listen to the wind pass through the trees. I only turn to look when Mum points up at the sky.

'Did you see that? A shooting star!'

Even now, I think she was lying. But still, I turn to watch the stars materialise slowly, as though someone is dimming the switch on the night sky so that each shining dot grows brighter and brighter. Pointing upward, Mum locates a spot of light and asks us to stay with it. Emily, trying to see, sits up, and from the corner of my eye I see her long, dirt-blonde hair charged by the trampoline as the night erupts.

The trampoline, and all of us on it, crackles with a sudden burst of static electricity and *I see it.* In the darkness, static flares in a tiny lightning storm, sparks flying from the ends of Emily's hair. There are so many zaps, so quick, you'd think we were living in a constellation. The fallen stars are quickly forgotten in favour of this new discovery.

We all scramble off the trampoline in order to skate our hands across the taut fabric that becomes a sheet of light as our fingers produce a shower of sparks loud enough to be heard all over the garden. What long fingers my mum has, I remember thinking, like the wands in fairytales.

I feel electrified, sparked, fizzled. Down here, where life has been hanging like a heavy, suffocating cloak lately, I can't remember feeling so ignited.

I think about coming out in that moment, taking something I am so afraid and shameful of and shoving it into this magic, cosmic moment. Maybe then that would make my queerness something magic and cosmic too.

*

The key to witnessing any stunning celestial event – whether it's converging planets or a shooting star – is being in the right place at the right time for a perfect view of the sky.

It's 2017; we're the first ones up to the top of Red Rock, grabbing the best spot in Mum's small, blue Mazda to look out across both Lake Colac and Lake Corangamite and the plains further west and north. Despite being about 8000 years old, and being the largest volcanic plains in the world, the actual Red Rock itself is one of Australia's youngest volcanoes, a complex labyrinth of overlapping maars, scoria cones and small lava flows.

The weekend has been a back-and-forth pinball of catching up with Emily, Dad, Mum and my grandparents, the 'coming home' carnival where conversation treads the usual updates of how my writing is going, how work is going. There's a change this time:

Mum tells me the Leonids are passing us, and asks if I want to come watch with her.

Being one year out of uni and three years up in Melbourne, the promise of a sky I can actually see is near-intoxicating. We climb up onto the Mazda's bonnet, thermos of tea and a blanket shared between the two of us. A few other sky-watchers soon arrive, bringing with them large telescopes and infrared cameras. It's intimate though, only about six of us in the whole volcanic plain.

It would have been a magical night to come out, except that almost a decade earlier I had been one of the generation of queers who came out via Facebook status, although as many told me I needn't have bothered. I didn't need to make a grand statement or declaration; I just ... *was*. It was only once I officially came out that people started telling me I needed to leave. I was constantly told that if I had grown up in a city – Sydney, Melbourne, maybe even Brisbane – things would have been different. That in order to live a full life as a lesbian, I would need to leave the country as soon as possible. In the city I would be *among* other queer people, in a way I hadn't been before.

I feel very among with my mum on top of a volcano watching the sky fall. Since moving to Melbourne, I would imagine looking up into the night sky and seeing a star fade away. If you saw a star die, that's probably the first time after its death in years that it was really 'noticed'. Other stars would 'notice' it, the change in energy or a shift in gravitational force, I'm sure.

It's not dying stars that cause the Leonids.

Sirius and the familiar stars of Orion are recognisable near the southwestern horizon, and the meteors, when they appear, seem to head right for the hunter's belt and sword. The reason we see the Leonids at all is because Earth meets these meteors head-on as they travel through space in a direction opposite to that of our planet. Like me, the Leonids are just passing through.

We share the blanket, Mum and I, huddled together to keep away mozzies, to keep close. We talk about nothing memorable and just enjoy the majesty of the cosmos, of my home I so desperately ran away from but sometimes struggle to remember why. Under the moonless, starlit sky with my head turned upwards, my thoughts wander, scatter themselves.

Meteor showers are not like how they are in the movies, with dozens of meteors careening past. Instead, we see about thirteen meteors in total over our entire time out watching.

On 17 November 2017, just a couple of hours or so before sunrise, bright white meteors flash through clear pre-dawn skies and I think of Melbourne – where everything fit and felt right and felt safe, except for the lack of stars in the sky with which to mark my place.

*

One of my new hobbies that I took up in the year 2020 is to go out at night and walk, past the houses, down the footpaths, ducking under the orange streetlights, to try and find patches of darkness where I can stare up at the night sky.

I don't have time to do this on my latest trip back to the Otways.

In Yeodene I am surrounded by paddocks of cattle, dirt roads, and the Otway Forest rising up on all sides. In this township there is a small fire station, and a combination tennis court and town hall that is rarely open to the public. From almost every vantage point, you can see kilometres of Australian countryside and bush, hear bird calls and the distant roaring of bulls. My childhood home is situated on the top of a small gully, at the fork of two dirt roads, barely in sight through the thick tree cover.

I feel as though a part of me is folding in on itself as I drive into town. The sun is out but I myself feel dim. My queerness feels dim. I don't think it will ever be easy to stand in the places that remind me of who I once was. There will always be pieces of me that hurt, pieces that regret. Pieces I have outgrown and ran from and hidden away. But these memories of who I was and where I lived are important to me. They are something that will forever be a part of this place, for me.

I could not have been more familiar with the stretch of tar that is Colac's main street, humping towards the 'city centre' with shops lining either side. Shops that weren't empty last time I came down. Every second store on the street seems to be closing down, or already closed. Although a few footpaths have been made more accessible now, the longer I stay the longer I realise something here is deeply wrong.

I walk past the old bowling alley and see nothing on either side except for the pet-grooming store and the old community radio hut. There are at least half-a-dozen newly renovated houses so at odds with the sheds next to them, and I feel surrounded on all sides by construction workers who don't actually seem to be constructing anything. There's a layer of empty all over the town, like nobody loves anything here enough to look after it.

'We're getting a 7-Eleven,' Emily tells me over a cup of coffee when I catch up with her on her lunch break. She sounds excited, I just feel bemused; unable to imagine something so quintessentially *Melbourne* coming *here*.

'I'm going to absolutely drown in Krispy Kreme,' she says.

It's silly, but one of the things I like about living in Melbourne is that when Emily comes to visit she always insists on heading out to scavenge a fourteen-pack of Krispy Kreme doughnuts, like it's a special treat for herself. Something she's been looking forward to.

'That's weird,' I reply, gesturing about as though I'm swatting flies. 'All of it, all of this, is weird.'

*

It took me until twenty-five to realise that while I'd been changing up in Melbourne – growing into myself, being kinder to myself – where I grew up had been changing too. Memories play over my eyes like ghosts. The tree behind the bike shed that I had my first awkward heterosexual kiss under has been torn out by its roots.

Both my primary and high school are unrecognisable. A garden has grown over the place I once had a breakdown, crying and vomiting mid-panic attack. The bench I escaped to outside Woolies when I convinced myself I was worthless, the night I came out, has been taken away. The Maccas I spent more time in than was probably healthy has been completely renovated – a strange snippet of Melbourne transferred into southwestern Victoria.

It's all changed without me, the place where I struggled to be a child, and then to be a teenager, and then to be at all. Maybe for the first time, I am seeing this town the way outsiders do. Maybe because after being away for so long, *I* have become an outsider.

That night, when I lie awake on the couch in my mother's house, all I see outside the window is the hazy, orange glow of the new streetlight outside.

If Someone Took You, They'd Soon Bring You Back

Gay Lynch

Returning to country feeds my mother's longing to lie beside her mother in a paddock of towering red gums, shifting skies and ancient swamps. Settlers unknowingly damaged that fragile environment, cleared it for cloven-hooved creatures, diverted potable water out to sea and disturbed – edging towards annihilated – the traditional custodians and their ways. My mother remembers Boandik people crossing family land as if she were fixed and they were not.

She dies in Adelaide during a Covid-19 outbreak; perhaps she would have anyway. A circle of women, my two sisters, my brother's wife and I, keen over her body at a funeral parlour, just hours before government eases a hard lockdown and relinquishes her body to her prepaid Penola plot. A generation earlier, her mother, my Scottish-descended then seventeen-year-old grandmother, rode her horse to work as a parlour maid at Yallum Park, Penola, where original William Morris wallpaper still covers the walls of formal rooms. I am named after a Yallum manor lady.

During my mother's dying days, I play a set of Strathspeys on my phone that launch her into vivid childhood memories.

'I'm wearing black gillie shoes and my kilt,' she says, without prompting. 'Dancing with Josephine down Church Street in a procession.'

I imagine her and her sisters, her brothers too perhaps, cutting their feet to ribbons on swords. 'Is Johnny there?'

'He's leading the pipers at the front.'

'And Lachie too?'

'No, not Lachie,' she says, as if I am an idiot, unworthy of her last difficult breaths. Lachie is long dead.

I squeeze her hand.

'It's New Year's Eve, we're dancing,' she mulls. 'No, not New Year's Eve. After that.'

In Naracoorte, most nights, after a skinful of whisky, our neighbour Paddy pipes around the crescent, bringing my mother to her feet to fling, hornpipe and jig. When she dances, shyness leaps away. I curve my joyful arms to join her, lift my chin and chest, backstep and rock. We dance like startled deer.

'Where are you now?' I ask her on her deathbed.

A final chord of the Strathspeys groans out of my phone, the cue for a low bow for men, a curtsy for women, and my mother closes her eyes.

'I'm crossing Rymill's paddocks,' she whispers. 'Climbing through the fence to go to my mother.' A glad look flits across her face. I hear no mention of her father, although he is buried there as well.

A light horseman in Palestine, he dies young of tuberculosis contracted at a horse sale, leaving behind his Sarah and six kids. From age eleven my mother walks from their farm across Rymill's paddocks, through swampy water and probably past tiger snakes, to sit by his grave. I imagine her mass of dark hair lifting in the wind, her long dancer legs folded sideways, a book in her bag or open in her hand, tears, as she confides her longings and troubles to him. Can she win the school reading prize a year-long subscription to the Institute Library, for a third time? If not, how will she cope? Paltry and poultry cash sometimes come her way, courtesy of her youngest brother selling eggs, rabbit skins, wild geese and swans. Shillings to buy boiled aniseed humbugs and ribbons.

Aged twenty-two, my mother marries my father and travels north. For a lifetime, she moves with him from one country town to another.

'It must have been hard,' he says at her funeral, 'for a girl like her.'

Ten months after their wedding, I join them in Kapunda, a copper town. Absent from my birth, the norm then, my father waits until after a hailstorm washes out the B-Grade football match and then, when the weather clears, captains the A-Grade to victory before he meets me. Photographs of damage after an earthquake to the old Institute building in which we live feeds my sparse memories of the town.

Aged two, I have moved to Burra, a second copper town. A sensitive, squalling brother turns up. By then I'm on my feet, seeking solace in the landscape, a dirt road, a creek that runs in front of the house, and a dusty eucalypt canopy, through which I gaze at northern skies of flawless blue or exploding black clouds. I talk, talk, talk to anyone, strangers who pass the gate.

'She tells lies,' my mother tells them.

Our family follows my manager father from one country appointment to the next, lives mostly in old sandstone bank premises with cellars, maids' rooms off the kitchen, chained doors into the offices where business is done behind solid cedar counters.

Aged six, I arrive in the verdant wine valley of Clare and walk alone past the main street shops to the infant school on the far side of town. When the bell goes, I set off for home with another new girl, edging past the Blue Moon café, where it is rumoured at recess-time, that gypsies gather. Surely not like Enid Blyton's horse-stealing, fire-dancing beauties, I ponder. For months, the Ngadjuri girl and I are like gypsies, both new to town and outcasts – until she and her family disappear.

Two years later, our family move south to a town near Penola, where we resume pilgrimages to my grandmother's weatherboard cottage. Round as a steamed pudding, with floury, freckled arms, she presides over choux pastry and scones straight from the *Green and Gold Cookbook*.

On weekdays, I cross Naracoorte from south to north, through a stone cutting to the main street, and ascend the chalk hill to the school, where I skin my knees on asphalt play areas studded with sprawling pepper trees. A long lone walk for a smallish eight-year-old. When a neighbour beckons me into his car during a deluge, I reply, 'No, thank you,' and squelch slowly home.

'She wouldn't get in,' he tells my mother.

'Quiet to the point of disinterest,' my school report reads. I *am* quiet, reading books, held under my desk. But not *un*interested. Nor impartial. About anything really.

My new friend's father manages a park of limestone-eroded waterways and caverns. At her birthday party we play games and scoff cake and red cordial, beneath the collapsed ceiling of Victoria Cave, a massive, murky ballroom space. Bats flip and whir above us, as we run shrieking across the uneven surface and crawl into fuggy side-tunnels. I read about Becky Thatcher but, unlike her and Tom Sawyer – or the giant marsupials and unknown cavers whose skeletons remain there – we do not get lost in the caves or attend our own funerals.

On weekends at my aunt's soldier settlement farm, I run wild with her six kids between machinery shed and bull paddock. I wait third in line to slide through greasy bathwater; I tear up newspaper to wipe my bum over the long drop toilet; before bedtime, we huddle around kerosene lanterns, slapping at clouds of insects, yarning and shouting with laughter. Their stepfather slits the throat of the Sunday roast, trussed from a beam in the shearing shed. I can hardly bear to watch him slash out the poor beast's insides and see them splash on the slatted floor. I feel as far away from my constrained religious family life as I can imagine. After dinner, he cuts up sides of beef and mutton on the wooden kitchen table. My aunt roasts and stews the meat, lifts trays of pastries, cakes and puddings from the wood oven. The room feels warm and moist, noisy and aromatic. My cousins stand on the furniture, bang doors, shout and quarrel, bunk from the house into the yard to sort things out. To be part of this drama excites me. To be loud.

They must think me odd – small, quiet, book reading – and when the boys make fun of my clothes or my language, my aunt reins them in. 'Leave her alone and get outside. She's my pet.' And lights another cigarette.

We move north again, to Yongala, the coldest town in South Australia. Water pipes explode on the fence tops and frost ices the lawn until morning teatime. In a ten-kilometre radius I possess one female friend, make do with boys, who nickname me Spitfire because I hit them back and receive the cane. I roam or lead my younger brother on bikes and on foot.

'If anything happens to him,' my mother says, 'don't come home,' pressing into my hands a packet of Arnott's biscuits. 'Be back before dark.'

We carry balls in our pockets like weapons, pound them against hard surfaces everywhere we go. While I know we are not the first to walk the land, and that we are small in the scheme of things, we feel contained and entitled to traverse it, crumbling ruins, hilltops, quarries, railway lines, stony creeks and the half-heartedly forbidden rubbish dump, from where we bring home treasure. Redolent of growth and ruin, land north of Goyder's Line reeks of desertion and pestilence, old cemeteries repopulated by trapdoor spiders and wild spring mushrooms. I search for gold among the freestone walls of the long-deserted Chinaman's Garden in the foothills and fear for flocks of emus ricocheting from fence to fence on the plains.

We have no fetish for carrying water. On picnics, we bring a canvas bag with a cork, on the back of the truck and, on arrival, hang it by wire from the branch of a tree. In town we are simultaneously the bank manager's kids and no-one's, invisible unless noisy, or if something goes wrong. After dark, I enter the ideal world that is fiction. Deep in Steinbeck or Hemingway, courtesy of my family's *American Readers' Digest* subscriptions, I only half register the raucous, sunset shrieks of galahs in gums outside my window, the night wailings, and scratchings in the cellar below my bedroom.

Then our family travels to a fertile mid-north valley, where customers speak Deutsch at home, where the school canteen cuts up slabs of strudel cake for recess, and writers Geoffrey Dutton and Colin Thiele present academic prizes. On voting days, the line for 'S' – Sagenschnitter, Scholes, Schutz, Schultz and Schupelius – stretches out the door. My blue-eyed, blonde-haired friends are Eberhards, Eckermanns, Geisters and Thieles. My conversation reflects their half-satirical idiom – 'yes, already' and '*domkoff*'.

I read a letter my mother leaves on the kitchen table, in which she confides to *her* mother that I am now 'a little woman'. For all the good it does me, this becoming while still a girl, contused with blood on the court, the oval and in the pool, butting against my father's double binds, barricading myself into a literary headspace.

Now that I badly need to roam, the domestic world – all female – closes in. My friend's mother makes public confession at the altar during Lutheran church service and is shamed by the pastor for bonking a bank manager – not ours. My mother gives birth the week we arrive in the Barossa Valley and again two years later, the week before she leaves for the next place. I become adept at raising babies, hosing shit from swanskin nappies pegged to the back fence, rocking the bassinette, dipping the soother into the pot of honey and then into the wailing child. I sing, 'High on a hill stood a lonely goatherd' and inhale the sweeter baby smells.

I am an awkward girl who cannot take instruction from men – who are always right even when they are wrong. Why do I create this trouble for myself? I stay on my feet through row after row. I take the strap without crying. I apologise to neighbours corralled into a search party after I am deemed missing.

'I am sorry. I will be more considerate,' I repeat.

'Do not worry your parents again,' says another hard, religious man.

Over and over, I flee into the steep hills behind our house and along the railway line, most often on foot, sometimes with a friend sharing her pony. Land and skyscape console me, swallow me up.

We retreat to the city in my mid-teens, where I find a new best friend but am, nevertheless, drawn to country students, enrolled from schools without senior education. I *get* their openness and good-natured irreverence, their boisterous lunge for courts and rackets during breaks, their refusal to embrace the imagined *ennui* of dream cities. Their reliability and fearlessness in a fight. Do all country kids burst from the womb shouting, 'That's not fair,' and then get on with life? Likely a myth, like city sophistication and urban violence. Like country bumpkins.

A friend, working on-air for regional radio, remembers how, newly graduated with her slick city degree, she returned to her country town and broached the bar of her local pub.

'Got a degree,' a bloke says. 'What's that mean?' He rotates his head for a laugh. 'BA. Bugger All,' he adds.

Newly married, brimful of education, I also go back to the bush, bizarrely as a teacher, with my city-man medico. The crack and crunch of gum leaves underfoot, the reek of eucalyptus, the gnawing of cockatoos, the hot northerly winds trigger memories. While I can still enter the landscape within a minute, on horseback, or dragging the baby after me, I am also now cowed by adult rural knowledge – domestic violence, gun accidents, incest, murder, suicide – that add another layer to stories I only partly understood while eavesdropping as a child. I meet buck jumpers, netballers, miners, railway folk and roo-shooters, who probably wouldn't invite my parents for a counter-tea. I like high-energy raconteurs but I'm wary of crossing men whose women I befriend and defend. I return to the country, a writer stumbling into memories, with all the conflicted feelings they engender.

At first, I fear digging in the backyard of our historic, pharmacy dispensary home, rented before us by a loner doctor accused of murder and later by an artist who painted the ceilings with menstrual blood. Bent or mad. Transcribing long-abandoned gravestones for the local history club, I weep over drought-stricken families who lost most of their children in one hit to diphtheria, measles or scarlet fever; over a university laid out but never built because the settled north-east became a wasteland, decimated by disastrous natural events.

'I shall return,' said, US General MacArthur changing trains at nearby Terowie in 1942, referring not only to our land but to Bataan and the Battle of the Philippines. I sense ghosts of historical figures but never encounter him or any other until I build a sprawling home in the Inman Valley. I want our children to know animals, birds, river walks and waterfall hikes, away from the newly wed and nearly dead in our nearby town. Past midnight, many times, I lurch upright in bed to face a menacing presence hovering high in the doorway.

An elderly water diviner follows his forked stick around the house yard and locates the best site for a bore. My dowser great-grandfather shared this gift and I have faith in it.

'By the way,' he reports afterwards, 'I removed the bad water from around your bedroom.' The aura moves on. Not long after this, the diviner dies. Just as my medico man deduced was on the cards after a modern blood test.

Over the summers before my grandfather Jack died, he drove six kids in his truck to wait on the beach for cray boats to come in.

Asked about food for her wake, my mother returns to her memories, of tearing apart her own small cray in her lap, cross-legged on the rocks, sharing a glass of shandy. 'Crayfish and shandies,' she says with conviction.

There's a certain moment when I take the last turn-off to Penola for her funeral when my consciousness shifts. Heart full of flat land and big gums, lagoons and swans, I enter land and memory-scape in a rush. A local cousin phones by way of funeral RSVP and I mention my mama's wish for the wake, ask about the lobster season.

'Boat's just gone out,' he says, all country brusque and brevity. 'See you Friday.'

I swing past the sign to Bool Lagoon, where he bells me back.

'Got the crays,' he says. 'Fisherman client.'

'I'll get the beer.'

'Got that too,' he says.

Joy rushes through me. That I still love my cousins. That I talk to every maggie up the Murray and every brolga on the swamp.

'You've got too much of what the cat licked itself with.'

Guilty, Mother. Yes, guilty.

Even though she saw too much talking as a fault, she indulged herself. Even though my father talked like a two-bob watch but preferred me quiet, invisible, because he thought I'd get things wrong.

Oversharing with my cousin – I call it conversation – brings largesse on a platter, glistening white flesh and red spikiness to crack and suck, for the wake at Ruby's Cottage, where old people nod in the lounge room, and others yarn in the yard. Ten inside and twelve outside – Covid-compliant. Add the talking cure, for sorrow and continuity. As sweating men in black lower my mother's coffin into the ground, a sulphur-crested cockatoo sweeps in from the west, grandly circles and cries out, as if remembering, decades earlier, a long-legged girl mourning her father, now returning home. I imagine Mother's spirit soaring away with the bird, over the dried swamps and red gums, through the haze of a forty-degree day, to join her brothers and sisters, perhaps to receive belated instruction from the first custodians. She had always been clear about where *she* would find rest.

A storm surges across the state from the Adelaide foothills where my father grieves, to all the lands of my childhood, north, south, east and west. Sleepless, he worries that Mother feels as cold in the ground as he does in the low, dark hours of a city night. Waiting in the south-east cottage for the Covid border to open, my sister and I take comfort in the beating benedictive rain, the shriek of birds seeking shelter, the rattling of eucalypts, the catapulting of their pods on our roof. Soon, my father too will return to this country, hers not his, his gesture towards fidelity.

'You should come with me now,' my mother berates him over weeks. 'We can both go to sleep. We're no use to anyone.'

And as he baulks and her temper frays, she asks, 'Why would you want to put the children through the expense and bother of two funerals?'

I still her restless hands. 'I don't think Dad's ready to go yet, Mum.'

She shrugs. 'Whatever.'

And her brothers, she believes, would agree with her, and tell him to 'stop buggarising around'.

Country talk. Under duress, she slips back into it, quoting rather than speaking because she is a 'country lady'.

Few people these days prefer burial to barbecue. Where should family strew my ashes? Land spirits sing along trellis wires in wine valleys, dance in the wind across vast northern plains and sclerotic creeks, burble in knee-deep sludge between the interlocked ponds of the Inman River, and lament in the eery cry of the bittern in south-east swamps. Sea susurrates in my ears as I hang out washing in the country town ports of Lincoln and Victor Harbor.

I seek revelation in books and find it in natural perils and splendours. From walk-writing the land, I infer the presence of people who came before us and present still, their stories lived and handed down, and retold. To know birds and waterfalls, rivers and scarps, unblemished skies and stormy seas is to belong.

The Devil and the Far North-West

Cade Lucas

I'd been sent to the principal's office again. Not actually inside the office and not actually to meet the principal, but just to sit in the foyer out the front. It was the usual location for classroom troublemakers whom teachers had grown sick of, and I was one of its most frequent visitors. There were chairs and a coffee table on which my fellow serial miscreants and I could do the work that we weren't doing in the classroom, and being right outside the principal's office with the looming threat of further punishment – the dreaded cane – ensured that we actually did it.

That was the theory, but this particular day exposed its failure in practice. It was early 1990 at Smithton Primary School in Tasmania's far north-west. It was approaching lunchtime and the whiff of warm pies and pasties was wafting in from the nearby canteen. Two girls – they were always girls – who'd finished their work early had come to collect me ahead of the break. Alarmed to find out that my worksheet remained untouched, they hurriedly set about filling it in for me lest I drift ever closer to a dose of corporal punishment.

Among the answers they helped me with was one that would prove prophetic: add. I couldn't spell the word 'add'. A simple one-syllable, three-letter verb derived from the noun 'addition', it was too difficult for me, but absolutely no problem for them. We were the same age and in the same class, yet at that point it dawned on me that we were very different: they could read and write, and I couldn't. I was seven years old, in Grade 2 and illiterate.

The amount of time I spent out of the classroom, combined with my usual piss-farting around while in it, meant I'd fallen well behind my peers and couldn't do schoolwork even when forced to. The word that demonstrated this to me would years later also be identified as the root cause: attention deficit disorder (or ADD). By the time my diagnosis was made, the definition had been broadened to include hyperactivity and so ADD was now ADHD and my story was slightly ruined. Whatever the acronym or definition, it finally put a label on behaviour I'd been exhibiting since I could walk, but which growing up in a remote and poor corner of a remote and poor island both exacerbated and obscured.

*

Though only an hour or so down the highway from Burnie, a large town of 20,000 and the regional centre, the isolation of Smithton and the surrounding municipality of Circular Head is as much metaphorical as physical. It's the end of the line. The chain of towns that make up Tasmania's north-west or 'The Coast', as it's commonly known, ends at Smithton and there's nothing beyond it save for farmland, thick bush and scrub, and then the Southern Ocean stretching across the globe to South America. The winds that rip across this vast expanse of ocean are known as the Roaring Forties and give Circular Head the cache of having the cleanest air on earth, along with the somewhat less marketable 300 days of rain a year. It's great if you're a farmer or logging contractor, but less so if you're a young family moving in from out of town. It's cold, wet and windy, and apart from log trucks and milk tankers there aren't many people passing through, and those that do tend not to stop.

We moved there in 1985 when my dad got a job driving fuel trucks after leaving his previous occupation: running a pub. Fourteen years my father's junior, Mum was a young housewife in her mid-twenties, and they had two kids under five and another on the way. Australia was between recessions, Bob Hawke's Labor government was in the midst of reforming the economy, and the 1987 stock-market crash was still a couple of years away. Conditions were relatively good; so good that a man in his late thirties – whose education ended midway through Year 10 when he hopped off the school bus outside a sawmill, asked for a job and was promptly given one – was able to buy a large weatherboard home on a single income. It was an awkward square-shaped place on the side of a hill at the edge of town, with an old cemetery across the road and an abattoir round the back. A trophy home it wasn't, but there was plenty of space for a growing family and an adventurous boy with a wandering and inquisitive mind, and legs that would carry him wherever it demanded.

As Mum tells it, I learnt to walk one day and ran the next. For the next few years I barely stopped: from one end of the beach to the other; up and down the aisles of the supermarket; in and out of the cupboards and wardrobes of homes we were visiting, my mother's bemused friends watching on as she trailed in my wake. My perpetual motion made sitting down a rarity and it was only seatbelts, food or the threat of Dad wrapping a stick around my arse that could make me stay put. To compensate for the lack of movement, my internal monologue – always humming away inside my head – would hit overdrive and so would the fidgeting that sprang from it. If it was a football game or sporting event playing out, my hands would flap and I'd snap my thumbs and index fingers together, while heavy breathing would emulate the roar of the crowd. If it was a conversation, the snapping fingers would still be there, but the heavy breathing would be replaced by my mouth miming the words. Music had me grinding and gashing my teeth, creating the backbeat to the latest track I'd seen on *Rage* or one I'd simply made up. If these options were exhausted, I'd fall back on an old favourite: stick my hands down my pants and play with my dick.

It was always likely then that school would be a struggle, yet, as is the way with ADHD, the symptoms are so obvious that their broader impact can remain hidden in plain view. For my first couple of years at school, I was considered just another rowdy little boy with an especially large colony of ants in his pants, and in a classroom full of seven-year-olds, that hardly made me Robinson Crusoe. What seemed to set me apart, though, was that when the teacher restored order, the other kids returned to their times tables or spelling, while I kept going, and going, and going. I couldn't stop. Eventually the exasperated teacher – it didn't matter whether they were new to the caper, like the attractive ex–TV weather girl Miss Wiggins, or had decades of experience dealing with unruly schoolboys, like my kindergarten teacher Mrs Medwin – would resort to the same course of action and banish me from the classroom.

Owing to her experience, Mrs Medwin would at least make sure I put my excess energy to good use and had me run laps of the school football ground in the hope that when called back in, I'd be too knackered to continue being a nuisance. For the less experienced teachers like Miss Wiggins – no doubt wondering why she left a career in front of the cameras for the purgatory of a public primary school in one of the country's most disadvantaged regions – it was off to the foyer in front of the principal's office with my classwork and pencil case to do my work there. Whatever the approach, the focus seemed to be more on preventing my bad behaviour rather than what that bad behaviour was preventing in me.

Even the realisation that I was functionally illiterate after four years of schooling added more confusion than clarity. Not being able to read or write stood in stark contrast to many other learning skills where I was not below average, but often well above. The paradox of ADHD is that hyperactivity can become hyperfocus when a subject of interest comes along, as it did whenever there was news or sport on the TV, or when there was a newspaper, atlas or encyclopedia lying around. I had a huge thirst for knowledge and even if I couldn't read properly I had an unusual ability to absorb and store information. It must've been a strange experience for my parents to arrive at parent–teacher evenings and learn that their son, who could name the four US presidents on Mt Rushmore and discuss sport, politics, geography and history at a level beyond many adults, let alone other children, was the same boy who couldn't write anything beyond his own name.

At the urging of a child psychiatrist, my parents concluded that the attention deficit lay with my teachers and the public-school system rather than me. The public system's open-plan classrooms and relaxed teaching style were designed to stimulate student creativity, but in my case they indulged hyperactivity, providing ample space for rolling on floors and climbing up walls. Mum and Dad thought I needed a more traditional approach, with teachers who would treat me as a student who needed to learn, rather than a problem that needed to be managed, and assumed this was more likely to be found at a private school than a public one. Fortunately, they didn't have to look too far. A new Christian school had recently sprung up next door to Smithton Primary, and with both my older sister and younger brother staying put, it made sense to keep us as close together as possible.

The move was made at the beginning of Term 2 in 1990 and paid almost immediate dividends. The Christian school had no open-plan classrooms, no room for rolling on floors or climbing walls, and there were no laps around the oval or trips to the principal's office. The principal, Mr Eagling, doubled as one of the teachers, and he and his colleagues (which included his wife Mrs Eagling) practised an old-fashioned chalk-and-talk style of teaching that kept me sat at my desk and forced me to channel at least some of my energy into learning. From a low base I made noticeable improvements and by the end of the year I was able to read and write. In order to consolidate, however, the school thought it would be wise for me to repeat Grade 2 the following year, meaning that for the rest of my school days I would be a year behind my age group.

Like many remote outposts, Circular Head is a serious Bible Belt with Circular Head Christian School at its epicentre. The school was closely attached to a church called the New Life Centre, which had recently built an impressive new premises just down the hill from our house. It was a big barn-like building with a fancy auditorium inside; an early '90s pre-curser to today's Hillsong Church and Assemblies of God. They held big tub-thumping services there every Sunday evening that were the hottest ticket in town. There was loud music, impassioned sermons, speaking in tongues, baptisms, whooping and hollering, the full gamut. Most of my friends from school were there with their families and I was able to ride my bike down the hill and join in. I loved it. I was hot for Jesus by this point; my first few months at the Christian school had not only seen my literacy improve, but my heart given over to the Lord as well. My ADHD was serving as a gateway drug to the world of Evangelical Christianity.

My newfound passion for Christ put my parents in a bind. They could see the educational benefits the Christian school had on me, but they had misgivings about following me down the hill to the New Life Centre. We were members of the local Uniting Church congregation, so were notionally part of the same community, but soon realised that the quiet Protestantism of the Uniting and the fire-and-brimstone evangelising favoured by the school were both Christian in the same way that fish fingers and caviar are both seafood. It was noticeable that no-one in the Uniting Church sent their kids to the Christian school and nobody at the school seemed to consider churches like the Uniting to be sufficiently Christian.

On that front they were probably correct. The truth was that my parents weren't especially religious and neither came from churchgoing families. The only reason I can think of why they attended at all was to meet people and make friends, and as new arrivals in an isolated town in the mid-1980s, it was one of the few places where that was possible. The congregation was mostly made up of elderly and middle-aged farmers from the broader region, who were much more welcoming than people in town. Despite the age difference, we became friends with many of them and in some cases their children and grandchildren too. Like us, none seemed especially religious, and the theology of the Church was very light-touch; the Lord's Prayer, some hymns, the odd Communion and then it was off to someone's farm for Sunday lunch. Everyone would bring casseroles. It was a social club.

But by the time I moved schools, the Uniting had become much more than that, with my mum, in particular, depending on the support network it provided. She'd become close to Margaret, an elder at the church who lived with her husband, Graham, on a dairy farm at Nabageena, a farming district about half an hour outside of town. It was like a mother–daughter relationship: Mum the struggling, lonely housewife in her twenties and Margaret the wise, compassionate farmer's wife well into middle age. Mum's own mother was still alive, but Nan, like the rest of the family, lived an hour or two away and at this stage of her life was more concerned with looking after Pop than worrying about her many children, most of whom were much older than Mum anyway. In her stead, it was Margaret who'd often be on the other end of the phone listening to Mum sob; it was Margaret who'd bring a casserole to help mum out with the cooking and it was Margaret's daughter, Kaylene, who'd come around to babysit and give my parents a rare child-free night. Despite this and other friendships that had developed after half a decade in Smithton, Mum was more in need of support than ever. Dad was still working long hours and Mum was still stuck at home looking after children, the only difference being that there were now considerably more of them.

*

The loneliness and isolation of life in Smithton meant my parents weren't just keen to meet new people, but to make them as well. After arriving in '85 with me and my older sister, Erin, my younger brother, Dirk, was born early the following year, sparking a breeding spree that was more Catholic than Protestant or

Pentacostal. Another sister, Kira, arrived in early '88, followed by a third sister, Romy, eighteen months later in October '89. As the new decade dawned, Mum and Dad took a year off before normal duties resumed in '91 with the birth of my youngest sister, Peri. In the space of five-and-a-half years my parents had four kids and it became more common to see Mum pregnant than not. She almost single-handedly kept the maternity ward at Smithton Hospital open and I would often pop in to visit her and my latest sibling when walking home from school. We had arrived in town driving a Holden Camira but now got around in an eighteen-seat Toyota HiAce. It was an ex-army troop carrier and painted dark green. It stood out and caught the eye of the locals, not least those in charge of the Christian school.

From the moment I arrived, the school set about reeling in the rest of us, too. The big green van full of kids, most of whom were now school age, was a tantalising prospect for a school that had just built a new campus and needed enrolments to pay the bills. And getting us out of the Uniting Church and into the New Life Centre was just as enticing for a school where evangelising was every bit as important as educating.

In normal circumstances, attempts to woo us would've involved a degree of charm and the promotion of the school's teaching. After all, I had arrived illiterate and months later was reading and writing at somewhere near normal standard. But for evangelical Christians, fear and shame are far more powerful motivators, and my family and I presented an ideal opportunity to use them.

While the stricter environment had improved my marks, it failed to have the same effect on my behaviour. Being forced to sit down and apply myself for longer in class only ensured that the outbursts, when they came, were louder and wilder than before, and the deeply religious environment made them even more conspicuous. The laughing, shouting, fidgeting and fits of anger borne of frustration placed me at odds with the other kids who were largely mild-mannered and came from good Christian homes. If they didn't go to the New Life Centre they went to one of the other Pentecostal churches in town or they'd been at the school long enough and had sufficient standing in the community to not arouse suspicion. Me and my family, on the other hand, were different. I came from the heathen public school next door, my parents were from out of town, were poor, and went to a church the New Life viewed with suspicion – how could the Uniting be properly Christian if I didn't even know to close my eyes and keep my mouth shut during prayer or that yelling 'Jesus Christ' instead of shit or fuck was not better, but actually worse?

The Eaglings were concerned that I was still acting in such a way even after Mr Eagling himself inducted seven-year-old me into Christianity by holding a prayer service in his office. To them, this wasn't proof of ADHD or any of the other maladies it was often confused for in those days; it spoke of something much darker. Urgent intervention was required and so, rather than arrange a meeting or forewarn my parents, they rang Mum one afternoon while she was at home looking after my younger siblings. There was problem at school: I was possessed by the Devil.

Mum was petrified. Already battling loneliness and drowning in a sea of soiled nappies, she now had the people entrusted with teaching one of her children politely informing her that he was the embodiment of Satan himself. She'd grown used to complaints about my wild ways – she found out about the trouble my Smithton Primary teachers had controlling me when she overheard one of them complaining to our next-door neighbour – but this was far worse.

Not only was it something they didn't believe in – the Uniting Church eschewed such literal interpretations of scripture like miracles or Satan or God taking control of a person's body – but it didn't chime with who they knew me to be. People with ADHD can experience emotional intensity that not only leads to bursts of anger and despair, but also kindness and empathy. While I was frequently in trouble, I would always be wracked by guilt afterwards and apologise profusely, even when I hadn't done anything wrong. My anxiety would extend beyond worrying about myself to looking out for those around me too, leading to a conscientiousness that was unusual for boys my age.

A prime example of this occurred just after my arrival at the Christian school, when one of my new classmates in Grade 2, Peter Shearer, fell off a swing in the schoolyard, injuring his neck. I saw it happen right in front of me and was so concerned that later on, after school, I rode my BMX around to the hospital to check if he was okay. Alas, unlike my mother, Peter wasn't giving birth and with no Emergency Department at Smithton Hospital, he wasn't even there. So, I then rode down to the offices of the *Circular Head Chronical*, the local weekly newspaper where Peter's dad, Les, was the editor. Somewhat taken aback by the presence of a scruffy kid he'd never heard of before, he told me that Peter had been taken to the hospital in Burnie and was okay. He'd been given a neck brace and would be back at home the following day if I wanted to come around and visit.

The Shearers' place was only a few hundred metres up the road from ours, but we were separated by a demographic chasm. Les was not only editor, but owner of the *Chronical* and carried a lot of clout in the local community, with a home to match. It sat atop the same hill we lived on, but whereas we looked out over an old graveyard, the Shearer's looked out over the entire town, the mouth of the Duck River and out to Bass Strait.

Pete and I soon became fast friends and spent most afternoons and weekends up at his place on the hill, where the extra space and lack of little kids running around allowed us to indulge our shared passion for wrestling.

This was back in the days when WWF referred to the World Wrestling Federation rather than the World Wildlife Fund, and the likes of Hulk Hogan and the Ultimate Warrior ruled the ring. We'd practise body-slams and headlocks in their newly built rumpus room, and when tired, put on one of Pete's many *WrestleMania* videos instead. Wrestling was almost tailor-made for ADHD: it was loud, physical and intense. Matches were absorbing but never long enough to be boring.

Our enthusiasm for it extended to the schoolyard, where the Eaglings took notice. They told my parents that it was my interest in wrestling that convinced them I was in the Devil's possession. Strangely, though, their concerns didn't extend to Pete. Apparently, the youngest son of a wealthy and influential family was immune from the Devil's charms, but the eldest son of a large, young family was at his mercy. This contrast wasn't lost on my parents whose suspicions were confirmed when the school offered their solution: we needed to completely give ourselves over to the Lord. All the kids needed to go to the Christian School and our family had to worship at the New Life Centre. Only total commitment would do.

My parents knew they were being taken advantage of, but also that they had nowhere else to go. The only other option was taking me back to Smithton Primary where I'd struggled before. Trying to maintain the status quo of me at the Christian School and my siblings in the public system was only going to invite more pressure from people who'd already demonstrated the lengths they would go to, to get their way.

At the beginning of 1992, my parents relented. Erin, Dirk and Kira joined me at the Christian School, though they drew the line at the New Life Centre. It was a victory for the Eaglings but one which proved pyrrhic. That winter, Dad was transferred back up the coast to Devonport for work and we left Smithton for good. The wind, the rain and the isolation were behind us, but the influence would be lasting. We remained in the Christian school system, I remained wedded to my faith, and my neurological deficiencies would continue to be mistaken for moral ones.

A Grey Cat in a Sunset Town

Dr. Karen Lowry

My uncle knows a person who knows a person whose cat just had kittens. We don't know them, but we're new to this town. They live on the other side of Bluebush Road, less than a five-minute drive. I peer under their daughter's single bed and see six kittens tumbling over each other like lint balls in a dryer. Their small bodies are in a constant state of agitation. A tortoiseshell kitten runs past me, bouncing off the ground like it's a trampoline. I miss the trampoline we had in Perth, and the playground just across the road. The tortoiseshell cat is the colour of every kind of cat I can think of. I wish that I could be made up of the best bits of every kind of person. Instead, I'm not smart enough to be a vet, I can't act well enough to be in films, and my asthma stops me from being any good at sports.

The tortoiseshell kitten has been promised to someone else, so I get the grey one. Grey is a colour I don't see often out here. We are seven hours inland from Perth and an hour down from Kalgoorlie, which is the next biggest town. The skies are always blue and vast. Each day they are a contradiction, looking both over-saturated and empty, much like the inside of the toy chest I have at home. I'm not used to owning many things, having moved, and moved again, to several different country towns. Each time we move, we sell our things in a garage sale. My toys get lined up on concrete driveways. My mother's handwriting says they're $1 each. It's only the books I get to take with me.

The grey cat looks almost blue against the red and orange of this town. Even the grey tin roofs have a thin layer of dust on them, tinging them the colour of sunset – the town stuck in dusk. It's why, as children, my brother and I are allowed to roam unsupervised; here it never gets dark.

The cat is the same colour as the dead grass out the front of our house: grey, almost white in places, though the cat has a soft underbelly the lawn seems to be missing. Our lawn is hopelessly dead and balding, the bright orange skin apparent underneath. We keep the cat inside in case the hot weather that turned the grass grey and callous might also infect her.

Our white house looks flimsy from the outside. It has a grey tin roof that stretches out over a small pergola on the left, where we discard our bikes at the end of the day. The large bricks that make up the walls are painted white, though it does little to brighten the space. The living room is dark, which eases the heat of the sun. The cream couch gives the cat something to scratch her claws on. My father waters the back lawn to keep it green. We rarely use it. Instead, my brother and I ride around the streets on our bikes – our playground made up of bitumen, empty carparks and an old concrete skatepark. My brother never wears his helmet. I watch him disappear around suburban corners, past painted green sheds and palm trees with drooping limbs.

My room has brown carpet the same colour as most of the trees. There are darker patches in the corners where the cat likes to pee. I am the one who toilet-trains her, locking her in my room and getting up late in the night to take her to her litter tray. I walk down the hallway at eleven p.m., late for a seven-year-old. The house is still up, the music in the backyard a dull murmur down the hallway. It's normal to see beer cans on the kitchen bench, some crushed, some half-full in the sink. I put the cat in the litter tray and quietly celebrate as she pees. Afterwards, she claws at the flyscreen door. I carry her back to my room, unseen.

The next day, my best friend sneaks around the side of the school to smoke. I don't follow her. Her hair is longer than mine. My hair sits above my shoulders; I cut it for the heat. I wear the school's teal polo shirt, a shade of green that seems optimistic.

Green is the colour of overcrowding, of dense forests where you cannot see the sky, of places you can get lost in, even though the road is only a few hundred metres away. This place is not green. It's the colour of vast deserts and dehydration. It's the colour of the sun setting on this landscape, this small town, forgotten in the twilight.

My brother and I can ride around this town in less than half an hour. We are turning onto our street when a policeman gives him a warning for not wearing his helmet. There isn't much traffic here; just the odd beaten-up sedan with faded, peeling paint. You can always identity the miners; their utes, sometimes a four-wheel drive, only two years old, paint still glinting in the sun.

The streets here are all named after trees; eucalypts with drooping leaves, long and slender, unlike me. Their tanned trunks shed bark, revealing a pale skin underneath. It looks the same as my sunburn: pale underneath when I peel. The banksia leaves have serrated edges. Much of this town feels like it's trying to push you out.

The local pub is our oasis in this desert. The staff know us all by name. We go every weekend and my parents give my brother $2 to play on the racing machine. He usually makes it last about half an hour. One time we were gone so long, we came home to find the cat had torn up the lace curtains in the kitchen.

My cousin and uncle usually meet us down there. My cousin is two years older than me and listens to music. I'm too young to be able to focus on the lyrics. For me, music is pointless, the words meaningless. It's something I have to sit through, like homework or church sermons. I don't like that it stops me moving. I don't see how she can sit there and not get bored. I learn the words to her favourite song anyway. I ask my parents for the CD, desperate to grow up and shorten the space between us. My cat rubs up against the speakers. She runs off if I turn the volume up too loud. I listen to 'Bye, Bye, Bye' while playing with the microscope I got for Christmas.

At the pub, my cousin puts on 'Why Don't You Get a Job?' by The Offspring. The song feels grown-up and my parents let me sing the swear words. The man behind the bar laughs. We get another $2 each for the jukebox. Dad drives us home. The local police know to look out for our car. They stop him in the cul-de-sac we live on, one door down from home. Dad's taken down to the station. We walk the rest of the way, watching the cat watch us from the lounge-room window.

My cat sleeps on my bed every night. One day, I get second-degree sunburn while swimming at the lake. My chest and back blisters. The blisters are clear, but the translucent skin looks almost white against the raw red skin around it, white like the heart of the sun, like the skin on my pelvis, where the burn doesn't reach. Mum takes a week off from cleaning toilets in the mines. She wets towels in the sink and wraps me in them. The cat sleeps at my feet.

We leave the small mining town after twelve months. I'm too young to be told why. The drive back to Perth is seven hours. The cat is in a moving box that has airholes poked in it. My parents won't let me lift the lid to pat her, so I spend the seven-hour drive listening to her meow. I can now see why my cousin listens to music.

Irrigation

Jay Carmichael

The road from Waaia out to the river drew a straight line through farmland. It was a pot-holed bitumen road, and went right to the forest's edge, where it was stopped from being so authoritatively direct by the forest's dense undergrowth. Here, the road became a dirt trail. This new path swung and looped around bulbous trunks and was littered by fallen branches. The trail gave access to several common camping spots: Black Stump, Snake Bend, Nookes Lagoon, Tongalong. You could hear the river before you saw it. The water and wildlife, as well as its unassuming bathers. During the endless heat, people sometimes got caught in the river's undercurrents, sometimes got dragged into waterlogged branches beneath.

Our family went camping at the river Murray most holidays, usually taking up a spot at Black Stump or at nearby Tongalong Beach. Those damned cockatoos always woke us. Echoing caws reverberated off the river's surface, bounced up, cracked open my eyes. Once I caught a silver bream. Pulled that strong, defined body from the muddy water and clasped it round its belly. When it kicked, I wanted to toss it back but someone shimmied round me and took it from me. A wet crack: the bream's blood squirted on the sand. The same bream was had for dinner. One New Year's, another family camping nearby had fireworks. Shot several out across the water at midnight. Vermillion, chartreuse, navy, lemon. A million sparks.

While I grew up in Waaia, you grew up in Numurkah. Despite my town having about a population of seventy and yours having about 4000, we shared a landscape of pure irrigation country. Because we lived on irrigation country, channels stretched as if points of a compass between us. Systems connected to main channels, Dethridge wheels and drop bars. Systems marked out and maintained by fathers, brothers, uncles, sons. Systems named after fathers, brothers, uncles, sons. Systems interrupted and interceded by roads and cattle and dairies and crops. A system prone to leakage, evaporation or inaccurate metering.

Despite that countryside we shared, us being from different towns made us inherently tribal – whether we bought into those tribes or not. Not only through our peoples' loyalty to local footy clubs or the ties that bound our families to a patch of earth since its surveyance, but also to the actual structure of your place compared to mine. The cruel secret of our particular patch of countryside wasn't that we did not have the opportunities afforded to those based in larger cities and regional centres, but that the countryside itself governed us more than we ever gave thought to.

Most adults in Waaia were married, so too were those in Numurkah. (Back then, marriage was defined as being between a man and woman, to the exclusion of all others.) You could be married in Numurkah in one of five differently denominated churches; Waaia had none. While most married couples had children, those in Numurkah could provide more easily for their kin: the median income was about two grand, compared to less than 600 bucks for the same cohort located in Waaia. Hardly anyone in either place had been through tertiary education, but the range of jobs in your town was much wider than in mine. In Waaia, you could expect to work in various ag industries: farming, manufacturing, freight. In Numurkah, the world was your oyster: hospo, retail, finance, teaching, real estate, health. There was even a V/Line connection where you lived.

While I hung out at the river, you and your mates swam in Broken Creek, which divided Numurkah in two. Intermittently, it overflowed – in 2012 a high flood knocked out the hospital. You swam beneath a bridge with a drop bar. It was deeper there because of the cascading water above. Some weekdays after school, while I sat on a vinyl bus seat – stuck there by the backs of my thighs – I'd see you as we drove past. You let the freshwater rush over your pale skin.

This water system drew its vitality from a greater system: the Murray–Darling Basin. An enormous squiggle of rivers, creeks, dams and wetlands. You could find it contained on a big map in an atlas. Murrumbidgee. Lachlan. Goulburn. Loddon. Murray. So on. Surely one body of water did not belong to one area? An area defined not by our understanding of each body of water but by some long-dead navigator who'd cast eternal ink across cartographer's parchment. Water moves. Not only by sloshing stupidly on a river's bank, but also by deep currents and the natural undulations of the local geography. We could move water mechanically, but if let free it knows the landscape better than any of us ever could. Water fell and collected, flowed into a creek and joined the river at a junction; the river rushed into another river and the two, combined, hurried into the ocean. Water replenished, flowed, combined, refreshed. No single body of water was a body at all.

The creek you swam in could be any creek; I wanted to be its water. Swimming was the closest I'd been to being immersed in another body. I suspected that within you ran strong undercurrents – not so visible from the outset, but eddies that momentarily swirled across your facade.

We'd gone to different primary schools in Numurkah: you to the public, me to the Catholic. We first met at high school. Quickly, you asked me if I was metrosexual. I didn't know what that was. You explained. You told me you were metrosexual. You cared for your skin, your hair, your clothes. You asked: *Are you metrosexual, too?*

During high school, we did not have smartphones; if we owned a mobile phone, we could only text message for twenty-five cents a pop. We did not use laptops for our studies – to use a desktop computer, our teacher had to book a computer lab. There was no Snapchat, Instagram or Twitter, and Facebook only came in somewhere towards the end of our secondary schooling. This was a time of Jacaranda atlases, Myspace, *Encyclopaedia Britannica*, MSN Messenger and, of course, the millennium drought. When we grew up, 'Wear It Purple Day' did not exist. In fact, the notion of safe space did not exist. Nor did organised charities dedicated to improving the lives of young people, such as Minus18 or headspace. I don't even think I knew what the rainbow flag was until I left high school – I never saw one at our school or on display anywhere in Numurkah or Waaia. We never learnt about LGBTIQA+ or about homophobia, biphobia, transphobia, or prejudice and discrimination based on sexual orientation. One sex-ed teacher had us list all the names we could think of for penis and vagina. Purple-headed yoghurt slinger. Cheese trap. Schlong. So on. Perhaps listing nicknames for genitals was uncommon, but sex ed defined by a penis/vagina dichotomy was mandated. It was within this place – school – where I saw you most. On excursions, in classes, at camps, during special presentations.

In Year 11, we had to do phoney life coaching. I sat at the back so I didn't get picked for audience participation. You came in late. You turned down the row I was in, and I moved my legs to let you pass. For a moment I thought you were about to sit by me, but instead you went down the aisle and sat beside those boys, your mates. I could still smell you even after you'd passed me. That day, the sharp fluorescent lights in the assembly hall cut your arms into sculptured articles. It almost feels like I could reach out and touch your biceps today, if I really focused.

Once, you were next to me, half-naked, in bed. I glanced at you. I let my eyes fall on you. Your back murmured liked the ripples on the river, moving in a mystic rhythm. The limp morning sun through the moth-eaten curtain cast orange onto your skin. We were not in the same bed – of course we weren't. We were sharing a room on Year 8 camp, that's why I could see you. But it was your choice to remain in the room with me. And as I looked at your sleeping body in the bunk bed across from me, I wondered if I could look you in the eyes and say *thank you*.

You had decided to stay in the room after six other boys deserted us because they didn't want to share a room with me in particular. I didn't really understand it all then. I just knew that I was in a room with you, and you were the messiest person I'd ever known. There were your things flung, strewn, tossed and fluttered all over the floor, the door, the bunk, on the bunk you were not using, and on my bunk too. There were towels – wet, dry, dirty – and jocks, socks, shirts, shorts and shoes scattered at random across the room. You were sleeping on the bottom bunk, and on the bunk above slept a mountain of clothes. Perhaps to show my gratitude for your choosing to stay, or to express something more unspeakable, I remember how, while you showered, I got out of bed and cleaned up your things. I folded your clothes and placed them back in your suitcase. I hung your old towels over the bed rails. I made your bed. And when you returned – how you laughed. Smiled. You said *thank you*. I wonder if you looked at me; I wouldn't know because I couldn't bring myself to do the same. I felt your presence beside me. I felt your voice vibrate in my chest when you spoke. Afterwards, you told everyone that I'd packed your bag for you. You spoke as if you were proud of me. *I'm not stupid*, I had thought, *I can hear it in your voice*.

Everyone made fun of me for doing what I'd done.

I didn't mind. I'd chosen to sit in the back row at the life-coaching shitshow because I'm not the outgoing type and I wanted to see if you'd come to me. I'd chosen to clean up your mess because it made me feel important to you.

The second-last time I saw you, I'd sat with some or another book open in front of me – I was in an art class, but I wasn't listening. I looked out the windows to where a group of boys, our age, were standing on the wooden verandah just outside the art class. They were probably wagging.

If asked, I'd say I was looking at the whole group, but I was only looking at one boy. Those other boys were scabby little pissants with dirt under their fingernails and mangy stubble on their chins. I wouldn't be able to say any of their names for sure, except if I was guessing. I could only name one of the boys – one name, for sure, that I could put a face to, and a body, and an image, all that I've since held thereafter: you.

The same sun that gave heat prickles to my forehead gave you a bright silver line all round your body. It shone brightest in your scruffy hair – unruly strands and tufts. You stood side-on to me. You stood with both hands grasping your sky-blue school shirt at your hips; because of this, the material was taut across your back. You flexed your elbows out as if you were trying to touch them together behind you. This made your shirt also taut over your flat stomach and chest; taut so that I could see the definition of your torso as clearly as if you had taken your shirt off. You could have let the sun rush over your pale skin as you would have the water from Broken Creek. You squinted when you laughed and bent forward, lifting one leg about a foot off the ground. What I liked most about this was that as you did so, you kept all the rest intact. You held yourself. You remained solid, true.

But you are not intact anymore. You and three mates were mucking around in a car after a party, just south of Numurkah, when the driver swerved to avoid a fallen tree, rolled, and crashed. You were thrown from the car and died; the other three boys were uninjured. You were seventeen. I was seventeen.

Those mates you hung out with, an ebb and flow of between four and five others, were a group of tormentors. They'd stride across the school grounds, smoke rollies behind the bike sheds, slap each other's arses. The boys belittled anyone unlike them. You were different. I never saw or heard you belittle anyone – though that doesn't mean that you didn't. All I know is that when you were with them, you were different than when you were alone.

Those boys marked me as different, pointed out the way I spoke and the way I held my body: my wrist, my voice, my walk. You likely noticed those things about me too, but you never said anything about them to me. Those things about me never explained why my eyes wandered to you. Pointing out my body, my wrist, my voice, my walk, didn't explain to me the what, the why, the being, the thinking. Rather, those words – and often worse words and worse actions – were silencing: they silenced my body, my wrist, my voice, my walk. Silence exuded from the people around me, sometimes from people who I cared deeply for and who cared deeply in return. It was as if their silence drew greater attention to my difference, and their non-defence of me a sign that they didn't want to be associated with me. Such silence made my existence more isolating than the geographical distance between our two towns.

The most frustrating thing about this is that many people probably don't think that anyone deserves to be treated this way, but I suspect that some, if not most, people wouldn't defend someone who they saw being treated this way if they sensed there was a level of risk to getting involved.

Someone told me later of how an SES van, which had arrived first at the site of your crash, had flown past a party on the night you died – orange lights and wailing siren. I was meant to be at that party, but I'd chosen to be alone in Waaia. It was raining. I sat up on the couch, earphones in with my MP3 player on. I had decided to forego the party in Numurkah because I wasn't the outgoing type. In the morning, my mother told me you'd died. I could have puked. I could have ripped my heart out and shown it to her. But no-one knew I thought about you as I did, so I said *oh* and carried on with my day.

The drink I drank, increasingly drank, afterward seemed to do more than just flow through me; it seeped past the boundaries of my veins and arteries, poisoned my organs and fatty tissue. I got lost in that numb feeling. I could have fallen back into the river, got caught in an undercurrent, got dragged to a waterlogged canopy submerged beneath. That feeling was sometimes so strong that I thought about what it would be like to smash the bottle-green glass and take a slice across my forearm. It would not be the veins that controlled how the blood got out from me, no – I would decide where and when, and I'd control and I'd determine that sweet-metallic liquid's flow from me. Of course, I'd have these thoughts at night, only to wake in the morning with a head heavier than I cared to carry, and I'd run my fingers, tingling, over my arm. Each time, I found that my skin had not been touched.

The very last time I saw you was after the last bell on the last day of school before the Easter holidays. I wasn't catching the bus home that night. I was meeting my mum in Numurkah because we were going straight to the river for our camping trip. You and I walked beside each other – you on the art-wing verandah and I on the pavement below. I smiled at you when I saw you looking at me. You had nothing with you, just you. When you reached the end of the verandah, you jumped down in front of me, spun on the balls of your feet and then continued walking ahead of me. I watched you from behind. Your shoulders shifted under your school shirt. Your heels never touched the dirt. Your hand stroked back through your hair. When we got out of the school grounds, I turned left down the main drag and headed into town. You crossed over the main road – there were no cars – and headed to your home.

Homesick

Cassandra Goodwin

I held my breath, and reached carefully for the handle on the front door. I had to be as silent as possible, for fear of waking anyone sleeping in the overstuffed house. Pausing for a brief second, I wondered if I was doing the right thing. I had no idea where I was going, no money, and only a couple of friends. It's never a good idea to make big decisions when you're angry.

But I was so beyond angry.

Driven by furious determination, I shook off the doubt and stepped out the door. I closed it slowly behind me, gripping the cold metal handle so tight I could feel my blood thumping in my fingers. There was a gentle click as the lock slipped into place, and I winced, waiting for a light to go on or a voice to echo down the hall. When nothing happened, I let my breath go and slung my backpack over my shoulder. I walked away, into the night, as fast as I could.

Tensions at home had been building ... well, all my life, I guess. I was in my last year of high school when I finally decided to leave, which probably didn't help. Doing well in the final exams meant I got to go to university and get the fuck out of my rural hometown that I despised. Doing badly meant staying there, and staying with my family, and staying under the constant pressure from my mum to do better, be *more*, excel at absolutely everything at all times, no matter the cost.

When presented with an essay I'd scored 98 out of 100 on, she would never miss the opportunity to ask, 'What happened to the other two marks?' Ninety-eight was better than any of my classmates and, most importantly, good enough to get me out of town, so that was more than okay for me. But not for her. My dad didn't care about my marks, or anything I did, really. But Mum was relentless. Perfection was expected at all times, because I was the 'gifted' one. Mum had been deemed 'gifted' too, when she was a teenager, with all the accompanying expectations that she would do something important and impressive in her life. But then I'd come along, and there was no time for university in between caring for and working to support a child.

Instead of living out her plans to go to university and become a poet, she passed those big expectations down to me. The only problem was that she was never impressed – no matter how hard I tried, I couldn't live up to her standards. In hindsight, I wonder if anyone could have possibly achieved enough to soothe the loss of an imagined future she never got to live out.

While I hated hearing that I was never good enough, her criticism became even more hurtful when she drank. As I got older and was able to help out with my siblings more, her drinking steadily increased. The fights escalated, and the verbal barbs became increasingly vicious over time. She never wanted to talk about these fights afterwards, so the hurt built up. We would fight and scream and say horrible things to one another, and then the next day she either didn't remember or pretended she didn't. Everything festered and simmered under the surface, until she finally said something I couldn't bear.

'You never loved me,' she'd accused. 'Not even when you were little. I love you so much and you've just never loved me back. I wish ...'

Her words had trailed off into ragged sobs, and I couldn't make out the rest of what she'd said. Not that I could really focus on anything other than the rage that was burning through me.

A hundred nights listening to her slur along to her favourite songs. A hundred nights of her weeping about the sister and brother she'd lost, so consumed in her own grief that it never occurred to her that I missed them too, and desperately needed it acknowledged. Several nights when I was told family secrets no teenager should have to carry. But that night, it was just too much, and too far. Normally my anger is explosive, tearful and all-around embarrassing. But that night I was so incensed by her accusation that I went past all that fire and rage, and instead everything went cold and smooth and perfectly crystal clear. That was enough. I was done. I was ready to leave.

*

A couple of blocks away from my parents' house, I slowed my anxious strides and took a moment to think about the enormity of what I was doing. After daydreaming and planning and wishing for years, I was finally running away from home. Suddenly I was a tiny little girl all alone in a place that had never wanted me there. During the daylight hours, the ten blocks that made up my hometown formed a bitumen cage that confined me. But now, alone in the middle of the night, there was nothing but empty, enormous silence in every direction. A thought suddenly struck me – when my parents found me gone, Mum would want to call the cops. In fact, my dad definitely would call them, since he knew them all on a first-name basis from work, and running away was definitely a big enough move to get him to take notice of me for once. I had to get off the streets. I tried to think of who or where I could run to.

Of course, I decided to go to my best friend, Tess. She was the kindest person I knew, and she was the first who'd had the patience to teach me that it was okay to let someone hug you when you were sad. She was also incredibly clever, and knew so much about the world outside our town. Our classmates mostly aspired to work at the local supermarket or try to get out of town by any means necessary. But not Tess. She was going to be an environmental lawyer, and she was smart enough and determined enough to make it happen. She'd always wanted to do something good with her brains, achieve something important that made a difference to other people. That's just the sort of person she was. My fondest memories of adolescence were our sunlit afternoons sprawled on her bedroom floor, her head of soft white-girl dreads fanned out across the carpet, while we listened to our favourite songs over and over, perfectly comfortable and at peace. Safe.

I was alone with my thoughts while I walked – the town was deserted at this time of night, and since I hadn't been chased down yet it was fairly safe to assume I hadn't woken anyone when I left. I ambled down the main street, or rather the street with all the shops on it. When your whole world is only ten blocks wide, you get to know every millimetre of it, and memories get layered over the top of the landscape like special effects.

I passed the church where Dad would drag us every Sunday because it was 'good' for us, despite his complete atheism six days a week. I wandered past the showgrounds, where I'd had my first kiss. Past rows of suburban houses full of people who would avoid me on the street because I was 'too weird'. Past the supermarket where they refused to hire me because I was 'too smart'. Maybe they'd been right about that one though.

When I snuck out that night, I made sure to pack my uniform and textbooks, determined to keep up my attendance at school. The constant fighting with Mum had fucked up a good chunk of my life so far, but I wasn't going to let it stop me from getting out of that town and making a life for myself.

The steady thud of my footsteps reminded me of other, older sounds that lived in my memories of this town. The crunch of gravel on my ex-boyfriend's driveway as I walked away from his house for the last time. The delighted chirruping of birds commentating from the trees as Tess and I picnicked in the park. The satisfying clang of the schoolyard gate, especially satisfying when you were using it outside of school hours or to slip away from class.

I got so lost in the memories and the sensation of my feet on the road that I heard her before I saw her. She was older than me, maybe late thirties, and she was wandering down the street in my direction, barefoot and wearing only a white slip, sobbing uncontrollably. It was her unrestrained howls of sadness that broke me out of my reverie. She obviously hadn't seen me yet – no-one ever cries like that when other people are around. I'd certainly never seen anyone cry so hard in real life before, and it was utterly heartbreaking to witness. I stopped dead still, having no idea what else to do.

As she got closer, I determined from her smeared makeup that she'd been crying for a while. When her eyes finally drifted towards me, her head snapped up and her hands curled into clenched balls. Her sorrow was hastily shoved inside as she put on a composed front. As she passed me, she seemed to be holding her breath to keep from crying, and I wondered if I should do something to help ... I just had no idea how. By the time I decided to at least say something, she had already continued on her way and disappeared into the night. I sighed, taking a moment to recollect myself, and started walking again.

Soon, the rhythm of my steps and the silence all around lulled me back into a warm, comforting bath of memories. Past the flat where another friend of mine lived, who let me play *Doom* on his computer sometimes since we didn't have one at home. Past the McDonald's where Tess and I had walked through the drive-thru pretending to be cars, keeping a straight face the whole time. Past the crumbling little weatherboard house under the abandoned railway tracks, where I'd put together my first zine with my little band of fellow 'weird' kids. I tried not to think about the distressed woman I'd seen.

*

When I got to Tess's house, I stealthily made my way through the overgrown front garden and knocked on her window to avoid waking her mum. A very confused face under a mess of tousled dreads appeared, muttering something about letting me in. I scuttled from her window to the front door as quietly as I could.

When Tess opened the door and peered out, the moonlight washed over her face and I could see the concern in her soft, hazel eyes. I was so happy to see her, and so relieved to be somewhere other than my house or our big empty town, that I just collapsed, weeping, into her arms. Without asking what had happened in order to bring me to her door in tears, Tess held me tight with one arm, and with the other gently shut the door to the outside world behind me.

Shallow Crossing

Tom Plevey

Maybe I wish I had more to say. Maybe I wish I had something scandalous, salacious, titillating. That small-town gothic that sells so well, echoed in the words of Tim Winton, Cold Chisel, The Hold Steady. You know: nights huddled with a high-school girlfriend swearing you'll get out, someday. The seamy undercurrent of the rural drugs trade, the families Who Everyone Knows Are Bad. Bikies blowing in and out in midnight runs in burner cars, the rotting corpse of dead local industry, and the whispered gossip of people living close, maybe too close, to each other – who's screwing who, who's bashing who. All that good stuff.

I've read enough books about where I was born, or places like them, where I grew up, written by those who've never been there, never saw it. Never smelled the scent of dust and cypress and whitebox on summer's afternoon, heard the ratcheting whirr of grasshoppers as you walked, parting the tall yellow grass, along the cattle country in summer, towards the base of the mountains.

I wonder if these writers know that the dirt along the roads in Bingara runs in pink and orange stripes.

I know why those stories are written, to subvert the tropes of quaint rural goodness, because there's always a tale in finding a seedy underbelly and ripping it open.

My truth's a bit more boring, but it's mine.

But that hasn't stopped people from trying to take it back.

*

Bingara is a small town, 2000 people, in north-west New South Wales, maybe an hour or two from the Queensland border. Alan Cunningham, winding inland on his explorations, named it because it was the only place he could ford the river on his journey north to the Darling Downs.

Cunningham named the river 'Gwydir', after a river in the original Wales. For the place where he crossed, he took the name from the language of the Kamilaroi. Bingara: 'shallow crossing'. It's famous for being one of few places in Australia where diamonds were found, and for being the childhood home of Channel 7's Europe correspondent, Hugh Whitfield, who I probably could've been nicer to in the playground back in my school days.

It's infamous for being the site of the Myall Creek Massacre, where white settlers chained up and shot the local Indigenous people who gave the town its name. A tragedy – but also the first massacre where settlers were put on trial for such an action.

I grew up there.

*

I pulled catfish from Halls Creek, the stream that ran in front of our house and the reason Dad chose that block of land to build our house on. Dad gutted them, peeling them from their skins with a pair of carpenter's pincers, dredging them in flour and frying them in the Sunbeam plug-in frying pan for breakfast.

I trudged for miles over a rocky, dry river bed, a rifle slung over my shoulder, eight years old, hunting goats with the old man, on a thirty-degree day. Bottom of a valley, with the steep sides of the mountains rising up left and right, sunlight dappled on the still and stagnant pools between the rocks, filtered through the tea-tree leaves.

We had a farm, a modest one, on the edge of town. A hundred hectares, maybe.

I earnt a lifelong distrust of horses after they made numerous attempts to kill me. Droving our cattle out to the common on

269

the edge of town and back, choking on dust, our heeler crosses nipping at their hooves.

The smell of singeing hair and Dettol and the iron tang of blood when we brought them in for branding, dehorning, castration. (We never liked having bulls. Steers and cows only. It was much easier to let your neighbours keep the bulls, and when they inevitably tore down the fence to knock up your cows, you simply complained to your neighbour and he rebuilt the fence. Free fence, and free semen.)

We owned a farm, but weren't farmers, certainly not cockies. We weren't townies, either. Dad earned a living from work for Telecom, later Telstra, wiring up everywhere from Collarenebri to the Sydney CBD, travelling home every weekend.

Mum was a Darwin girl, an Australian-born Chinese who travelled Australia in the wake of Cyclone Tracy, where she met Dad. Darwin is one of the biggest of Australia's small country towns, second only to Brisbane. If you lived in a small country town, and have been to Darwin and Brisbane, you'd know why.

*

Like most, I suspect, I treat my time growing up there as ... normal. I have no revelations of the heartache and the hurt readers are looking for in these words.

The Other doesn't see themselves as the Other, not until they're exposed to those who consider themselves normal.

It was perfectly normal, to me, up until I left.

*

Small towns are islands, defined by their boundaries and those willing to transgress them. Those who stay and those who leave.

*

The Great Dividing Range isn't just geological; it's also a feature of our human geography and social tectonics. And it's a barrier more often crossed by those going west to east than the other way around – if you want an education, medical treatment, or a job beyond a certain wage level, you go east. You end up in Sydney, Newcastle, Melbourne or Brisbane.

Transgressing those small-town boundaries means ending up there.

I did.

For a nation that prides itself on projecting a global image of Banjo Paterson and Mick Dundee, four-fifths of our population is urbanised. And I wonder how many of those have ever left their cities.

I travelled north, to Brisbane, partly because it's closer, partly because no one in their right mind wants to live in Sydney, but mostly because I won a scholarship to a boarding school north of the border – the less said about those years, the better – and it was easier to get into a Queensland university.

*

'Be nice. Tom votes for the Nationals, don't you, Tom?'

At the QUT Kelvin Grove Guild Bar, the conversation had turned to left-wing politics, as conversations among students tend to do.

We were out on the terrace with the smokers and the endless stream of tradies in hi-vis polos and Redback boots, who were churning out the new buildings of a uni perpetually under construction.

The revelation of my political preferences was surprising in two ways. One, the Nats were so far from my political compass I couldn't even get a bearing on them, and two, at that stage I hadn't even registered to vote.

The pre-emptive defence of my theoretical political leanings came from a nice enough person: a hippie earth-mother type, right down to the West End address. A mature-age student, she was our little group's matriarch, and I knew she meant well. She was wearing her op-shop jeans and a loose turquoise blouse, but at that moment I could imagine her in hi-vis, paving the road to hell.

'I don't vote for the Nats,' I said, with perhaps a little bit too much acid.

'Oh,' she stammered, 'It's just that … aren't you from The Country? I just thought, well, I thought you would've.'

'Why would you think that?'

She didn't have an answer.

You learn to live for those moments when their shoulders sag, almost imperceptibly, and a light goes out behind their eyes.

Oh.

You have to or you go mad.

As much righteous ire as a Nats voter would draw from the urban, urbane enlightened, a greater sin, it seemed to me, was to be someone who denied them a chance to demonstrate their empathy, or to nobly convert a heathen – or, at least, to fight gloriously in defence of their beliefs.

But I was already there, as open-minded as the rest of them, just with different experiences. It wasn't so much the specific assumptions they made about my background that irked me; it was the fact that they never bothered to try to find out what I was really like.

At first, it bothered me that it was so very clear I didn't belong; as I got older, I realised I never would, so I stopped trying.

Like all youth, I longed for a sense of belonging and an identity but lacked the means, the wisdom, quite just yet, to make and nurture my own.

*

For all the wider experience we ascribe to people from the city, compared to the parochial, provincial bumpkin-ness of people from the country, it didn't take long to run up against the limits of their worldliness. I was surrounded by people who had left Brisbane and travelled the world, people familiar with the cultures of London, Los Angeles or Tokyo, but who never looked internally, who did no geographic introspection.

By the standards of kids who were living only the next suburb over from their childhood home (or who had never left it at all), I was poorly travelled. The privilege of the urban Australian, the city-slicker, I soon learnt, was having a higher social and cultural value. Their judgements were held in higher esteem. They didn't have any experience of my life, but with their superior cultural intellect they were, somehow, able to extrapolate an accurate picture of people like me from incomplete information – clichés, myths, stereotypes and other bullshit.

I was not, of course, extended the same privilege. City people are smart; country people are dumb, sure as the sun rises. City people can judge rurals, but rurals can't judge city people.

The Aussie cultural cringe means we are perpetually looking outside; the lack of internal travel, our apathy towards ourselves, is a metaphor for our national psyche.

*

As a rural who had moved to the city, 500 kilometres away from home, to study a fine arts degree in writing, I was a puzzle to those who assumed all left-wing, hoity-toity, arty-farty things were verboten in the bush, or at least unheard of.

But there I was.

As a rural Chinese-Australian, I may as well have come down from a wall on Mars. It was a combination that few could come to terms with – the redneck and the Asian were such diametrically opposed concepts, a chimera they could not comprehend existing in the same body.

If I was a terrible bumpkin, for the purposes of the city-slickers, who were looking for a rube to charm and repair into a proper human being, I was a worse token Asian. I don't speak Chinese.

I'm allergic to seafood. I didn't come from some exotically cool conclave in the city, like Sunnybank or Hurstville. I couldn't show them the delights of my cool culture. I couldn't take them to that little gem of a Chinese restaurant where all the real Chinese go. I don't even expect guests to take my shoes off in my house. (Of all the assumptions people make about being Chinese, that's the one they always go for first. It's always been amusing.)

The Chinese side of my family has been kicking around this wide, brown, occasionally on-fire land in some fashion for decades, way before the parents of the people who feel I'm the outsider here stepped off the SS *Orcades*.

These newcomers still felt they had to invite me in. My Chinese grandfather went to school at Nudgee College (our family had money back then, legend has it) in the 1920s; his classmates there asked him constantly if he knew kung fu. The more things change, eh?

Well-meaning, all of it. But frustrating.

*

In a Chinese restaurant just off the Mall in Fortitude Valley one Friday night at the end of a semester, we set out to line our stomachs for the evening ahead. As with all properly hardcore Chinese restaurants, the row of fishtanks along the wall wasn't there to add to the ambience. They were food storage. And next to the lobsters and the mudcrabs was a small tank filled with something familiar from my childhood – slate-grey oval fish, with fine cross-hatched scales, hunkered together and awaiting their fate.

As we walked past, I said, 'Hey, cool, silver perch.'

'Oh is that what they are?' replied and one of my drinking buddies, an ash-blonde private schoolgirl, still living with her doctor mother and banker father in Ascot. 'So that's one of your traditional Chinese fish?'

*

Why couldn't I be homophobic, racist, ignorant and a right-winger?

Why couldn't I be a nice Token, one of those second-generation immigrants who exist as fashion accessories for benevolent whites, who still had enough of the Old Country in 'em to be interesting to the gwailos but with enough of a grasp of English to be easy to deal with?

They had boxes. I didn't fit in any of them. I couldn't bring myself to bow and scrape and break my bones to do so.

But I came to relish that at times and learn to live with it at others.

Truth is, uncomfortable as it seems to many except myself, I never had a problem until I went to the city. I don't recall being made to feel left out in Bingara; I never had the problems of race or class or postcode until I travelled to the more enlightened city.

I never experienced racism back home, and that truth seems to hurt others more than it ever affected me. The first time I got called a fuckin' chink was on Adelaide Street in the Brisbane CBD. (It was amusing more than anything – in fact, I was kind of impressed he pegged me for Asian.)

I've blown many a city-slicker's mind with the revelation that there was a chain of department stores in Moree, Warialda, Inverell and Texas called Hong Yuens, run by the Ping Kee family. A lot of bushies have fonder feelings for the Chinese than people in the cities do.

And the objectification – being treated based on what I am, rather than who I am – may have been done with the best of intentions, but it was still just that: objectification.

The Other doesn't see themselves as the Other, not until they're exposed to those who consider themselves normal. My childhood and background in rural Australia only ever became a thing when I was an adult, when I was exposed to the more 'enlightened', to my supposed social betters from the grand and noble metropolises – or at least Brisbane.

But not fitting into those boxes defined by others is an identity in and of itself, a better one, because it's one you forge yourself, by yourself, for you. My childhood setting was a farm on the edge of town, but not our main source of income – we weren't townies and we weren't cockies. And I'm grateful for that. The comfort from growing up in that interstitiality really helped; I move in the spaces between. I can and have crossed the Great Divide, in both directions – something few Australians will ever do.

I never really thought about my childhood, about growing up, until I had to defend it. That's lucky, in a way. I never thought it special until it was thrown into high contrast against those who are considered the Norm, the Mainstream.

You are who, not what, you are. People who think they know you better than you know yourself will try to claim it, to take it from you and change it, but the only real mortal sin is letting them.

it is all before us

Alaina Dean

It is all before us.

This is a line from a book of Alan Gould's poetry I borrowed from the uni library – it's scrawled on my wardrobe door. I'm sure it's from a poem about a river, but it reminds me of standing on the edge of our hill, at the place we call 'The View'. Here, where the hill falls away into the lucerne flats, you look out over the whole valley: the patchwork of paddocks, my uncle's, Grandma and Pa Kearney's, the shearing sheds, my other uncle's, the snaking road, the dip where the town is nestled, and out across to the Nangar Range. Standing there is like standing on the edge of our childhoods, our whole lives. Standing there, it is all before us.

*

When I was a child, there was this red-eyed rat that watched me when I slept. I swear.

When I was a child, there was a swagman camping out in the shearing shed. An aunty left a note on a wool bale that read: *Please move on, you're scaring the children.*

When I was a child, pagers beeped at a cousin's birthday party and our fathers rushed for their firefighting gear.

When I was a child, my uncle left a dead snake on my grandmother's back verandah, and my mother screamed when we skipped over it, oblivious.

When I was a child, I slipped off my pony and the buckle on

the girth ripped me from the top of my ribcage to the bottom. It now looks like a neat surgical scar.

When I was a child, a sow careened out of the piggery and my father bellowed at us to get out of its way. My sisters stepped behind me, shielded.

When I was a child, we attempted to herd a calving heifer up into the yards. The calf was stuck and swinging lifeless.

When I was a baby, my parents were gifted an olive tree and they planted it outside my bedroom window. When we eventually moved onto their block of land (a wedding gift from my grandparents) they dug out the entire root system and moved the olive tree with us.

*

I grew up in the Central West of New South Wales on Wiradjuri country, 18 kilometres from a town of 400 people, with my three younger siblings – Abbey (ecologist), Claudia (artist) and Oliver (diesel mechanic) – and a gang of cousins. We grew up on the back block of the family farm, up in the hills near where the cleared land meets the nature reserve. It's windy up there, the gums bending and sometimes breaking, the clothes whipping and cracking on the clothesline (a length of wire strung between a few trees).

I am finding this difficult to write! I don't know where to start, what to include, how to thread a theme through these snippets and vignettes so they make up something worth reading. I want to write more about my childhood, about growing up, but I am baulking at that. These paragraphs seem half-finished (probably because they are) and –

I am conscious that this may be published and if it is published everyone will know, and everyone will read it, a copy will circulate around town, and I will have written something wrong. I will have written something that offends someone (or a lot of people), or I will have not written enough for other people. I will have written something that makes my parents sad or makes my siblings go: 'That is NOT what happened.'

I get a coffee with a friend on Chapel Street and tell her I can't write this piece. She says, 'Well, of course it would be hard, it's your whole life you're trying to write down.' I don't write a word for weeks after because this is an impossible task.

*

My parents are young. They were younger than I am now when they got married. Mum is the youngest of eight and grew up on the farm outside of town. Dad is the fifth of seven children and grew up in town. Not to get hyperbolic, but we are related to almost everyone in the district. As a child, this was idyllic. I mean, what's better than the bulk of the primary-school population being your siblings and cousins? We'd all pile onto the school bus chattering and planning our next big adventure and be dropped off in instalments along the road, waving over our shoulders as we lugged our schoolbags up to our houses. Sometimes we'd all get off at our grandparents', and Grandma would be waiting at the end of the lane under the tulip tree. I wouldn't say we grew up communally, but we definitely grew up collectively. The back doors were always unlocked, and we never called ahead when we dropped in on each other.

As a teenager, in that awful, self-conscious, who-am-I-and-why-am-I-here stage, this was suffocating. I hated it. I'm mad that this makes for such a cliché story, but I did. I found my peers small-minded, my community backwards, and prospects for a fulfilling career slim. Girls were – and are – treated differently to boys (much like everywhere). My sisters and I were constantly being asked to make our deb, so they would have enough girls to justify having a debutante ball. We flat out refused to take part in the archaic spectacle. It was incredibly difficult to grow into your own person when you've known everyone around you your whole life; it was incredibly easy to stagnate.

The closest I've ever come to breaking down in my life was after swimming training at the local pool. I'd argued with a boy I'd grown up with and … snapped. I ferried my siblings and probably a few cousins home, stormed into the house and collapsed on the floor of my bedroom. By the time Mum came in to see if I was coming to have dinner, I was distraught – sobbing, gasping for air and unable to explain why. I just cried and cried. Mum crouched beside me, put her hand on my back and whispered, 'You're so close to being out of here. You're so close.'

And I was. I followed the tried-and-true path of many country kids who'd *gotten out* – I studied like a possessed woman, topped all my classes, copped a stupidly high ATAR and a place at the University of Melbourne. I deferred the course, but left home almost immediately.

*

I left the Central West of New South Wales on 31 December 2015. I'd never been to an airport, let alone on a plane, but I was out of there and off to London for a year. Mum still holds it against me that I didn't look back as I walked through the departure gates. I watched the New Year's Eve fireworks exploding over Sydney Harbour as the plane took off, my forehead pressed against the plane window, the cliché of it all not lost on me.

I had no comprehension of how big London would be – I spent my first week walking around my new swanky neighbourhood in my Redback boots with a lump in my throat, convinced I made the wrong decision and desperately homesick. Slowly, slowly, I fell in love with the grey, heaving city (and bought new boots to match).

But I could never shake the need to leave – the need for green space and clean air and aloneness was hardwired into my brain. Before I even noticed what was happening, I had a pattern of jumping on a train one weekend a month, leaving the city for the impossibly green fields of South England, the tiny villages in the Scottish Highlands, the looming Welsh mountains.

Now that I live in Melbourne, going on six years out of the Central West, I rarely leave my inner-city bubble. That yearning for space is less frequent, less intense, and usually held at bay by an occasional week back at home.

*

When I was at uni, I'd go home for most uni breaks. I'd write essays on the eight-hour journey, my laptop bouncing on my knees as the XPT rattled up through the belly of Victoria and into New South Wales. At Cootamundra I'd get off, drag my bags across to the coach and sleep the rest of the way. The coach would pull up right outside my mum's post office and she would be waiting to collect me. We'd usually drop off parcels or news-papers to neighbours on the way home.

My childhood was defined by the post office. I hated it. It felt like it was us four kids versus the post office. We'd walk there after school and hang around the back, reading magazines that were too old for us and begrudgingly serving customers. Or we would nick off to Nanny and Pa Dean's where we'd watch cartoons until Mum pulled up outside.

The post office is the beating heart of this little town – it's the only shop left, more of a general store than a post office. My paternal grandmother owned it before Mum took it over when I was ten. If I help sort the mail in the morning when I'm visit-ing, locals will lean against the counter and say, 'So, when are you moving back to take over from your mother?'

I think only half of them are joking.

*

For a kid who grew up in the millennium drought, I had a lot of water-based fears. I would lie awake at night in the bedroom I shared with my three siblings, fretting that sea levels would rise so much that we'd have to wade out to the school bus that picked us up from the end of the driveway. I was convinced a tsunami would wipe us out every time we went to Sydney to spend a weekend at the beach. I was worried that a flash flood would gush down the dry creek bed just as we were crossing it and we'd be swept away, struggling to keep our heads above the rushing water.

I was worried that we'd run out of tank water and we'd have to drink water trucked out from town. I can't drink the town's water, not even as an adult.

I wonder if I'd grown up in a city would I be this prone to anxiety? Would I self-analyse to the point of paralysis, would casual comments echo in my head months after I've said them? Would I be able to name every person who probably has a strong dislike of me and outline the reasons why it would be valid?

I still check over both shoulders before I talk about someone. Even in Melbourne, in this leafy park on the edge of the city, the nearest picnic blanket metres away – I still check. My friend who grew up in the city laughs and says, 'Why do you do that every time?'

'What if they're behind me?'

'Why would they be?'

My other friend, who also grew up in rural town, says, 'Don't worry, I do the same thing.'

I check over my shoulders again and lower my voice as I speak.

I don't think I will ever outgrow this, the constant assumption that I am going to run into someone I know, someone who will recognise me by my face that looks like my family's and report back that they saw me – Alaina Dean who moved away – and I was gossiping in a park in Melbourne.

No-one knows how small the world is more than small-town kids. Growing up, we're convinced that all we've got to do is get out of our hometown, and the rest of our life will start – in complete anonymity and with the ability to shape it any way you want. But I've stepped off a tram, on the phone to my mother and complaining about a friend, only to have that friend reach across the footpath and pull me into a hug. In the neighbouring town to the one I grew up in, I've had an old woman grab me by my chin and say, 'Now, which Dean do you belong to?' I sighed, long and slow, and explained. Abbey and I once checked into the cheapest hostel in Edinburgh only to have the receptionist look at our place of birth on our passports and say, 'There's a guy working here who was born in the same hospital as you – grew up in some tiny town that no-one's ever been to!' Disbelieving, I checked Facebook. We had more than twenty mutual friends.

There are other things from my childhood that I probably can't outgrow. The need for all my friends to know each other. The inability to drive on a highway (or in the city, or suburbia) – traffic makes my thighs seize with adrenaline, and I can't overtake without deep breathing and encouragement. The jolt of panic any time it starts bucketing down, asking myself: *Are there any small animals that need moving if the rain keeps up?* Before talking myself out of a panic: *You live in an apartment and you don't have any pets, just close the bedroom window.* The fully stocked pantry of unperishables and the three-minute showers (we're in a drought!).

There are things I'm unlearning from my childhood, things I've been turning over and over like a piece of gristle in my mouth. There isn't just one way to lead a valid life (leaving a small town and only coming back for Christmas and funerals). It's okay to disagree with people, to call them out on their bullshit even if it disturbs the peace (assertiveness is a crucial skill you weren't modelled growing up). Most people aren't actually keeping tabs on you (you aren't the centre of the universe, get over yourself!).

*

While I have my own gripes with the Central West, I won't let anyone else talk flak about it unless they also grew up there.

Here is proof: a letter to the editor of a certain Murdoch-owned newspaper who printed a story about how the Central West is being revived by the sweat, tears and style of Sydney-siders seeking a tree change. It was grossly edited for 'clarity' but the full version is a pretty comprehensive summary of how I feel about people talking down about rural Australia.

To the Editor,

The celebration of gentrification in ARTICLE NAME REDACTED had me cringing. The Central West of NSW, just like every other part of regional Australia, is a network of small towns and regional cities that rely on each other – distinguishing Orange as 'much less bogan than other towns' speaks volumes about the mindset of both the writer and his interviewees.

As a Central West kid now living in Melbourne, I can assure you that the opportunity to rub shoulders with Sydney's elite in Orange while eating fresh basil (!) pesto in these uppity restaurants is the last thing that would entice me home.

The narrative of cultured city folk revitalising regional areas is boring, elitist and often disrespectful to the communities that have endured here for generations. WRITER REDACTED should've asked the 'daggy' towns if they actually wanted to join the 'X-Factor gang' – I'd wager that the answer wouldn't be the enthusiastic 'yes, please!' that the writer has imagined.

I rejoice at the growth and opportunities popping up in the Central West, but to paint this a wholly due to the innovation of people crossing the mountains for a tree change is false. I was expecting a more nuanced article from a writer who grew up in a town like mine.

Kind regards,
Alaina Dean

I will fight tooth and nail to destroy the idea that country Australia needs saving from itself. Country Australia is flawed, sure, but so are these metropolitan centres I now exist in. If anything, our entire country needs to take a good, hard look at itself.

I have so much to thank the Central West for. I am indebted to it.

I am the writer I am because I grew up there, surrounded by the best storytellers I've ever come across. I wish I could spin a story as well as my parents and their friends do over a few beers out in the back shed on a Friday night.

I am the woman I am because I grew up there, surrounded by strong women who raised families on the land in the endless drought.

I am the citizen I am because I grew up there, deeply immersed in a community that demonstrated the importance of connection, hard work and kindness.

I am the person I am because I grew up there, with parents who fought to give us more freedom and opportunities than they were ever afforded.

I acknowledge that my experience of growing up in country Australia is a privileged one. I grew up in a loving family with parents who went above and beyond in ensuring we could leave and function in the big, wide world if we wanted to – Mum once took us to Sydney and made us ride around on buses so we got used to public transport. My privilege as an educated white woman with a family who supported me is the only reason I could leave – that option isn't available to so many country kids, no matter how hard they may be wishing to get out.

Is this coming across the way I want it to? Are you getting that I exist with both a deep and unwavering love for that bit of our country and a simmering resentment of it? Can you understand that I wanted to write something much more scathing, more critical than this? And that I also wanted to write something more affectionate than this?

I may never get down in words how I feel about growing up in country Australia. Not how I want to, anyway.

*

When I was a child, I sat at a dying campfire and listened to a baby fox's cry echo through the gully. Dad said, 'City kids would be scared by that noise, you know.'

When I was a child, my grandfather rode over on his quad bike and killed a snake in our backyard with one crack of the whip. My mother had wanted him to bring a rifle.

When I was a child, I learnt to drive my father's manual ute, in case of emergencies. I can't drive a manual anymore, I've tried.

When I was a child, almost everyone had a stash of illegal fireworks and set them off every long weekend.

When I was a child, a feral pig came out of the nature reserve and wandered up the driveway as we ate breakfast. Oliver chased it despite being only half-dressed in his school uniform; the rest of us went back to our bowls of cereal.

When I was a child, my father walked us around the yard and showed us where to put the sprinklers if a fire came racing up the hill and we were home alone.

When I was a teenager, we used to wade into the creek and wait for leeches to latch onto us. We'd watch them engorge themselves on our blood, then pick them off and throw them back into the stagnant water.

*

Rewind to when Abbey and I met the boy from one town over on the other side of the world. We'd never crossed paths at home, but I knew his name because he'd gone to primary school with a good friend of mine. And here he was in Edinburgh.

He was so excited. I was secretly exasperated – how can the world be *that* small?

It was Christmas Eve, and like good, wholesome children who grew up on good, Catholic farming country, we went to Mass.

Down we went into the old town of Edinburgh, wearing heavy coats against the coldest Christmas we'd ever had, and he was practically bouncing. 'I am so excited that there are people from home here!'

I was already imagining our running into each other being chatted about over the post office counter or in line at the butcher's.

He moved back to the Central West this year, for a job an hour further west of where we grew up. I didn't think he actually would because … how? How can you go back after years in the city? How do you be an adult in country Australia when you've only ever been a child there?

A friend cocked her head at me and said, 'But doll, you go back too. You go back because you need to.'

And I do. I go back because I need to walk across the paddock to The View and I need to stand there, with that air in my lungs and that wind in my hair. I need to look out across the valley until life reorganises itself into manageable chunks. Breathe in, breathe out, watch the colours fade to purple as the light leeches from the sky.

I go back when I've spent too much time in my head in Melbourne, and I need my cousins to drive up the road for afternoon tea and a game of cards.

I go back because, there, it is all before me.

An Ogmore Story

Melinda Mann

I grew up in a country town, a town on Darumbal Country.

I have two sisters and three brothers. My parents were born and raised in Central Queensland, as were their parents and many generations before them.

Falling on either side of the north–south railway tracks, Ogmore is a small town in Central Queensland. In its heyday, when the mines were operating – in the '40s, '50s and '60s – thousands of people came and went, but by the time I grew up there in the 1980s, the population had dwindled to several hundred. Now only a hundred or so residents live there.

Until I was ten, we lived right by the railway line, just a few metres from the tracks. The times of day and the days of the week were marked by the arrival and departure of diesel engines and what we knew as 'motors' – the small mechanical trolleys the workers rode. The railway was the main source of employment for the men, while most of the women were stay-at-home mothers. Some of the women, though, worked at the small state primary school I attended with twenty-three other students, or worked at the town's only general store, which included a post office or on the cattle properties.

Ogmore is located at the northern end of Darumbal Country. When it was first established, it was called Harley, but in 1933 it was renamed Ogmore, after a town in Wales.

The rivers and creeks around Ogmore are significant Darumbal waterways. Darumbal Country is where my Ancestors have lived for thousands and thousands of years. It is where my father and mother raised me and where I have raised my children. I have shared this space with thousands of cousins, aunts, uncles, Darumbal countrymen and -women, other Aboriginal and Torres Strait Islander people and non-Indigenous people who have come to live on Darumbal Country. There are places here that cause us unspeakable pain. Places where we know Darumbal people were executed and where Kanakas were brought and bought.

Some of my great-great grandparents and a great grandfather were among 60,000 Kanakas 'blackbirded' to Queensland. They were taken from Gaua and Ambrym Islands in Vanuatu and brought to Darumbal Country in the late 1800s. Here, they were forced to work on the sugar cane plantations around Yeppoon. The owners of these plantations worked lands stolen from my father's people. My South Sea Islander old people eventually took up residence at Joskeleigh, and some in 'Kanaka Town' on the northside of Rockhampton, along Moores Creek, all of which are on Darumbal Country. In our local South Sea Islander community, we are connected most strongly to 'Josko'. My mother and her siblings maintain a large block of land there, passed down from their father and his father before him. There we spend days and weekends together, sharing time with our cousins and their children doing the same on their parts of 'the block'. Our family built a shed which has been extended on to accommodate in-laws and many grandchildren and it nestles on the western side of a small ridge under the shade of a gigantic mango tree planted by my great-great grandfather. Josko is a place that many South Sea Islanders refer to as a specific community of Islanders but for those who have lived there or who, like me, get to camp there regularly it is a truly special place. However, I live not far from Kanaka Town, and my children attend a high school situated a short walk from where many Islanders created community.

But back to my childhood in Ogmore – we spent so much time in the freedom of living and being on Country. We walked on the same ground, hunted in the same hills and fished the same creeks that our forebears a thousand generations before us did. I can still smell the muddy banks along the 'Back River' in Ogmore where we learnt to fish and swim and – at the same time – keep an eye out for crocodiles. Even now, in my forties, I love to listen to my cousins, my parents, and my aunts and uncles share memories from Ogmore – we all have our own story with this special place and so many of these stories centre around our beautiful grandparents, Johnny and Shirly Mann.

I remember the excitement of seeing my dad, Robert Mann, walking down the road from the railway huts at the end of a long day. Opening his big tucker box and clearing out any leftover meat sandwiches, which were doused in black sauce, before rushing to mix the feed for the pigs in the stye with him. We had pigs, dogs, chickens, and a beautiful chestnut horse we called 'Judy Diamond'. The pigs, though, were never pets; we never thought to give them names. We knew they were for food and that at some point the uncles would come over and the old bathtub kept near the lean-to shed would be filled with boiling water to scald and scour the pigs before they were cut up and bagged in deep freezers.

We would sometimes pick up butchers' meat from the next town north on the railway line, where Mum's parents, Wicky and Betty Warcon, and siblings lived in St Lawrence. Or Dad and Mum would have a quarter of a bullock sent up on the train from Rocky. There was no butcher shop in Ogmore when I lived there, so meat would often come from the land and the creeks and we had a huge veggie garden and my parents would blanch and freeze the fresh produce to make it last months. Dad would make our own pressed meat mostly from pork, and boney bream would be minced with bread and garlic to make fish cakes. We never went hungry. Dad shot or caught a lot of our food, taking us out in the cool of the afternoon to hunt or my grandfather would take us to set and check traps for wallabies. Dad could spot a kangaroo or a pig hundreds of metres away. When my parents whispered 'shoosh, now' to us kids, we knew to be absolutely still. The shot would ring through the air and we would wait for Dad to say 'got 'im' or 'nah, missed'. When it was the former, us kids would jump out of the car and run through the grass, over logs and divets, keeping our distance from the wounded animal in case it attacked us. The silence of my father's movements as he prepared an animal to be our food will always stay with me. There was a deep reverence involved in his taking of food from the land, creeks and sea – today he remains an advocate for responsible hunting and fishing rights and practices. This was life and is still the life for many of us.

When Dad worked on the railway there were dozens of Aboriginal, Torres Strait Islander and South Sea Islander men in the gangs between Rocky and Mackay, and similar railway gangs worked across northern Australia. They toiled for long hours in searing humidity. After work or on the weekends, Dad also worked for white station owners. They burned Country and took special care in doing so. He would often get called on to break in horses, drawing on skills he learned as a young boy and adolescent working on stations in western Queensland in the '50s and '60s with his parents and siblings. Dad was a terrific cricketer, too, and I went to many of his games when Ogmore boasted a cricket team. Cricket was the favourite pastime of the family; inspired by the West Indian cricket players of the '70s and '80s.

After Ogmore, we moved a little further north, to Carmilla, where Dad was promoted to the railway ganger position – a team supervisor. He was the boss of the Fetling gang and became renowned for standards of excellence in his team's work and for being a hard worker and expecting the same of his men. The job itself came with a house, which had running water, a landline phone and a septic toilet. We thought we'd been transported to another universe!

When I was about seven, I found ring binders of paperwork that belonged to Dad. There were pages and pages of calculations of lengths and angles of railway tracks for hundreds of kilometres of work. I was mesmerised by Dad's genius. Later in life, he told us about doing the training course in Rocky in the early '80s to become a supervisor. He would sit alone during breaks frustrated with the lack of opportunity that afforded him only minimal Year 4 school education. This was not of his or my grandparents' choosing but government policy at the time which did not permit Indigenous students to progress beyond Year 4. He may not have been able to read or write well but he could calculate measurements and construct all of the materials required to lay miles of railway line with nothing more than pencil and paper.

Mum (Mae Mann) was a young woman in her early twenties when we lived in Ogmore. Like Dad, she had minimal schooling. She did high school via 'correspondence' (distance learning) for a year but doesn't remember if she finished that year or not. In our old, blue two-storey Queenslander, with a huge water tank which had unfiltered creek water pumped into it twice a week, an outside toilet at the back of the yard and where it was common to use kerosene lights regularly, she filled our home with love and joy. Mum could whip up a delicious meal one minute and be staring down a brown snake the next. There was always a shovel handy to protect us from something venomous, which Mum wielded deftly.

Each afternoon around three p.m. she would start the outside fire and place two large tin boilers on hanging hooks that she filled with the water from the tank. When the water was steaming hot, she would carefully carry the heavy boilers to the house and up the back stairs to the bathroom. The smell of hot water in the bathtub, soap, damp wood and washcloths made from torn-up bedsheets will always be one of the most comforting scents for me.

Mum was my first teacher and taught me to read before I started school, enrolling me in a pre-school correspondence program and set up a classroom for us in a small room under the house. She baked amazing chocolate cakes, scones and dampers. She would chase us outside because she didn't want our running through the house to make cracks in the cakes as they baked in the oven. I don't know if it really would have or not, but we spent an awful amount of time outside while cakes baked, babies slept, adults talked and floors were cleaned. There was always a reason to make us play outside and we found ourselves spending full days in creeks, catching crawchies with cotton thread and meat, building rock weirs to herd fish into, walking around town visiting our families, getting chased by magpies, following our grandfather's dog into the long grass to catch echidnas, sifting through rubbish at the tip to find stuff for our cubby houses and building rafts to paddle in the small dams dotted around the town.

After my pre-school correspondence course, the excitement of starting at Ogmore State School was overwhelming. Mum tells me I insisted that my older brother not look after me because I could look after myself. In my defence, there were three other students starting in Grade 1 – one was my favourite cousin, and the other two students were kids I already knew. The school staff consisted of a principal and a couple of teacher's aides and the school itself was a two-storey building, with a long, open verandah and stairs on both sides and the tuckshop underneath. Uniforms weren't mandatory, shoes were optional and we never wore hats. At lunchtime, corn on the cob from the tuckshop was a treat and we had 'parade' every morning before class started. We sang 'God Save the Queen' and marched up the stairs to the classroom while the older students belted out 'The Grand Old Duke of York' on their recorders.

The end-of-year school break-up was a community fun day. There was always a 'lolly man' – someone would stick lollies to a hessian bag split open down the sides with a hole cut for someone's head to go through. The lolly man would run across the schoolyard and we would give chase. The poor guy always ended up being violently tackled by one of the older kids, much to everyone's amusement. There were chickens and piglets to win if you could catch them. Once I caught a rooster by accident, which was scary because I hated birds. It ran straight at me and the cheering of the crowd caused me to panic: I reached out and picked it up as it tried to run past me. I was about six at the time. Mums threw broom handles and dads competed in the wood chop. We made a lot of great memories on these days.

My parents' work ethic inside and outside of their home is something I strive to emulate but will probably never achieve because they come from the old-school ways of working (and working hard) every waking moment. They're in their mid and late sixties now and work harder than people half their age. I admire them because being of service to family and community is how they show love and care for others and how they bring joy to themselves. Even in their moments of 'rest' they would spend hours in conversations at the kitchen table sharing stories of families, places, politics and sport. These active pauses resulted in my siblings and I being grounded in our identities; knowing who we are, where and to whom we belong.

*

Our relationship with the white people in Ogmore was different to what we experienced in other towns. In other places, I would describe those relationships as purely transactional. My world was Black – the people, the food, the language, the stories, the priorities. It was an Aboriginal, and to a lesser degree a South Sea Islander, world, where white people barely featured except in public spaces such as school and church. But in Ogmore I remember genuine friendships forged by strong Black and White families. Ogmore families prided themselves on being hard-working and trustworthy. There is a sense of safety in having genuine relationships with other families, it comes from working side by side and respecting boundaries and people like my dad always reinforced those boundaries. Throughout my entire life I've always known my parents to be the first ones to pull someone up if boundaries are crossed, someone doesn't follow cultural protocols or someone speaks when they haven't been asked. Trust between residents is an important quality of healthy towns, but it isn't easily achieved because so much has been done to undermine trust.

As difficult as it is to work in regional places as an Indigenous person, I am reminded regularly by my Elders that it is an important part of exercising our custodianship of Country. Regional and rural towns in Queensland are notorious for excluding Aboriginal people, Torres Strait Islanders and South Sea Islanders from their identity; many barely acknowledge whose lands the towns are built on. The erasure and exclusion that occurs in these places can be paralysing.

I love regional, rural and remote places. My life is forever shaped by the thirty plus years I've spent living in these types of settings. If my upbringing has taught me anything about leadership in regional and rural towns, it is that it has nearly always excluded the very ones who know these places best. It is not a matter of inclusion but a matter of moving aside so the excellence that exists amongst Indigenous people can come to the fore. Reimagining 'country Australia' is necessary as the nation moves towards climate action. Indigenous leadership in regional and rural areas will be a critical factor for success.

Regional and rural people pride themselves on being 'resilient'. But this description is limiting and doesn't explain the experiences of Aboriginal, Torres Strait Islander and South Sea Islander people where I'm from. We have held tightly to our histories with unwavering determination to cement our identities into the fabric of country places, despite the exclusions we experience. It strengthens us to maintain the ways of our old people and to raise our children with the same fortitude.

Aboriginal people, specifically in country Australia, are not 'resilient' but 'continuing': continuing our responsibilities to Country and continuing the oldest living cultures in the world.

Notes on Contributors

Editor

RICK MORTON is a writer and journalist who grew up in outback Queensland. He is the author of three books including the critically acclaimed, bestselling works *One Hundred Years of Dirt* (MUP 2018) and *My Year of Living Vulnerably* (Fourth Estate 2021). Rick's debut memoir, *Dirt*, was selected among the long or shortlists for numerous prizes including the Walkley Book Award and the Victorian Premier's Literary Award. It was a finalist in the 2019 National Biography Award. He is also the author of the book-length essay *On Money* (Hachette 2020). Rick is the senior reporter for *The Saturday Paper* and lives in Sydney.

Contributors

TONY ARMSTRONG is an Australian journalist and former professional Australian Rules footballer. He is an ABC *News Breakfast* host and a sports producer with ABC radio and television.

CLAIRE BAKER is an author and researcher living and working on the lands of the Bundjalung nation. She is the author of *A Sociology of Place in Australia: Farming Change and Lived Experience*.

LECH BLAINE is the author of the memoir *Car Crash* and the Quarterly Essay *Top Blokes*. His writing has appeared in *The Monthly*, *Guardian*

Australia, *The Best Australian Essays*, *Griffith Review*, *Kill Your Darlings* and *Meanjin*. He was an inaugural recipient of a Griffith Review Queensland Writing Fellowship.

TIM BOCQUET is part of a fantastically odd family, from beautifully crafted surrounds, writer of cheerfully befuddled prose, with a handsomely supportive man and a reasonably middle-aged dog.

JAY CARMICHAEL is the author of *Ironbark*, which was shortlisted for the 2019 Victorian Premier's Literary Award for fiction.

LILY CHAN's parents were Chinese migrants who settled in the Atherton Tablelands and opened a Chinese restaurant. She and her sister helped at the shop from a young age. After completing university in Brisbane, she moved to Sydney for work, where she currently lives with her husband and young family.

JOO-INN CHEW works as a doctor in general practice and refugee health in Canberra. She has had stories and poems published in *Growing Up Asian in Australia*, *Growing Up Queer in Australia*, *Inside Out*, *Sunday Magazine*, *Press: 100 Love Letters*, *First Time Mum*, *These Strange Outcrops* and *First*. She edited *Heart Murmurs: Stories by Canberra GPs*.

ANNABEL CRABB is an ABC writer and presenter. She is the host and creator of ABC shows including *Kitchen Cabinet*, *The House with Annabel Crabb* and *Ms Represented*. Her books include *Losing It*, *Rise of the Ruddbot*, *The Wife Drought* and two Quarterly Essays, *Stop at Nothing: The Life and Adventures of Malcolm Turnbull*, which won a 2009 Walkley Award, and *Men at Work: Australia's Parenthood Trap*.

ALAINA DEAN grew up on Wiradjuri land, and now lives and writes on Wurundjeri land. She won the 2020 Grace Marion Wilson Emerging Writers Competition, has been published in *Galah* magazine and is currently writing the next great Australian novel.

JACINTA DIETRICH is a Melbourne-based writer and editor. Her first book, *This Is Us Now*, was published in 2021.

FARZ EDRAKI is an Iranian-Australian writer based in Sydney. She is a deputy editor at *ABC Everyday* and is studying literature and creative writing at Western Sydney University. She has worked as a TV producer on *Tonightly with Tom Ballard*, *The House* and *The School That Tried to End Racism*.

SAM ELKIN is a writer and radio maker living in Naarm. His work has been published in the *Griffith Review* and *Kill Your Darlings*. He is a co-editor of the forthcoming anthology *Nothing to Hide: Voices of Trans and Gender Diverse Australia*, and he is working on a debut memoir.

JO GARDINER is a writer of poetry and fiction who lives in the Blue Mountains in New South Wales. Her novel, *The Concerto Inn*, was published in 2006.

CASSANDRA GOODWIN is a writer and crafter, originally from rural NSW and now happily residing in Sydney. She spends her days wrangling words and resin into amusing shapes, and can be found online far too frequently.

ADELAIDE GREIG is completing a Master of Arts thesis, looking at child-bearing bodies in medieval Arthurian romance.

OLIVIA GUNTARIK, originally from Borneo, is a descendent of the Dusun-Murut Indigenous hilltribes of East Malaysia. She spent her teenage years in Bendigo on Dja Dja Wurrung Country, before returning to her first homeland to work as a writer. She teaches popular culture and music at RMIT University in Melbourne.

BRIDIE JABOUR is the author of *Trivial Grievances* and *The Way Things Should Be*. She is the opinion editor at *Guardian Australia*.

JES LAYTON is a writer and artist whose work has been published in *Junkee*, *Voiceworks*, *Kill Your Darlings*, *Archer* and elsewhere. Her story 'Chemical Expression' was published in *Underdog: #LoveOzYA Short Stories*.

SAMANTHA LEUNG is a Fremantle-based writer, editor and storyteller who grew up in North Queensland, Darwin and regional Western Australia. She performs at oral storytelling nights and works in events and marketing in arts and education.

DR. KAREN Lowry is a freelance writer, graphic designer, baker and digital poet. Her publication history includes work in *The Digital Review*, *The Guardian*, *The Conversation* and *Australian Poetry Journal*. She currently works as a sessional academic at Curtin University.

CADE LUCAS is a teacher, writer and broadcaster living in Melbourne. Originally from Tasmania, he's written for *The Guardian*, *The Age*, *The Jakarta Post* and *Crikey*, been a journalist at the ABC, driven delivery vans and taught English in China and Indonesia. He has ADHD.

GAY LYNCH writes essays, novels, papers, reviews, and short stories on unceded Boonwurrung land and adjunct to Flinders University. Recent works include *Unsettled* (2019), an Australian historical novel and 'On Work,' a Covid-inflected essay in *Meanjin* (Winter 2021). South Australian rural landscapes shaped her thinking and her writing.

MELINDA MANN is a proud Darumbal and South Sea Islander, who has forged a career advocating for equitable and accessible education. She is an adjunct professional fellow at CQUniversity.

LAURA JEAN MCKAY is the author of *The Animals in That Country*, which won The Arthur C. Clarke Award and The Victorian Prize for Literature 2021. She is also the author of *Holiday in Cambodia* and a lecturer in creative writing at Massey University.

EDIE MITSUDA is a young woman born and raised on Wilinyu/Nhanagardi Country, Western Australia.

FRANCES OLIVE is a writer from Stanmore, New South Wales. Her writing has appeared in journals and anthologies in Australia, the UK and the US. She holds a PhD in philosophy and is currently completing a Doctorate of Creative Arts. When she isn't reading or writing, she moonlights as a potter. She lives in Sydney with her greyhound Pegasus.

DOROTHEA PFAFF is a short-story writer interested in the resilience of the human spirit. She has travelled widely around Australia and currently works as a psychologist in Perth.

MA PLAZZER is an audio producer, writer and creative collaborator. The co-founder of SquareSound, she works with authors and actors to bring stories to life.

TOM PLEVEY is an Asian-Australian writer and journalist, born and living in New England, New South Wales.

CARLY RAWSON currently lives, works and studies on the unceded land of the Wathaurong nation. Her work has been published in *Verandah*, *ACE II*, *Chart Collective* and *The Big Issue*.

BENJAMIN RILEY is a freelance writer, journalist and researcher interested in radical queer histories and texts, class politics and the cultural legacy of AIDS. He works as a policy advocate for issues relating to HIV and sexual health and has a decade of experience in queer community advocacy and activism.

MEG SATTLER has been published in media and journals in Europe, Australia and North America. Her writing explores the everyday, often women's relationships. She lives between Europe and Central Victoria and is working on her first novel.

YOUSSEF SAUDIE is a journalist from Naarm. He grew up in Mparntwe and has a passion for telling stories. He has just completed his bachelor's degree in journalism at RMIT University.

SAMI SHAH is a multi-award-winning comedian, writer, journalist and broadcaster.

HOLDEN SHEPPARD'S debut novel, *Invisible Boys*, won the 2019 WA Premier's Prize for an Emerging Writer and is now in development as a TV series. In his spare time, Holden is a gym junkie and plays Aussie Rules football. He lives in Perth with his husband.

ANGUS THOMPSON is a journalist and emerging writer.

FIONA WHITE is a writer and teacher who lives in the Macedon Ranges. Her work includes children's stories, short stories and articles.

JESSICA WHITE is the author of two novels, *A Curious Intimacy and Entitlement*, and a hybrid memoir about deafness, *Hearing Maud*. Her short stories and essays have appeared widely in Australian and international literary journals. She is currently a senior lecturer in creative writing and literature at the University of South Australia.

MICHAEL WINKLER is a writer and reviewer. He has been published in *The Sydney Review of Books*, *Australian Book Review* and *Meanjin*. His most recent publication, the non-fiction novel *Grimmish*, was described by Nobel Laureate J.M. Coetzee as 'the strangest book you are likely to read this year'.

www.ingramcontent.com/pod-product-compliance
Lightning Source LLC
Chambersburg PA
CBHW032344280326
41935CB00008B/442